HITLER'S FINAL PUSH

HITLER'S FINAL PUSH

THE BATTLE OF THE BULGE FROM THE GERMAN POINT OF VIEW

EDITED BY DANNY S. PARKER

Skyhorse Publishing

Visit our website at www.skyhorsepublishing.com.

10 9 8 7 6 5 4 3 2 1

Library of Congress Cataloging-in-Publication Data is available on file.

Cover design by Rain Saukas

Print ISBN: 978-1-63450-530-7
Ebook ISBN: 978-1-63450-833-9

Printed in the United States of America

Typeset by DP Photosetting, Aylesbury, Bucks

Contents

List of Illustrations and Maps

Preface

By Danny S. Parker

Immediately after the cessation of hostilities in Europe following the Second World War, U.S. Army military historians seized upon a fleeting opportunity. As victors, they had the ability to interview prominent enemy commanders being then held prisoner in various locations within Germany. The European Theater of Operations (ETO) Historical Section saw this as a remarkable opportunity to provide historical data of great importance for future documentation of the great conflict. The project was first initiated by Colonel William A. Ganoe, but the use of interviews with German participants in the Ardennes operations was begun by Colonel S.L.A. Marshall and Captain Kenneth W. Hechler. Colonel Harold Potter turned the operation into a fully-fledged program with the assistance of a group of able young officers. During 1945–9, this was performed with great enthusiasm and dozens of interviews and written accounts were composed on a variety of campaigns. However, no conflict elicited as much in the way of interviews, commentary and analysis as the Ardennes Offensive – known to the Allies as the Battle of the Bulge.*

The reason for this interest in the Ardennes was simple: in no other campaign had the enemy so dramatically embarrassed the Allies with their cunning and sheer ferocity as in this final great desperate gamble in December of 1944. Some confident American G-2s went from predicting impending collapse of the German war machine to pondering whether the enemy might somehow have developed some new weapon of unprecedented destructive power. Top secret espionage missions were again repeated to ensure that no further German progress had been made in the area of atomic research. After the war the Allies remained understandably curious about the nature of the German attack. Much of the collected data was instrumental in providing information for the U.S. Army green books – the official histories of the various campaigns. Until now, however, this material has largely been available only to military historians with a budget to see or reproduce the source documents. I have always seen this as unfortunate, given the insightful quality of many of the manuscripts which I

---

* The codename for the secret German offensive was *Die Wacht Am Rhein* (Watch on the Rhine). The source was a German patriotic poem of 1840 by Max Schneckenburger, set to music by Karl Wilhelm. With a defensive sounding name, *Die Wacht Am Rhein* lent itself admirably for use as the cover name of the greatest German attack in the West since 1940.

have had occasion to review over the years. Since many of these were composed
by the German commanders without access to their official records, or maps,
there are inevitable errors associated with memory. Yet this series of manuscripts, composed so soon after the end of the war, provides a compelling
snapshot of the German view of the Battle of the Bulge.

In the companion volume to this book (*Hitler's Ardennes Offensive*, Greenhill,
1997), I provided perspectives on the offensive as seen from army level. This
second book instead deals with the battle as it was seen from the highest levels
of the German high command, starting with Adolf Hitler himself. The available resource material paints a remarkable portrait of German intentions and
operations within those desperate days of late 1944. In composing this volume I
have tried to assemble the most illuminating manuscripts from the many that
are available from German headquarters. Additional documents describing the
offensive from corps and division level are left for a possible third volume.
While space precludes the inclusion of the majority of material, I have nevertheless made an attempt to select the best and point out relevant documents
that are not reproduced within these pages. Most of the original source
documents are available at the National Archives Modern Military Branch in
College Park, Maryland, in Record Group 338. Many are also available at the
U.S. Army Military History Institute at Carlisle, Pennsylvania. Other documents, prepared specifically for U.S. Army historians as part of the R-series, are
maintained on file at the Office of the Chief of Military History (OCMH) in
Washington D.C. The editor is indebted to the assistance he has received over
the years at these institutions: at the National Archives, George Wagner, John
Taylor and Robin Cookson; at Carlisle, Dr. Richard Sommers and Michael
Keogh; and at OCMH, Ms. Hannah Zeidlick.

As much as possible, the editor has left the original record intact. However,
in some instances, translation, grammar or brevity has dictated alteration. In
other cases, the editor has taken the liberty of correcting the flawed phonetic
spelling of the American interviewers. And, of course, there are factual errors in
the German testimony. In cases which the editor has information conclusively
showing entries to be untrue, these are footnoted for correction or explanation.

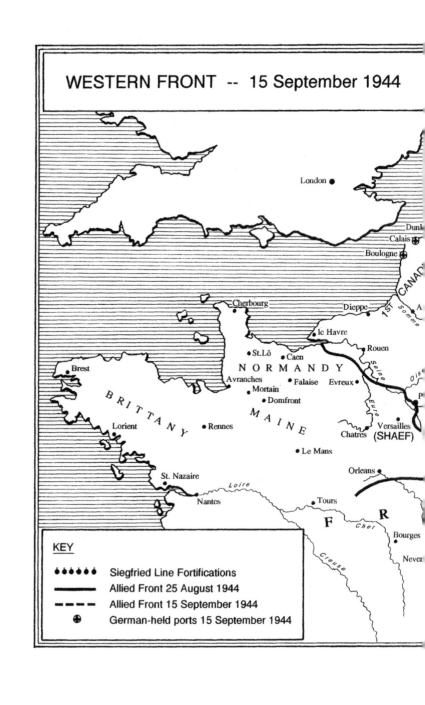

WESTERN FRONT -- 15 September 1944

London

Dunk
Calais
Boulogne

Cherbourg
Dieppe
1ST CANAD
Somme
le Havre
Rouen
St.Lô Caen
NORMANDY
Seine
Oise
Brest
Avranches Falaise Evreux
Mortain
Eure
BRITTANY
Domfront
MAINE
P
Lorient
Rennes
Versailles
Chatres (SHAEF)
Le Mans
Orleans
St. Nazaire
Loire
Nantes
Tours
F R
Cher
Bourges
Never
Creuse

KEY

♦♦♦♦♦♦ Siegfried Line Fortifications
─────── Allied Front 25 August 1944
─ ─ ─ ─ Allied Front 15 September 1944
⊕ German-held ports 15 September 1944

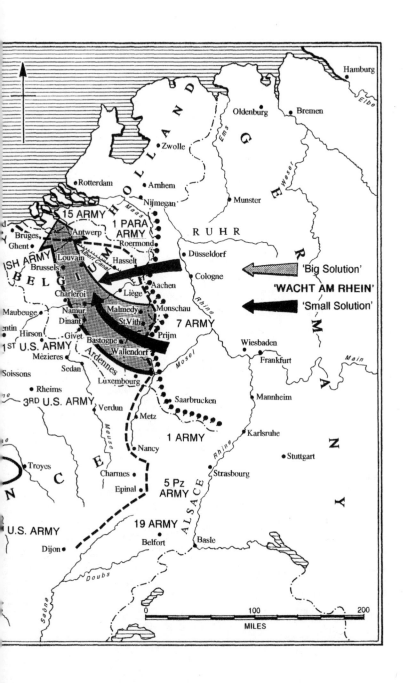

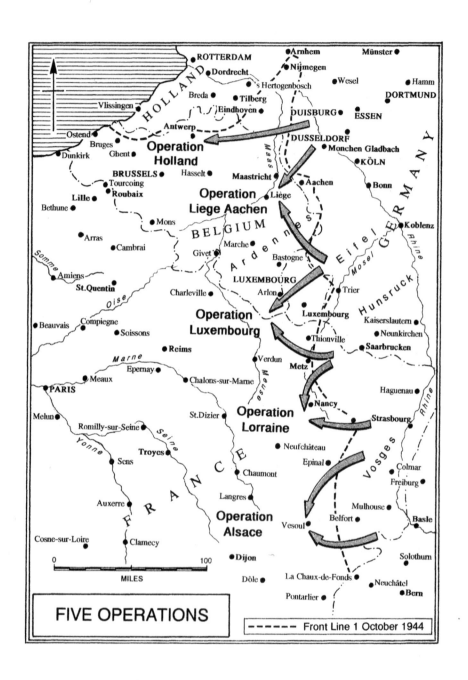

FIVE OPERATIONS

– – – – – – Front Line 1 October 1944

1

Hitler's Speech to his Generals
12 December 1944

Editor's Introduction

In early August 1944, while bedridden, Adolf Hitler confided in his most trusted assistant, Generaloberst Alfred Jodl, that it might be possible to strike a sudden blow against the Allies to reverse the tide of the war in the West. Although frequently at odds with Hitler, Jodl did not cease to be impressed by his master – even late in the war:

> Hitler was a leader to an exceptional degree. His knowledge and intellect, his rhetoric, and his will-power triumphed in the end in every spiritual conflict over everyone. He combined to an unusual extent logic and clarity of thought, skepticism and excess of imagination, which very frequently foresaw what would happen, but very often went astray. I really marveled at him in the winter of 1941–1942. By his faith and energy, he established the wavering Eastern Front; for at that time, as in 1812, a catastrophe was imminent. His life in the Führer headquarters was nothing but duty and work. The modesty in his mode of life was impressive.[1]

By late fall of 1944, even amid ultimate calamity, Hitler and his generals had fleshed out an ambitious plan, codenamed *Die Wacht Am Rhein* – a final great gamble designed to win a war that was lost. In December, this plan resulted in one of the great conflicts of the Second World War – the Battle of the Bulge. But what did Hitler himself, the architect of the plan, think about his brain child? Known as Fragment No. 39, the following text is the only surviving record of Hitler's speech to his generals on the evening of 12 December 1944. Major Kenneth Hechler, with the ETO Historical Section, describes his impressions on first examining these records:

> I have a very vivid recollection of going through the unburned portions of the stenographic minutes of Hitler's situation conferences with Sgt. Beck. Unfortunately, such a small percentage of these minutes were salvaged and reconstructed by the stenographers at the Führerhauptquartier that they were of little practical value. We were particularly impressed by the minutes of a conference during October when Hitler's intelligence officer briefed the conference on the disposition of the various American units on the V and VIII Corps front [in the Ardennes], noting the 80 km width of the front held by each division. Hitler interrupted, asking the briefing officer to repeat the distance, then after the officer had gone on to some other subject, Hitler kept interjecting, as if thinking

to himself, '80 kilometers . . . 80 kilometers.' It sounded almost as though he was at that point planning the offensive.[2]

Two months later Hitler's plans had all been translated into reality: a final tremendous gamble in which the German leader was staking everything. In the speech at his Adlerhorst headquarters on 12 December, the Führer spoke before two dozen high-ranking officers — army, corps and division commanders with their chiefs of staff. Hitler spoke without a script for a period of three hours, the surviving typescript being composed from the stenographic record produced at the time. It is a candid view of Hitler's penchant for military action to invoke political change, and his view of himself as a Nietzschean savior of the German people in search of historical miracles.

The original fragment contains barely half of Hitler's address (the rest was lost to fire) and I have shorn off a further third for reasons of space and interest. However, I have preserved enough of the original to provide a sense of Hitler's rambling, long-winded style. Three days later, on the evening of 15 December, Adolf Hitler conveyed the following message to General Walter Model, in charge of Army Group B:

> The final decisions have been made; . . . everything points to victory. The magnitude and the scope of which . . . depends entirely on the handling of the situation; . . . if these basic principles for the conduct of operations are adhered to, a major victory is assured.[3]

Notes

1. *Trial of Major War Criminals*, International War Tribunal, Nuremberg, 1948, vol.XV, p.302.
2. Major Kenneth W. Hechler, 'The Enemy Side of the Hill: The 1945 Background on the Interrogation of German Commanders', Historical Section, Washington D.C., 30 July 1949. On file at the U.S. Army Military History Institute, Carlisle, PA.
3. Walter Warlimont, *Inside Hitler's Headquarters*, Prager Publishers, 1964, p.485.

Hitler's Speech to his Generals, 12 December

Fragment of the Address
of the Führer to the Division Commanders
on the 12 December, 1944 at
Adlerhorst

Begin: 1800 hours.

Der Führer:

Gentlemen! A battle like the struggle in which we are involved today, fought with such a boundless bitterness, has naturally a different goal than the quarrels of the 17th or the 18th century which dealt with small inheritances or princely, dynastic differences. No people or nation will enter into a decisive war of life or death for a period of years if there is no deeper reason to be found behind such a struggle. It is not to be denied that the German nation had won for itself by numbers and merit the right to be the leader of the European continent during the Middle Ages, but from a political point of view, especially after the Thirty Year War, it was not in a position to realize this right, just as it was the purpose of the peace of Münster and Osnabrück to prevent a reestablishment of the German Empire's leading position in Europe by a unification of the German nation. Only through preventing concentration of the German people's powers, caused by the political confusion in Germany, could the British World Empire come into existence, could the American continent become English instead of German and France maintain her dominant position. Both nations have therefore taken every opportunity to oppose all possibilities of a political convalescence in Germany, which would mean a unification of the individual German states and tribes or even the construction of a German Empire in the sense of a unified state.

The policy of encirclement of Germany began, and war against Germany was proclaimed as some sort of a holy war. Churchill was its spiritual father and the international world Jewry was behind it for clearly understandable reasons.

This battle is continued today, not as a continuation of the World War of 1914 to 1918, as the press claims it to be at times, but actually as a continuation of the war of 1870–71, 1866, 1864. Because the so-called Wars of

Unification in contrast to the Wars of Liberation, had the goal of re-uniting the German nation. That this could only be accomplished in steps, and not at one big moment, is only natural. But the goal was clear. The final goal could only be, though not everybody was conscious of it, the complete unification of all Germans. To reach this goal was the purpose of my life. This goal must be reached out of the conviction that without it the life requirements of a nation of millions will not be met. Life without living space is unthinkable. Living space can only be secured under the assumption of the employment of corresponding political power. The employment of the political power is again dependent upon the object from which this political power emanates or should emanate. Germany can realize its life-right of living only if all Germans collectively and in a unified state defend this right to live. This became particularly clear to the others when they thought they could see the possibility of a unification of all German peoples, even ideologically, in National Socialism. Hence their battle, using all available means, against National Socialist Germany right from the moment it came to power, and even earlier, in which they were again supported by the international Jewry.

But there was another fact to consider, and that was decisive for me personally. I had to make some very difficult decisions in my life, some very difficult decisions. Only a person who is ready to give up his private life and so forth, and to give and sacrifice himself to only one thing, can make such decisions. I was of the conviction that there would be no man in Germany in the next 20, 30, perhaps 50, years who has more authority, more possibility to influence the nation, and more readiness to reach decisions, than I have. I also believe that time will prove that I have judged these things correctly.

I have therefore personally seen it as correct to reach the necessary clarification in the shortest number of years and by exploitation of the situation, not to get into this war but to find the security on which Germany will depend should she be attacked. This security was: 1) immediate establishment of conscription and complete armament of the nation, 2) reestablishing of German sovereignty for the purpose of the occupation of the Rhineland and reestablishment of sovereignty in the West by the construction of fortifications, 3) the immediate corporation of Austria, liquidation of Czechoslovakia, and finally the liquidation of Poland to put the area of the German Empire in a defendable condition. This was for the assurance of the maintenance of a future peace. Because peace can only be maintained if one is armed. And there is not only military armament, but there also exists, I would like to say, territorial armament, which without sufficiently large living space is very bad and difficult. You can see today that today's bombers can reach the heart of Germany from England.

A few conditions had to be fulfilled under all circumstances: reestablishment of German sovereignty, armament of the nation, reestablishment of general

Selective Service; and to this end also the occupation of the Rhineland, liberation of the territories created by the Treaty of Versailles, the Treaty of Trianon, and so forth, and creation of a territorial unit. If this led to war, this war would have to be waged at a time in which we were armed as never before. Otherwise, perhaps, we would have to face a time in which we will have lost this armament again. That through postponement a concern cannot be avoided was proven by the World War. Because, beginning with the year 1898–99, which was the first really opportune moment to settle the dispute, a number of years had been allowed to pass, always in the expectation of preserving the peace by giving in or by waiting for an even better armament situation, until in the year 1914, in spite of all peace aims, war was forced upon the German Reich. If one thinks over Moltke's desires of the years 1876, 1877, and 1878, when Moltke wanted to strike again, namely at France, to choke the resurrected France in the bud, and considers the political arguments which were brought against it, he will realize how wrong it was not to give in to Moltke at that time for political reasons caused by the internal parliamentary German situation and other difficulties within the country itself. We gave up the plan and finally still slid into war, and indeed at a very unhappy moment.

Gentlemen, that such things as world-historical events have their ups and downs is clear. He who imagines that entire historical epochs are only one great chain of successes, has never understood or probably never even read history; but it is clear that success and misadventure change. The palm of victory will in the end be given to the one who was not only the ablest, but – and I want to emphasize this – was the most daring. The construction of an empire, be it the Roman Empire, the British Empire, or a Prussian Empire, has been accomplished by toughness, stubbornness, and endurability, and less through a roaring singular genius or through singular energy which effervesces and disappears again, than through the tough insistence which in the first line helps overcome all crises. Rome would not be thinkable without a Second Punic War. England would not be thinkable without the crisis in England which they themselves conquered. There would be no Prussia without the Seven Years War. And the greatness of leading personalities, as well as of the people themselves, has not borne fruit in times of happiness but has always been proven in times of misfortune. History has shown that there is nothing special about people who can manage in happy times.

It is, therefore, understandable that a struggle which in effect sets about introducing a new world order in which it is absolutely necessary Europe should be preserved, cannot be run along the same lines as, let us say, a temporary battle to settle a small dispute, or an inheritance, but is dealt here with a year-round war which has its high and low points and in which he who lasts through, demonstrating the toughest endurance, will in the end be victorious. The objection that there could be moments in which technical advances will bring about a decision in the end, is completely negligible. For even from a technical point of view, this is not a question of superiorities which lie from the outset on one side, but it deals with superiorities which are once on the one, later again on the other side. Our present position is caused by a temporary lowering of our armament in certain technical fields, not numerical but only in value, by new inventions through which our opponents also gain. I have only to point out that one single invention, not made by the British but which they could unfortunately develop better than we could, namely the invention of an electrical locator, has wiped out our submarine war, which at one time was blossoming, and that we unfortunately lost bases of the highest value at a time when we were in the process of neutralizing this invention through new U-boat construction which we now have, and which I hope to commit this winter to influence our fate at sea in our favor.

The war is, of course, a test of endurance of all participants. The longer the war lasts, the more difficult will this test of endurance be. This endurance test will have to be suffered as long as there is some hope of success. As soon as hope of a victory disappears, the test of endurance will not be accepted with the same willpower with which, for instance, a fortress fights as long as it still has hope for relief. It is, therefore, important to remove the enemy's confidence in victory from time to time, by making clear to him from the beginning, through offensive actions, that the success of his plans is impossible.

This will never be as possible through a successful defensive as through a successful offensive operation. In the process of time we can, therefore, not hold on to the basic principle that a defensive action is the strongest component of a battle. It can favor the enemy. One should never forget that the total amount of men employed on our side is still as large as that of our opponents. We should never forget that a part of the enemy is tied down in East Asia against Japan, against a state which, even without China, has over a hundred million people and which represents a valuable factor in technical armament.

We still have to be clear about it, that overlong periods of exclusively defensive endurance will drag us down in the long run, and that they will have to be relieved by successful counter-blows. It was, therefore, my desire to make this war an offensive one, an active one, from the beginning, and not to let myself maneuver into a world war situation. If that happens anyway, then it is simply the result of the falling away of our allies which, of course, has operational consequences.

But the final decision in a war is brought about by the realisation of one or the other side that the war as such cannot be won. To persuade the enemy of this, therefore, is our most important task. The quickest way to persuade him is by the destruction of his living space through occupation of his territory. If one is himself forced to the defensive then it becomes his vital mission to make it clear to the enemy by ruthless strikes that he has, nevertheless, gained nothing, and that the war will be indeterminately carried on. It is just as important to enforce these psychological moments by not letting a moment go to waste, to make it clear to the enemy that whatever he does he will never be able to count on a capitulation, never, never, never! This is decisive. Even the smallest sign of defeatism raises the enemy's hopes for victory; his broad masses which have already lost all hope, will be filled with new hope and will gladly take upon themselves all sacrifices and all deprivations. The danger is in the publication of defeatist memoranda, as it was in the year 1917, or of documents of the kind which we had this year, and which, known by the enemy, still preserve the hope of a miracle, a miracle which would turn the situation round with one blow. The enemy must know that under no circumstances will he reach success. When the attitude of the people of an army and in addition to this the heavy setbacks which he receives make this clear to him, then he will find himself at the end of the day at the breakdown of his nervous powers. It will come to what Fredrick the Great in the seventh year of his war called the greatest success of his life. Do not object: 'Yes, the situation then was a different one'. It was not a different one, gen-tlemen, but all his generals, among them his own brother, were doubting the possibility of a success. His government presidents, ministers, came to him in delegations and begged him to end this war immediately; it was not to be won. The steadfastness of one man made it possible to go through this battle and find, at the end, the miracle that the tide of battle had been turned. Nor object that it would never have come to that if the Crown in Russia had not changed hands. For if they had capitulated in the fifth year of the war, the change of the Crown in the seventh year, two years later, would have been utterly insignificant. One has to wait for the right moment.

There is another thing to consider, gentlemen. Never before in history were there coalitions like the one of our enemies, composed of such heterogenic elements with completely contradictory goals. Those we have as enemies today are the greatest extremes on this earth: ultra-capitalist states on the one side, and ultra-Marxist states on the other side; on the one side a dying empire, Britain, and on the other side, a colony striving for inheritance, the USA. There is friction between these states even today about their future goals. And if one sits in his web like a spider and follows developments he can see how these contrasts evolve from hour to hour. If a few more very hard blows are delivered, then it might happen at any moment that this artificially-supported common front will collapse with one tremendous clap of thunder. Every party went into this coalition with the hope of realizing its political goals by pulling a fast one on the others, to gain something by it: the USA with its attempts to inherit from England; Russia attempting to gain the Balkans, to gain the Straits, the Persian oil, to win Iran, to win the Gulf of Persia; England trying to maintain its position, to strengthen its position in the Mediterranean. In other words, one of these days – at this instant it can happen at any moment, for history on the other side is also formed by mortal humans – this coalition will disintegrate, always assuming that this battle will under no circumstances lead to a moment of weakness on our part.

Now we, of course, have had our own great weaknesses from the beginning of the war, weaknesses which were caused by our allies. Our greatest weakness was that we did not have really strong nations, but weak nations as our allies. But at any rate, they fulfilled their duties for a certain time. We cannot complain and we cannot whine about it, but we must thankfully recognize that, for a time at any rate, these states fulfilled their purpose. We succeeded in holding the war on the periphery of the Reich for a period of years. Now we have partly been pushed back to the borders of the Empire. Partly we are still far away from the old borders. At any rate, we are waging this war now as before in a position which gives us every chance to last through, especially with the assumption that we can clear the danger in the West. I have now, gentlemen, taken sacrifices upon myself on other fronts – which would not have been necessary – to create the presumption here to advance again offensively. If I talk here about an offensive, then he who amidst the hardships of the battle suffers especially under the complete air-superiority of the enemy might be worried and say in advance, 'Can one even think about such a thing?' Not even the situation in the years 1939 or 1940 was such that everybody was convinced that this battle in the West could be decided offensively. On the contrary, gentlemen! I did not compose memoranda about this to break open doors, but I composed these memoranda to force open closed doors. It would not have been necessary to advance my thoughts about offensive warfare in the West in countless and repeated conferences at that time. I had to fight the official opinion which demanded a defensive war in those years. They still accepted the offensive war in Poland. But to make war against France and England offensively was taken for madness, for a crime, for a Utopia, for a hopeless attempt. Developments have not proven the opposite. Today we cannot even imagine where we would be if we had not liquidated France then. We also object that the difference between 1940 and now is in one respect a tremendous one: then the enemy army was not yet battle-tested, and now the enemy army is well experienced in war. This is correct gentlemen. But considering the strength, omitting the air corps – which, of course, is a very decisive factor – I will yet talk about it. The strength we employed then in the West in the actual offensive was a total of about 100 divisions, of 110 divisions; of them altogether about 86 divisions were offensively committed. These were not only first class divisions: a part of them were improvised, created within a few months, and only a part of them could really be called first class divisions. Not all the units at our disposal for the coming offensive are first class, but the enemy's units are not first class either. We have many exhausted troops; the enemy also has exhausted troops and he has lost a lot of blood. We have now the first official reports from the Americans. They have lost about 240,000 men within a period of hardly three weeks. These figures are simply gigantic and surpass by far what we thought he could lose. Technically both sides are equal. The enemy might have more tanks at his disposal, but we with the newest types have the better tanks.

2

The Preparations for the German Offensive in the Ardennes

By Dr. Percy Ernst Schramm

Editor's Introduction

That the German armed forces could, after five years of exhausting war, still deliver a stunning blow from the Ardennes against the Allies, will always stand as an astonishing military accomplishment. Perhaps more fantastic than the physical feat itself was the fact that it was achieved with complete secrecy – which is even more remarkable given that all encrypted German radio traffic was being speedily deciphered by the top secret Allied code-breaking project known as ULTRA.

As a witness to the groundwork which preceded it, Dr. Percy Schramm was uniquely qualified to comment on the German plan. In late 1944 he was the officer in Hitler's Wehrmacht Operations Staff charged with maintaining a detailed war diary during the preparations for the Ardennes Offensive. A professor of mediaeval and modern history at the University of Göttingen, and an officer in the Reserve Corps, from March 1943 onwards he worked closely with Jodl in the Armed Forces Operations Staff. Schramm remembered that:

> At the time, an expert was sought whose name would guarantee expert work. Jodl appointed me to the position at the suggestion of the deputy chief . . . I did not attend the Führer situation discussions or the internal conferences, but I did participate every day in the situation discussions of the OKW staff and every important document passed through my office during those two years.[1]

Schramm recalled his former superior with more than small respect. Five days after the abortive attempt on Hitler's life on 20 July 1944 in which Jodl, too, was almost eliminated, Schramm recalled that:

> The officers of the staff were called to our mess hall at short notice. We were told that the General wanted to address his staff. As not all the officers were able to attend, I was ordered to take notes . . . The General appeared on the scene with white bandages around his head. We were all most surprised that he should have recovered so quickly from the attempt considering that he had been standing right next to the explosion. I must say that, at that time, we were deeply impressed by the concentrated energy with which he reappeared before his staff and his moral attitude to such an attempt.[2]

Schramm was almost always at Jodl's side over the following months, leading up to the Ardennes operation. The professor freely consulted a number of other knowledgeable officers during the preparation of the important document that follows. The original manuscript is available from the U.S. National Archives as MS A-862.[3]

Of particular interest in this long piece are Schramm's perspectives on Hitler and his thinking process, as well as his view of the various German commanders who played major roles, both in the refinement of *Die Wacht Am Rhein* and in its execution.

Notes

1. *Trial of Major War Criminals*, International War Tribunal, Nuremberg, 1948, vol.XV, p.596.
2. *Ibid*, p.601.
3. Schramm's follow-on document is omitted from this compilation for reasons of space. Those interested in reading it can find the manuscript at the National Archives: Percy Schramm, 'The Course of Events of the German Offensive in the Ardennes', A-858. See also E. Halbband, *Kriegstagebuch des Oberkommandos der Wehrmacht, Band IV*, Bernard & Graefe Verlag für Wehrwesen, Frankfurt am Main, 1961, for Schramm's diary covering the period; and Charles von Lüttichau, 'The Ardennes Campaign Planning and Preparation' and 'Key Dates During the Ardennes Offensive', R-14 and R-11 respectively, both on file at OCMH.

The Preparations for the German Offensive in the Ardennes

INTRODUCTION

The problem

The offensive which the Germans commenced so surprisingly on the morning of 16 Dec. 1944, and the countermeasures of the Americans and the British, which had the result that the Germans only attained a part of their objectives, will always be of interest, because it is so instructive from various points of view. It will engross the historian to consider the offensive in connection with the following months, and to compare it with the last minute efforts undertaken by the Germans in the spring of 1918 in order to avert the threatening, fatal disaster. The military historian will above all be interested to know how, on the one hand, it was possible to produce such a powerful effort with an already exhausted army, and, on the other hand, how such a highly successful surprise attack was stopped in so short a time. This involves many individual questions of great instructive value to the military expert. For instance: that of the maintenance of secrecy; that of the concentration of troops hampered by the difficulties of the terrain, the weather and, above all, by the destruction of railways and roads; that of mid-winter battles taking place in a terrain which was difficult for both sides; that of the correlated actions of ground and air forces, and many other questions. Mention 'Ardennes Offensive', and a number of historical and otherwise significant associations of thought will emerge. The course of events can be reconstructed in every detail, even from the German side. It is true, that the war diaries and the files of the Wehrmacht have either been lost or were systematically destroyed at the termination of hostilities. But it has been possible to fill in the gaps by interrogating officers who had held key positions and who are at present in prisoner of war enclosures, and by consulting various records connected with the offensive. This applies also to the most complicated part – which is perhaps also the most interesting – namely the preparation of the Offensive. At the time, when the German command took the preparatory measures for the Offensive, the different stages of the preparations were clouded in a secrecy which was even more carefully guarded than was customary in such undertakings. The circle of the initiated which, since, has been much reduced by death, was very small, and written records were only retained on matters which absolutely had to be written down. Furthermore, the staff officers below the rank of army commander who were initiated in the plan, were only given a sectional view of the whole.

For this reason, the investigation of events, which only took place a year previously, produced difficulties which the historian otherwise only encounters when engaging in research concerning events deep in the past. The framework and foundations of the overall picture are based on records, taken from the files, and which may therefore be regarded as absolutely reliable with reference to dates and details. Nevertheless, they do not shed sufficient light on the determining factors and considerations which emerged from the preparatory discussions. Of assistance here are the statements and opinions of those who had taken part in the conferences. Although these statements can render very valuable services, they cannot be accepted without verification. Apart from the vaguaries of memory, which should always be taken into account, particularly in the case of officers, who had lived for years in an atmosphere of high tension, and who had experienced the shock of the collapse immediately afterwards, all subsequent statements are under the impression of the failure of the Offensive. They are therefore consciously or unconsciously distorted by the fundamental question of responsibility for the failure. There is a tendency in the mentality of the soldier in a high command position to see flaws in his subordinates because they did not carry out his orders correctly or with sufficient vigor. But if he only occupies a position on an intermediate or lower level, he tends to blame his neighbours to the right or the left, or else the wrong orders of his superior command for any failure. This tendency is not only human but particularly understandable in this case, because the persons involved are men who consider themselves called upon to judge in the name of long years of experience. On the other hand, how is it possible to expect a detached and unbiased judgement, if these statements involve not only one's own military reputation, but also the existence of the entire Wehrmacht?

It is therefore the duty of the research analyst to eliminate from all sub-sequent statements the facts which were established in the memory of their authors only after the failure of the Offensive. After this first process, the analyst has to take into consideration, how far statements were influenced by the fact that their author had been completely or only partly initiated in the plans, also whether he had held a position on a high, intermediate or low level, whether his utterances were made while he was still under the effect of the shock he had suffered as a result of the outcome of the war, or whether his conclusions were the result of objective consideration of the problems, and many similar questions. The facts, which remain after this process of eliminating distortions from the basic informations, may be inserted one after another, into the framework of the facts which already have been ascertained. This method is similar to that of a man who restores a work of art. By carefully examining and replacing piece by piece, he repairs a badly damaged mosaic, reconstructing at first the outlines and basic colors, then the more delicate lines until finally even the gradations and tints of the colors are blended into the picture.

This is the method which has been used in the following chapters. It is not to be assumed that additional evidence could be produced which could essentially enhance the result since, with the exception of A Gp B, all headquarters staffs, which had participated in the Offensive, have expressed their views. However, postscripts can still be added. It has not always been possible to clarify each individual point, and it is to be expected that inaccuracies have found their way in, despite all efforts to the contrary. But, in general, the picture may be considered as complete.

The clarification of the origin of the plan of an offensive out of the West Wall has been stressed particularly. Therefore, the attempts, which had previously been made to carry out a counterthrust from a retrograde movement and which failed each time, were also included in the report. For, only in this context can the reasons for the decision to undertake the Ardennes Offensive be clearly understood. Therefore, we commence with a survey of the operations which took place since the day of the Normandy Invasion, in order to clarify which plans the German Supreme Command had – between 6 June 1944 and the day the West Wall was occupied – elaborated to regain the lost initiative.

The Plans for a German Counter Offensive from a Retrograde Movement and the Failure of these Plans in Sep 44

As shown in the following pages, the plan of carrying out an attack of strategic dimensions in the West had by September 1944 already taken shape. This attack was to take place after thorough reorganisation of the Heer and was to be carefully prepared. Its line of departure was to be the West Wall and it was to strike a weak point in the enemy front. For these reasons, the Eiffel front had been selected as the area of the attack and Antwerp as its objective. Thus, the plan for the Ardennes Offensive was first outlined at a time when the chances of still taking the initiative during the withdrawal to the West Wall, grew dimmer and dimmer.

The strategic plans, which were being followed in Sep 44, and the Ardennes Offensive, which had to be postponed until Dec 44, were connected like links in a chain. The attentive analyst will discover more than one point of comparison in the drafting and execution of these plans, although they differed so widely in their structure. The main difference was, that in Aug and Sep 44 attacks were planned while the situation was fluid, while the offensive in Dec 44 was intended as a break through of a more or less fortified position, with the aim of again imposing mobile warfare upon the enemy. Therefore, we want to emphasize a number of points, which elucidate the subsequent operations, not only with regard to the drafting of the plan and the participation of the subordinate commands, but also with reference to the methods by which the plan was adapted to the necessities of the situation.

The reader will have observed, how much the German Supreme Command interfered with the decisions and functions not only of OB West, but also with those of the army groups, and even those of the individual armies. The independence of the immediately subordinate command was very limited indeed – and that not only on the Western Front.

This feature had not been as predominant during the early part of the war. But, the longer the war lasted, the more pronounced it became. This development was primarily determined by the personal characteristics of Adolf Hitler, who, because of his differences of opinion with the General Staff of the *Heer* and the top commanders, was driven towards controlling minor details in the execution of orders issued by him. By this method he wanted to prevent his ideas from being adulterated during their execution and to supervise that they were actually carried out according to plan. But there were also other factors which contributed to this tightening of the reins. Since the German situation had taken on the character of a besieged fortress, it had – more than ever before – become necessary to coordinate to the greatest possible extent the measures which were to be taken in the different theaters of war. These measures did not only pertain to the strategic aspects, but, above all, to the allocation, of men and materiel. The increasing shortage of men, weapons and equipment only contributed to increase the interference into details by the Supreme Command. As a consequence, the more the reins were tightened, the more changes were made in command positions. Naturally, there were two sides to this method: although the execution of plans, conceived by one central agency, presumes swift transmission of orders received from above, experience shows that exaggerated centralisation of military leadership tends to ignore local necessities. This tendency leads to arm-chair strategy and to conduct of battle based on maps. A further consequence is, that the subordinate commands are either forced to act against their better judgment or to do as they wish and conceal this fact from their superiors. In any case, this practice jeopardises their readiness to accept responsibility and impairs the atmosphere of trusting co-operation, without which no concept – however good it might be – can be realized. The inevitable result of this type of leadership is strong criticism of the higher command by those on an intermediate level. This theory was borne out by the course of the retreat in the West, as demonstrated by the frequent changes in leading positions which occurred during that period. The fact that Hitler's headquarters in the field was at that time in East Prussia, was a valid reason for differences of opinion on the situation. He could therefore obtain only indirect information on the impressions and experiences resulting from the entirely new methods of combat, which were being experienced in the West since 6 Jun 44, and particularly after 30 Jul 44. This did not correspond to his original intention. On the contrary, preparations had been made for an installation at Soissons from which the Führer had intended to command after a landing in the West. But, as a result of the Russian summer offensive, he decided, in Jul 44, to return from Berchtesgaden to his former headquarters at Rastenburg. He believed that his presence would reduce the shock which had been caused in the whole of East Prussia by the Russians approaching the border of this province. A move to Soissons was not undertaken, because this town was situated in the danger zone soon after 30 Jul 44. Now, the situation was truly grotesque: the Führer and commander-in-chief of the German Wehrmacht, together with the entire German Supreme Command, was sitting about 60 km behind the Russian front, that is within reach of a successful armored breakthrough, but as far away from the other critical front as he could possibly be.

Due to the modern means of communication and transportation, this distance was not a decisive factor in itself. On the contrary, the decisive factor was that some of Adolf Hitler's experiences in Word War I had developed in his mind into fixed principles. The most important was that every withdrawal would reduce the power of resistance and would bring about the danger of a retreat which would go further than originally intended. This concept was related to the ancient military principle, that attack was the best defense. For this reason, Adolf Hitler maintained that his personal authorization was needed for any withdrawal which was of more than local significance. For the same reason, he authorized requests for occupying a new position only under extreme pressure, that is to say at a time when events at the front had already forced a decision which corresponded to the previous request. Only too often, the authorization for a withdrawal and the report on the occupation of a new position crossed each other. The orders for counterattacks, which are measures evolving from the antithesis of the principles of withdrawal, fared correspondingly: they arrived, when the premises, on which they had been based, no longer existed. The Führer then received a report in reply, which informed him that his orders could no longer be executed or that they could only be carried out with several important modifications.

This method of leadership led to much criticism. But in quite a number of cases it resulted in fronts being held, which had been considered untenable, and in the success of counteractions, which, at first, had been regarded as impossible.

Now, the speed and the tactics, forced upon the German formations by an enemy possessing air superiority, and whose armor was not hampered by air attacks or supply difficulties, brought up the question, whether this method of leadership and the principles, on which it was based, could still be justified. The Commanders in the West felt that they had adapted themselves more rapidly and radically to the prevailing circumstances than the Supreme Command in

East Prussia. According to the opinion of these critics, the Supreme Command was dealing with factors which no longer existed and was therefore unable to draw inevitable conclusions at the right time. On the other hand, it made demands which were unrealizable.

It would be an over-simplification to explain these tensions by reducing them to the formula: 'The Supreme Command lacked contact with the front.' The differences went deeper than that. Adolf Hitler himself realized all the better how the war in the West was developing, because the battles of materiel of World War I had left an indelible impression on him and because he was interested in the technical developments of warfare as only few other people. But he was so convinced of the high quality of the German soldier that he believed that the most improbable would become possible, if only the lower and intermediate commands could be induced to do their utmost and if the will for initiative continued unabated. He considered his orders for counterattacks as necessary, if only to maintain the morale of the *Heer*, that is from a pedagogical point of view. Besides, dispassionate considerations also played their part in his plans. On the basis of information available to him, which referred to the enemy forces and the forces which Germany could still oppose to them on the Western Front in the way of men and materials, he considered a turn in the tide as possible. If events during the month of Sep 44 had shown that this no longer was possible in front of the West Wall, then the change in the situation would have to be brought about by an attack originating from the West Wall.

A. THE OPERATIONS PLAN

I. The Plan for an Offensive out of the West Wall: The Preparations at the Führer's Headquarters (Sep–mid Oct 44)

1. THE DEVELOPMENTS AT THE FRONT

It would probably be worth while to investigate how many offensives of World War II were planned, how many of them were prepared, and how many of them were actually carried out. In the third category the question would then arise of how many of these offensives started after considerable modifications of the original plan, which were the results of events intervening during the time needed for preparations, and how many had been converted into reality, as they had first been conceived on the map. Within this last category another breakdown would have to be made, separating those offensives which led to a complete success, from those which achieved only a moderate success, or failed completely, or those which had to be altered in the course of the battle because the fundamental assumptions had been overtaken by the development of events or because they eventually proved to be wrong. It would mean anticipating the results of the following chapters, if the Ardennes Offensive, which was being planned by the German Supreme Command in Sep 44 and which was begun on 16 Dec 44, had been classified according to the above mentioned method. But even so, this method of classification shows how important it is to briefly remember what was happening simultaneously on the Western Front before considering the development of the operations plan. To what extent was this plan from the outset determined by the events of the moment, and to what extent by the anticipation of further events? To what extent did the critical situations in the battle sectors determine corrections of the original plan during the weeks of preparation, and to what extent were these critical situations instrumental in disorganizing and modifying the preparations themselves? These are the questions with which we approach the course of simultaneous events. Resuming again from the end of the introduction, we commence with mid-Sep 44 and describe the period up to the first days of Nov 44 when OB West, A Gp B and the Army Commanders were integrated into the preparations for the Offensive.

By mid-Sep 44, it was already certain that the bulk of Nineteenth Army, which was fighting its way back from Southern France in the direction of Dijon, would reach the German lines on time. Furthermore, it was expected that at least the combat units of LXIV Inf Corps, which had been committed along the Biscay front, would succeed in their withdrawal. There still was uncertainty as to Fifteenth Army, which the enemy had cut off west of Antwerp. How many of these troops would be able to escape?

In any case, the losses suffered by the West Heer since the first days of the Invasion were enormous. On 29 Sep 44, OB West gave the figure of 516,900 men. In addition, a further 95,000 men were being employed for the occupation of the coastal fortresses, which were to deny the enemy the use of the ports. Besides this loss of over 600,000 men, there was also a qualitative deterioration, which was due not only to the fighting, but also to the long forced marches which took place almost entirely at night because of attacks from the air, and which were rendered more difficult by the shortage of motor vehicles.

On 9 Sep 44, OB West had calculated his actual strength to be as follows:

	Infantry Divisions	Panzer Formations	
		Divisions	Brigades
Full Battle Strength	13	3	2
Reduced Battle Strength	12	3	2
Battle-weary	14	7	—
Scattered	— 7	—	—
Undergoing Reorganization	9	2	—
Total Available	48?	15	4

Four of the infantry divisions of full and of reduced battle strength are not to be counted, as they were employed for the defense of the fortresses. This number was further increased when the Channel Coast was lost as far as the Maas. The Allied strength on 7 Sep 44, was calculated as follows:

In France: approximately 54 combat divisions, as well as a great number of service troops.

In England: at least 30 combat divisions

Total available: 84 or more combat divisions

It was also known that additional units were arriving from the United States.

Not counting the forces occupying the fortresses – some of which were only blockaded at first and were not under regular siege, and which therefore pinned down enemy troops of only inferior quality – a computation of divisions showed that approximately 60 German units were opposing about 54 Allied units in Sep 44. But, as the Allied units had been less weakened by combat and scarcely exhausted by marching, the German forces were now also suffering from a considerable inferiority on the ground. This numerical inferiority was emphasized by the considerable losses of heavy weapons and equipment, which had begun with the Battle of Normandy and which had since been multiplied during the retreat. The most important problem of the German Command, which overshadowed all others, even the preparation of an offensive, was therefore to equalize the unfavorable ratio of forces and materials – at least to a certain extent. The necessary measures were already under way since Aug 44 and were beginning to show results by Sep 44. In view of the serious situation, all interested agencies were endeavoring to do their utmost. For the time being, however, it still was a question of improvising and applying transitional and makeshift measures.

The number of combat troops was increased by incorporating into the battle-weary divisions, which reached the West Wall, the units which the *Ersatsheer* (replacement training army) had activated for the defense of the West Wall. Consequently, battle-tested, but exhausted soldiers were now standing shoulder to shoulder with men who had not finished their training, or, for reasons of age or infirmity, had not previously been called to the front. The performance of the newly arrived troops deserves recognition, and in some cases is even worthy of high praise; but these troops were still to be broken in and hardened to battle conditions before they could rightly be considered full soldiers.

Besides this inequality of purely military value, there was that of equipment and training. Here there was a shortage of machine guns, somewhere else there was no ammunition; here was a shortage of men who understood how to use their weapons, and there a shortage of officers who knew how to commit them. There was a general shortage of tanks, anti-tank weapons, guns and engineering equipment. There was a shortage of almost everything which makes a position defensible in modern warfare.

Under these conditions it was a very real advantage that the flanks of the new front were being supported by strong natural barriers – on the right by rivers and canals, on the left by the Vosges – and that the center was supported by the West Wall. The value of the so-called Siegfried Line – a name invented by the British – was perhaps to be found more in the field of psychology than in that of fortification. Even in 1939, it was unable to satisfy all the requirements of an effective defensive line, and since then the technique of warfare had advanced so much that the West Wall was already to be regarded as obsolete. Furthermore, the wire entanglements had been dismantled in the preceding years, armor-plate doors had been removed and used for other purposes, and other measures had been taken, which now had to be reversed with all speed. Nevertheless, it was still a fortified line. The enemy took this fact into consideration when he fanned out in his advance on the West Wall and made careful preparations before he began his first attack. Because of this, the defense forces were given the time needed to improve the West Wall, to repair the worst damage to its structure and to equalize the equipment of their units. This also had the effect of increasing the confidence in the fortified line, and the *Heer*, which in view of the never-ending air attacks had begun to feel that resistance against this type of warfare had lately become useless, regained faith. In this connection it is no exaggeration to talk about the 'Miracle of the West Wall'.

From Sep 44 on, a reorganization and regrouping of the entire West *Heer* was taking place, which, although it was impossible to reestablish its former value, brought it every week a little further strengthening. Similarly, the state of armament and equipment was improving as one shipment after another arrived from the Zone of the Interior.

However, this improvement was not evident on all sectors of the front, since the reorganization had to be delayed at all points where the fighting continued. A very considerable part of the reinforcements in men and materials, which arrived on the Western Front, was immediately consumed by the fighting which took place after the occupation of the new line. How the ratio of strength had developed by mid-Oct 44, is indicated in a report from OB West to Hitler's headquarters in the field. According to this report, he now had on the Western Front – which at this time was about 1,000 km long – 41 infantry and/or Volks grenadier divisions and ten panzer and/or panzer grenadier divisions. According to the calculations of OB West, the actual combat strength of these units could – despite the incorporation of reinforcements – only be considered equivalent to that of 27 entire infantry divisions and six and one half entire panzer divisions. According to the opinion of Genfldm von Rundstedt, the British and

Americans already had 48 infantry and 18 armored divisions, as well as 11 armored brigades available, with which they were opposing his forces. He pointed out, that the enemy would be able to maintain his forces at full strength as well as bring up reserves, whereas the German West *Heer* had lost about 150,000 men in the period from 1 Sep to 15 Oct 44. In the same period his own total replacements had been 152,000 men. But at the same time, 86,000 men had been withdrawn for the activation and reorganization of units, so that in spite of the large number of replacements the West *Heer* had been reduced by a total of 84,000 men during one and one half months. Genfldm von Rundstedt concluded from these figures that it would not be possible to hold the Western Front indefinitely with the forces at his disposal. Furthermore, it had to be taken into consideration that the enemy had not yet completed the assembly of his troops, and that his heavy airforce formations had not yet been thrown in. All the more urgent was the formation of adequate reserves, of which there were practically none. Over and above the forces, which he had already been promised, Genfldm von Rundstedt requested six additional infantry divisions and one panzer division for A Gp B and two infantry divisions for A Gp G.

Any consideration of a German offensive has to begin with an analysis of the question, whether and how the requirements of OB West could be reconciled with the assembly of forces needed for an attack. Additional units had already been promised to OB West, a fact which he had mentioned in his report; more units were to follow. He also received current replacements for the divisions which were already under his command. The disadvantage of temporarily withdrawing so many troops for reorganization behind the front, would certainly be compensated in due course. Thus, in spite of all the current losses, an improvement in the defensive situation in the West was to be anticipated. But, what was to be done with the divisions that had been withdrawn, when they were once more ready for commitment? And what about those units which had meanwhile been activated in the Zone of the Interior, or those which had been transferred from other theaters of war? If they were released to OB West, it was to be expected that before long they would be weakened by the attrition of defensive fighting. If, however, they were held in reserve for an offensive, there was the danger that the forces of OB West would be insufficient to prevent a breakthrough, and that the reserve forces, which had been set aside, would be thrown into the gap, division by division, which would result in the collapse of the plan for an offensive before it could be put into operation. The chances of regaining the initiative would be reduced, if the requests of OB West were granted; but if they were denied, critical situations might develop at the front. Therefore, the decision with regard to the commitment of each division had to be carefully considered. The same applied to every single *werfer* (rocket projector) brigade, every artillery battalion, and every *pionier* (engineer) battalion. A wrong disposal of units might spell disaster. On the other hand, the enemy superiority in men and materials, which now also existed on the ground, and the danger of further battles of attrition similar to the one which had just taken place in Normandy, would, in the end, result in a desperate situation, because Germany, pinned down on so many fronts, had neither sufficient men nor materiel to withstand this type of fighting. The greatest possible defensive risks seemed to be justified, if the pressure on the Western Front – the continual intensification of which was to be anticipated – could be reduced in some manner. Furthermore, the old principle, that 'attack is the best form of defense', can be amplified by experience to the effect that an attack which leads to mobile warfare results in fewer casualties than a purely defensive battle.

This is the key to the German methods of warfare in the West from the time the plans of the offensive were beginning to take shape.

In the beginning of this phase of the war, Belgium – including the port of Antwerp, which was considered as extremely important for the further conduct of the war – had fallen into Allied hands, but it had nevertheless been possible to blockade the mouth of the Schelde by building up a bridgehead at Breskens and fortifications on the island of Walcheren. Furthermore, the Allies were halted south of the Dutch–Belgian border, because it had been possible to build up a new front along the Albert Canal, which was extending further to the east along the Maas, thereby making use of another natural obstacle.

This line, which had not yet been consolidated, was in danger of suddenly being ripped open when the Allies, on 17 Sep 44, made their surprise airborne landings at Arnhem and to the south of it. These were coordinated with a simultaneous armored thrust to the north from a bridgehead across the Albert Canal. This move placed all the German forces near the Maas and Rhine deltas as well as those in western Holland in danger of being cut off.

The Germans succeeded in destroying the forces which had been landed in the vicinity of Arnhem, and were thus able to parry the strategic effects of this operation. But it was impossible to sever the neck of the salient which was connecting the enemy with the southern group of his airborne troops. On the contrary, the enemy was able to widen it so much that a blunt wedge was protruding northward from the canal into the former front line. Even though the Allies had only been able to realize part of their intentions, they had, in this sector of the front, created a situation which remained a strategic threat, and which above all, pinned down more German forces than before.

Therefore, it was particularly advantageous that during those days it had been possible to rescue the bulk of Fifteenth Army, which had been pushed back to the west toward the coast after the surprisingly swift fall of Antwerp. The army escaped to the north via the Schelde delta, and via Walcheren and Süd-Beveland, the islands adjacent to the north. By 23 Sep 44, 82,000 men and

580 guns had been rescued. Not only were these troops able to escape being captured, but a reserve of manpower was thus being built up, with which it was possible to feed the battle in the area of the Arnhem breakthrough, which, in the beginning, had to be fought with very heterogeneous and hurriedly assembled troops.

These elements of Fifteenth Army had been of no further use for the defense of the Schelde delta, because of supply difficulties. The defense of the sector to the south of the river had been left in the hands of a reinforced division which was able to hold out until 2 Nov 44. Meanwhile, the battle for Walcheren and Süd-Beveland had already begun. It ended on 8 Nov 44. From that time on, the Schelde delta was no longer blockaded, and therefore the port of Antwerp could be approached from the sea. It was now beyond doubt that the supply problem of the Allies would be eased in a very short time. There would be no further delay in the supply of men and materials, which had been caused by the absence of suitable harbors.

Meanwhile, the Aachen sector had developed into the most endangered part of the front in the A Gp B area. At the time of the airborne landings at Arnhem, the enemy was already so near to the town that it was within the reach of his guns. It was feared that the enemy would take the town by a *coup de main*. But, he first consolidated his lines to the right and left of Aachen. On 20 Sep 44, he penetrated into Stolberg, and thus entered the second line of pillboxes in the West Wall. A counterthrust, carried out by the battle-tested 12 Inf Div, succeeded in reducing the salient in the German frontline, but the threat remained nevertheless. As the line to the northwest and southeast of Aachen had now been withdrawn, the fine old imperial city, which had at one time been the center of the Reich, was a prominent salient jutting out of the German line. Against all expectations, the attack was further delayed, which made it possible to reinforce the endangered sector. Thus, the battle which commenced on 2 Oct 44, developed into a stubborn struggle, lasting almost three weeks. OB West made an evaluation of the situation on 9 Oct 44, in which he described the Aachen sector as the main danger point on the entire Western Front at that time. He threw in all the forces at his disposal, but these were not many. Day by day ground was lost, and the double envelopment of Aachen was clearly taking shape. On 15 Oct 44, the city was already surrounded except for a very narrow access. All efforts to bring up relief forces failed. On 21 Oct 44, the last resistance ended. The first major German city had fallen to the enemy – a fact which was not without psychological repercussions, both for the *Heer* and for the German people. A glance at the map made it obvious, even to a layman, that the enemy would sooner or later renew his attacks in this sector.

The front adjacent to the south and extending as far as Trier, which was supported by the West Wall, did not give any cause for anxiety to the German Supreme Command because the Americans had committed only weak forces in this sector. A surprise attack, which had looked dangerous at first, and which the enemy had succeeded in making in mid-Sep 44 in the region of Wallersdorf at the boundary between two corps, had been driven back by a counterattack, which further strengthened the confidence in the West Wall.

The sector of A Gp G began at Trier. Little need be said on its subject, because of the failure of the plan to carry out a thrust into the enemy flank. The attacks of Fifth Pz Army had led to only temporary success. We recall, how, contrary to the intentions of the Supreme Command, A Gp G had been pushed back toward Lorraine and into the Vosges, after Army Group had taken into its frontal salient the bulk of Nineteenth Army and the main elements of LXIV Inf Corps.

Until the end of Sep 44, and after First Army had been transferred from A Gp B to A Gp G, the front on the left wing of OB West was organized as follows: First Army on the right wing, Fifth Pz Army in the center and Nineteenth Army on the left wing. In view of the offensive, the staff of Fifth Pz Army was withdrawn in the beginning of Oct 44 and its sector was divided between the two adjacent armies.

First Army, which had been fighting its way back from the Paris area, was holding onto the Moselle line. But Army was now only holding the sector between Trier and Metz. In the vicinity of Metz there was a major bridgehead, which was reinforced by the antiquated, but still useful installations of the old fortress. At the end of Sep 44, the enemy was expected to strike here, as well as at Aachen. But here, major operations were longer delayed than at the critical point further north.

An attack on Metz must have appeared particularly inviting to the Americans after they had already obtained control of the Moselle line to the south of Metz, and were thus able to strike at Metz from the left flank via Pont-à-Mousson. At first, enemy pressure had made itself felt further to the south, that is to the northeast of Nancy and Luneville. To the right of Château-Saline, in the Nomeny area, where critical situations had developed in the past, and to the left in the forest of Parrey, both sides were engaged in bitter and stubborn fighting during Oct 44. It was obvious that the fighting in this sector was just a harbinger of more important events. If the enemy hesitated to initiate major operations along this front, which had not yet been consolidated, the German Command could only assume that he was first making systematic preparation. In the rear of this sector were several natural defense lines as well as the fortifications of the Maginot line, the *Saarhechenstellungen* (the Saar heights position), and also the West Wall. Should the battle-weary army receive adequate reinforcements, there was some prospect of preventing a breakthrough. But if Army did not receive these reinforcements, none of these fortifications would be of any avail. On 9 Oct 44, OB West reported that, according to his estimate, the enemy would now attempt to envelop and capture Metz from the south The Supreme Command, therefore, had to decide whether, in view of its plans for the offensive, it would take the risk of having First Army withdraw because of lack of adequate forces.

In addition, OB West also pointed out in his evaluation of the situation of 9 Oct 44, that the enemy would probably attempt to seize the Vosges mountain passes by an attack on a broad front between Luneville and Lure (northwest of Belfort). If it were possible to delay this attack, the German prospect would improve. Along the foothills of the mountains, the so-called 'Westvogesenstellung' (Western Vosges Position) was hastily being constructed in front of the main position along the ridge itself. It was to be hoped, that, with the coming of winter, the mountain sector would not be considered for an attack even by specialized troops. Thus, only the passes would constitute danger points. There were two main passes: The Saverne Gap in the north and the Belfort Pass to the south.

At the end of Sep 44, fighting was still taking place in the outpost area of the Western Vosges Position which was to enable the troops to gain time for its improvement. In mid-Oct 44, the German line had already been withdrawn into the Western Vosges Position or immediately in front of it. The Americans and French followed up, and stubborn local fighting took place for the important approaches to the passes. Nevertheless, at the end of Oct 44, the entire Western Vosges Position was still in German hands. At this time, there was no special indication that an attack on Belfort and the Belfort Pass was imminent. But, in view of the general situation, it was certain that it would come.

In view of this situation, the Commander of A Gp G, Gen Pz Balck, supported by OB West, insisted that the left wing of the Western Front receive reinforcements of men and materials. This request was constantly repeated and its urgency stressed by statements on the condition of the troops. The Supreme Command was supplied with harrowing details of the performance of the battle-weary divisions and inexperienced units, which had been brought up from the rear. But the Supreme Command limited additional transfers to the barest essentials, because it was of the opinion that the left wing could only be decisively assisted, if the initiative could be regained by the Germans at some point along the Western Front, and the enemy would thus be forced to reduce the pressure on the remaining sectors of the front.

This brings us to the end of our survey. It has shown, where critical points had already appeared on the Western Front, and where they had to be expected. It also will have demonstrated, how every single decision concerning the front, which was extending over 1000 km from the sea to the Swiss border, was connected with the plan for an offensive from the Eifel in the direction of Antwerp. This plan had meanwhile already taken shape, although it was only known to a very limited circle within the Supreme Command.

2. THE PRELIMINARY PLANS AND THE ORDER FOR THE DRAFT OF AN OFFENSIVE PLAN (END OF SEPT 44)

It is necessary to describe with a few words the situation at the Führer's headquarters in the field. As already mentioned, the Führer's headquarters had moved to East Prussia in Jul 44. It was located in a forest camp near Rastenburg and consisted of concrete shelters and wooden barracks which were surrounded by mined barbed wire entanglements. Due to the constant withdrawal of the front, the threat of air attacks grew proportionally. The concrete shelters were continually being reinforced and modern installations were being set up. Inside the camp there was a large enclosure for the *Wehrmachtführungsstab* (Wehrmacht Operations Staff), the security troops and similar units. There was a smaller enclosure for the top commanders, and inside this enclosure a very narrow space was reserved for the Führer and his constant escorts.

It was here that the attempted assassination took place on 20 Jul 44, which so nearly took not only the Führer's life but the lives of all his military advisers, since Count Stauffenberg's bomb exploded while the daily conference was in progress.

Because of the extraordinary distribution of the explosive power of the bomb, those present received injuries of widely differing degrees of severity. Apart from the four who were killed outright and those who died afterwards, there were several others, like Genfldm Keitel, who were hardly injured at all. Several persons were very seriously injured, a number of them received slight or relatively serious injuries, while with others the effects of the blast showed only after some time.

Adolf Hitler himself was among the slightly injured. He was therefore able to continue in his functions as head of the government as well as military leader. His external injuries and the damage to his ear healed normally. But, in Sep 44, a very marked deterioration in his general health set in. This was originally attributed to the after-effects of the attempt on his life. But later, the real cause proved to be Adolf Hitler's over-indulgence in a certain stomach drug. It had been prescribed by a doctor [Dr. Theo Morrell], of whom he had a very high opinion, but who was regarded by others as a mere charlatan. This treatment was stopped, but it was several months before his body had eliminated the accumulated amount of poison. Thus, Adolf Hitler was physically incapacitated from Sep 44 on. During the first weeks he was only able to get up for an hour or two at a time and could only receive very few visitors, who came to give him their verbal reports and inform him on the situation. However, there can be no question of his mental processes being affected, and there is no evidence that this critical condition of his health influenced his decisions in any way. On the contrary, the Ardennes plan was first formulated at a time when his physical condition was most affected.

Among those who had only been slightly injured was the Chief of the Wehrmacht Operations Staff, Genobst Alfred Jodl – a name which will often recur from now on. Since he showed no signs of after-effects, he was able to continue his duties in his usual intensive and harmonious manner, and to apply himself thoroughly to the detailed preparations of the offensive. Next to the Führer, he was the most important person engaged in these preparations. Although he was subordinate to Genfldm Keitel according to rank, he was the immediate adviser of Adolf Hitler on all strategic questions. The C-of-S of the Wehrmacht was fully occupied with all those questions which had been dealt with by the Secretary of War during World War I, and he did not have a decisive voice in the planning of operations.

The function of Genobst Jodl in the Führer's headquarters consisted of preparing – on the general staff level – the decisions the Führer made in his capacity of C-in-C of the Wehrmacht. Jodl also was responsible for their execution. But these were not his only duties. Whenever the Führer conceived a new military plan it was Jodl with whom the idea was discussed and closely examined. It was again Jodl who obtained the information necessary to transmute a vague idea into a workable plan. It was also he who raised objections and suggested his own alternatives to the Führer, and who trans-mitted the opinions which had been voiced by the immediately subordinate commands. These facts were so little known to the outside world, that the public scarcely knew Jodl, and that within the Wehrmacht – even among those in leading positions – he was mostly considered only as an executive tool, by some people even as too willing a tool. The view was widely held that the Führer did not accept any opinion other than his own. It was not recognized that, although Hitler in final analysis might only follow his own trend of thought, he acquired the inner assurance necessary for his actions by constantly discussing his intentions within the confines of his inner circle. For this reason, the Chief of the Wehrmacht Operations Staff was an extremely important figure in all strategic decisions.

Jodl's name immediately comes up when we try to find out, at what time – besides the plan of carrying out a flanking attack from a retrograde movement which was still predominant in Sep 44 – the new idea was conceived of first permitting the West *Heer* to consolidate a new line, to reorganize it, and then to pass on to the offensive by using this line as jump-off position. On 6 Sep 44, Genobst Jodl informed the Führer that a major offensive of this type would not be possible before 1 Nov 44. Until then an effort should be made to withdraw as many units as possible in order to reorganize them and make them ready for commitment. The Führer agreed with this evaluation. In this connection he also pointed out, that it was important to keep the front as far to the west as possible, since attacks on the Rhine bridges, made by fighter-bombers, might have serious consequences.

The first step toward the realization of this plan was made on 14 Sep 44, when an order for the organization of the staff of a new panzer army was issued. The panzer units which were to be withdrawn for reorganization, were to be subordinated to Army, which was designated 'Sixth Pz Army'. Obstgrf Sepp Dietrich, who had previously been the Commander of Fifth Pz Army, was appointed Commander of Sixth Pz Army.

It should be noted that the estimates, submitted by OB West [von Rundstedt] at this time, pointed in the same direction. In an estimate of his forces, submitted on 21 Sep 44, he declared that, in view of the present situation, he was primarily fighting for time, but, in order to eliminate the threat of invasion of German territory, a German counterattack was, of necessity, to be envisioned as final objective.

By this time it was already obvious that the orders, which had been given to OB West since the end of Aug 44, to execute flanking thrusts, could only lead to local successes designed to relieve pressure on the A Gp G front, but not to a major operational change in the situation. After one more week, the Supreme Command became resigned to the fact that this plan had to be abandoned.

The renunciation of this plan was facilitated by the fact that – in connection with Jodl's verbal report of 6 Sep 44 – the Führer had been pondering over the question of where and how an offensive could be undertaken after the reorganization had been accomplished, and that he was now able to visualize the broad outlines of an offensive.

The sequence of considerations, which went through Adolf Hitler's mind while he was lying on his sick bed in the East Prussian shelter, and the back and forth of subsequent discussions can no longer be reconstructed. But it is possible to render them by way of a systematic survey. The picture will not be distorted by the inclusion of one or the other consideration, which had not yet come up for discussion in Sep 44. The offensive, which was now being visualized, was to have a completely different strategic significance from the preceding counterthrusts. It was to implement the complete breakthrough of a position with the objective of penetrating into open ground. It was realized from the beginning that this offensive had no prospect of success unless it was carried out with the strongest forces and the largest quantity of materiel that could possibly be assembled. Therefore, such an operation could only take place at the expense of other theaters of operations which would then, of course, have proportionately smaller allocation. Did the situation on the other fronts permit of this? And above all, did a thrust in the West promise greater advantages than offensives in the other theaters of operations?

In Sep 44, the general situation was as follows:

a) The Eastern Front

The loss of Romania, which had resulted in the collapse of A Gp Süd, produced a critical situation at the southern end of this front. The German counter-measures – which included, among other things, the increased use of Hungarian forces for commitment at the front – were bringing about an improvement in the situation, which led to hopes that a front line could be held along the Carpathian salient.

After the collapse of A Gp Mitte, a new line had been built in the center of the Eastern Front, extending from Galacia along the Vistula and Narew rivers and along the eastern border of East Prussia. The dangerous Russian bridge-head across the Vistula in the vicinity of Baranow had been considerably reduced by counterattacks, but not eliminated. A Gp Nord in Kurland had been cut off by land from East Prussia but, nevertheless, the front had been stabilized here as well. This army group pinned down considerable Russian forces which could therefore not be committed on the East Prussian front, or further to the south.

The general impression was that the Russian summer offensive was now dying away. With the exception of the southern sector of the front, a relatively quiet period was to be expected until the start of a winter offensive.

b) The Northern Front
The loss of Finland did not result in any particular difficulties for the German forces in northern Finland. Twentieth *Gebirgs* Army was scarcely being disturbed by the enemy, and was now marching toward northern Norway. It was to be anticipated that a number of good divisions – particularly mountain divisions – would be released for commitment on other European fronts.

c) The Southern Front
Under the command of Genfldm Kesselring the army group employed in Italy had succeeded in rebuilding a stable front line after the withdrawal from central Italy. This line extended mainly in front of the Apennine Ridge Position, and it gave an opportunity for additional improvements in the defensive lines further to the rear. Here too, after a stabilization of the situation, a readjustment and reorganization of German forces was becoming possible.

d) The Southeastern Front
As a result of developments in Romania and the Mediterranean, the forces in the Balkans were in the process of withdrawing to Croatia in order to reestablish contact with the southern sector of the Eastern Front. This long drawn-out movement was made particularly difficult by flank attacks of Russian and Bulgarian troops – which were now being committed by the Russians against the Germans – as well as by the terrain, and by the fighting against partisans. Nevertheless, the withdrawal was being carried out according to plan, and there were no signs of any critical developments in the immediate future. Although further operations by the Russians and the Allies were to be expected on the

Dalmatian coast, it was not thought that they would be on a large scale. The danger, that sizable German elements would be cut off, was diminishing day by day. The forces, employed by the Russians themselves, remained limited in size. Those forces, which they were mobilizing in the Southwest, were of very unequal combat value. The operations, which the Allies were initiating from the Adriatic, were limited in extent.

e) The Home Front

The assassination attempt on 20 Jul 44 had exposed the danger which had been threatening the regime below the surface for a long time. The investigation which followed had not succeeded in uncovering all the threads. But whatever facts emerged were sufficient evidence to show, that in practically all military key positions, at the front as well as in the Reich, there had been officers who were prepared either to participate in the attempt or to condone the deed after it had been accomplished. In the civilian circles the net had neither been so extensive, nor so intricate. Nevertheless, this conspiracy was frightening; not because of the number of the conspirators, but because of the importance of their positions and because of the personalities involved. That so many men of such caliber should have conspired out of despair with the developments in the situation, for which they blamed the leadership – a leadership, which was now being considered a political as well as a military failure and which was also being rejected on moral grounds – should have been regarded as a writing on the wall. Its effect on Adolf Hitler was quite a different one. Instinctively, he had felt this opposition, but he had been unable to lay hands on it. After the assassination attempt, he felt relieved from something similar to a nightmare, since he was now able to put Himmler on the scent of those whom he called by the collective term of 'reactionaries', making him search all their hide-outs in order to render them innocuous. The fact that he himself had remained practically uninjured – which in itself is a physical enigma – was considered by him as divine providence and a confirmation of his mission. Therefore, the attempt on his life had in no way depressed him; on the contrary, it kindled the flame of his energies.

The attempted assassination had made less impression on the German people than one should have expected. They were not acquainted with its ramifications, and only received a belated and one-sided explanation of it. They were given the impression that it was the work of dilettantes, who had bungled their plans and who had placed the Reich in the gravest danger without any sense of responsibility. Therefore, when the government sought to parry the shock by demanding renewed and more vigorous efforts, the people responded willingly. Renewed efforts were made in order to prove the full power of resistance of both the Wehrmacht and the people by enlistments in the Volkssturm, by the employment of hundreds of thousands of civilians in the building of defense positions – particularly in the East – and by further conscriptions into the Wehrmacht.

The achievements on the Home Front were truly amazing, considering the ever growing fury of bombing attacks over the whole area of the Reich and the extreme physical and mental strain. A major part of the armament industry had succeeded in not only maintaining production rates, but in some cases – as in the production of guns, planes, and tanks – in actually increasing them. The indefatigable struggle of the armament industry against the effects of heavy bombing attacks, and above all the transfer of its most important sections to underground factories provided some hope. Particularly in the aircraft industry, the increased production of the latest, jet propelled types, which were superior to the most modern enemy planes, appeared to provide a stabilization of the situation in the air and a relief of pressure both at the front and at home.

Thus, the situation on the home front was an additional point in favor of taking the initiative by a special effort on at least one front, after having been submitted to a series of demoralizing retreats and an all-around defense with its accompaniment of gloomy fears. Taking the initiative would improve the morale of the armed forces and the home front, which was not only able, but willing to produce the necessary material conditions.

Once the fundamental question, whether there was to be an offensive, had been answered affirmatively, the next question was, where it was to be carried out.

a) The idea which seemed most obvious, was to carry out such an operation on the Russian Front. Its purpose would be to meet the danger, resulting from the collapse of almost the entire front. This collapse was threatening eastern Germany with its agricultural and industrial areas, which were of decisive importance for the continuation of the war. The Führer himself believed that carrying out such an operation on any sector of the very long front would in the most favorable circumstances only result in the destruction of 20 to 30 enemy divisions, and in strictly limited territorial gains. In relation to the size of the forces that the Russians still had at their disposal, such a success would have produced only a relatively minor change in the eastern situation and therefore a still smaller change in the general situation.

b) The Italian theater, which had lost much of its political significance, also appeared unsuitable for such an operation. Apart from the difficulties of supply caused by the Alpine valleys, the Po river, the Appenines and the very vulnerable railway net of Lombardy, the Italian climate with its long periods of fair weather appeared vulnerable to the enemy air supremacy. The assembly, and more still the commitment of forces of such strength without adequate protection from the air and without satisfactory supply facilities, seemed impossible. The Führer considered the plan of launching an attack in Italy with only five or six mountain divisions, and if possible a few good infantry and panzer divisions in support, as more promising in this theater of operations and wanted to undertake it. However, the necessary minimum of five mountain divisions as backbone of the attack was not available since these divisions were scattered on all fronts, and therefore, this intention was never realized.

c) The German forces in the North and the Southeast were in the process of being withdrawn. But even if this had not been the case, these forces would not have played any part in the current planning, as these two theaters were of less importance than the others.

d) A systematic examination of all the possibilities for an offensive, pointed therefore to the Western Front. However, it was questionable whether the conditions in the West were favorable for a large-scale offensive operation. The enemy had won the campaign in France with relatively small forces; this was due to complete air superiority, a high degree of motorization throughout the entire army, and a constant stream of weapons, munitions, POL (petroleum, oil and lubricants) and materials of every kind. By considering all these factors, one can explain how the Germans could have been forced to evacuate the whole of France and almost all of Belgium by an enemy employing only about 50 infantry and armored divisions, and about 15 armored and infantry brigades, some of which had even been without combat experience.

A change in these conditions was to be expected in the immediate future. According to an estimate of enemy forces made on 27 Sep 44, the American and British strength in France was now equivalent to 60–61 full divisions (35 infantry, three to four airborne and 14 armored divisions as well as three infantry and 13 panzer brigades). The strength of 21 A Gp was assumed to be equivalent to 27–28, that of 12 A Gp to $23\frac{1}{2}$, and that of 6 A Gp to nine full divisions About four Allied divisions were supposed to be employed on the Alpine front, but this force was considered too small for a major operation in difficult mountain country at this season of the year. All these units had been identified at the front, and therefore the German Supreme Command did not believe that the enemy had any important reserves available which could be used for surprise operations.

On the other hand, it had to be borne in mind that additional units were constantly being brought over from Great Britain. It was assumed that 14 British and nine American divisions as well as four divisions belonging to First Allied Abn Army were still in the south of England, in addition to five other divisions in the Midlands and Scotland, that is altogether 32 divisions. But, only part of these forces could be considered as reinforcements for the Western Front. In addition to bringing up reinforcements, the possibility of another landing in the rear of the German lines had to be taken into consideration. This possibility called for appropriate countermeasures on the German side.

There was an impression that the flow of forces intended for France was delayed by disembarkation difficulties, and that the same difficulties also hampered the bringing up of supplies in a way which made itself operationally felt. Since the fall of Antwerp on 4 Sep 44, it seemed probable that this situation would improve in favor of the Allies, unless Fifteenth Army succeeded in blockading the Schelde delta. (The full extent to which the Allies had been able to make themselves independent of harbor installations had not been realized at that time.)

On the other hand, no considerable addition of forces for the Western Front was to be expected from North Africa, as the bulk of the forces assembled in that area had already been transferred to Italy and Southern France, and the balance was needed for internal security purposes. About 39 additional divisions were assumed to be in the United States, five of which apparently had already been shipped overseas. Five more had to be taken into account for the month of Oct 44.

Thus, although the enemy did not have any strategic reserves at the moment, he would be in a good position to build them up in the future. From this point of view, a potential reserve of 39 divisions had to be considered for a future date.

The grouping of the enemy forces indicated a significant emphasis on the left wing (First Can, Second Br and First US Armies). The penetration area in Holland and the battle area on both sides of Aachen showed a particularly strong massing of forces. The points of main effort of the somewhat weaker right wing (Third and Seventh US Armies) were in the battle area of Nancy and on the southern Vosges front. In between, particularly in the Moselle sector from Metz to the west of Trier and along the eastern border of Luxembourg, the enemy front was occupied by relatively weak forces. On the basis of this distribution of forces, it was estimated that the enemy intentions – after reorganizing, regrouping and supplying the attacking forces – during the coming months, would be the following: a) To continue the attacks in the 21 A Gp area against the Fifteenth Army front. The frontal attack would be made by First Can Army, with a simultaneous flank attack by Second Br Army. This secondary thrust would be carried out from the penetration area Eindhoven–Nijmegen with the objective of both cleaning out the Schelde delta in order to open up the port of Antwerp, and pushing the German forces back to the area of the Rhine delta. After this operation, it was to be expected that the British forces would be shifted further east for an attack of the Venlo–Roermond sector of the German bridgehead across the Maas.

b) To resume the attacks in the First US Army area with the objective of breaking through the West Wall in the Aachen Sector in order to create favorable conditions for a large-scale offensive against the Rhine and the Ruhr area.

c) After these preparatory operations had been successfully accomplished, the bulk of the force of 21 A Gp and First US Army would be assembled in the

Aachen Sector, from Venlo to west of Cleve, in order to carry out the decisive breakthrough to the Rhine, and possibly into the Ruhr area. These forces might be reinforced by Ninth US Army which was reported to have arrived in Europe, but which had not yet been committed.

d) Third US Army would attack from the Nancy area in the general direction toward northeast, in order to push back to the West Wall the German front in this area and thereby create an immediate threat to the Saar area.

e) To reinforce the Allied right wing by inserting First Fr Army into the front, and to continue the attacks against the Vosges positions with the point of main effort in the Belfort area. The objective would be, to unhinge the Vosges position by a breakthrough into the plain of the upper Rhine.

f) After the failure of the landings near Arnhem, a renewed commitment of powerful airborne units was not to be expected for the time being. The German Supreme Command believed that elements of First Allied Abn Army would only be committed in connection with the large-scale offensive mentioned under c). It was estimated, in particular, that an airborne landing might be attempted with the objective of facilitating the crossing of the Rhine on the left wing, the area east of Goch–Cleve, and thus assist the British forces east of the Rhine to turn southward in the direction of the northern Ruhr area.

g) In the immediate future no large-scale attacks were expected on the Eifel and Moselle front. But the possibility of attacks to eliminate the German bridgehead at Metz and to form enemy bridgeheads across the Moselle had to be taken into consideration.

Since the planned offensive was to avoid encounter with the full strength of the enemy, but, on the other hand, was to upset the enemy plans, the above estimate of the situation gave some essential clues for the choice of an attack area. In determining this area, various other considerations had to be borne in mind. An examination of all the advantages and disadvantages, and of all the other factors which would influence the execution of such an offensive, resulted in the emergence of a very definite pattern for its execution. Among considerations of this type, the following are worth mentioning:

a) Considering the limited strength of the enemy forces in the West, particularly in full divisions, a successful offensive, which would shatter 20 to 30 divisions, would suddenly modify the whole situation on the Western Front in Germany's favor. Should this operation lead to the simultaneous destruction of large quantities of materials, a temporary stabilization of the situation in the West was to be expected which would enable the Germans to withdraw some of the forces in order to commit them in the threatened sectors of the Eastern Front. The complete success of such an offensive would upset the Allied operations plans for a considerable period. It was to be expected that even a partial success would delay Allied measures for at least six or eight weeks. The psychological effect of such a success was another factor which had to be taken into consideration. Regaining the initiative would not fail to make an impression on the German leadership, people and troops, not to mention the public opinion in the Allied countries as well as the effect it would have on the Allied troops.

b) However, the execution of such an offensive entailed the taking of great risks. The necessary attack units could only be obtained by weakening the front during the long period of preparation. The Western Front had to relinquish some of its panzer units during an extensive period for the purpose of their reorganization. The bulk of the newly organized *volks grenadier* divisions, which were badly needed both on the Eastern and Western Front to reinforce the battle-weary infantry divisions, would no longer be available for this purpose. Furthermore, the reorganization of the panzer forces would absorb a considerable portion of the current output of tanks thereby constituting a considerable reduction in the supply of tanks which were urgently needed, especially on the Eastern Front. Also, considerable restrictions would have to be imposed on the consumption of ammunitions and POL on all fronts. The probability that the Allies would start major operations of their own before the conclusion of the German preparations, further increased the risks.

c) Additional disadvantages for an offensive arose from the fact that the enemy had almost complete air supremacy on the Western Front. The attack could only be carried out at a time when the prevailing weather conditions would be a considerable handicap for the enemy air forces. The month of Nov 44 appeared to be the most appropriate for this purpose. But an offensive at that time of the year would of necessity entail unusual terrain difficulties, because the mobility of large tank units would be considerably reduced due to the condition of the ground.

d) Thus, certain limitations were placed upon the execution of the offensive from the first. In addition, the state of training of the troops also had to be considered in the selection of the attack area. The troops had only just been given their first breathing spell, and their losses had been equalized by replacements most of whom were both lacking experience and unsuitable due to their age. A frontal attack against an enemy area, which was being occupied by strong defensive forces organized in depth, would be doomed to failure from the very beginning in view of the limited number of suitable divisions, the lack of experience in the execution of large-scale attacks, and the non-existence of air support. The German offensive in Russia of Summer 43, which had been carried out under much more favorable conditions, constituted a warning example confirming this theory. After about two weeks of stubborn fighting through Russian defense lines organized in depth, the German attack forces were, in spite of good air support, so exhausted that a complete success had become an impossibility, and the offensive had to be discontinued. A rapid breakthrough could therefore only be obtained in a sector of the front which was occupied by only weak enemy forces.

e) Even there, a breakthrough could only succeed, if the greatest possible emphasis was laid upon secrecy and surprise. It was therefore a question of preventing the enemy from prematurely observing the concentration of troops, which would enable him to bring up last minute reinforcements to the sector selected for the breakthrough. All the disadvantages connected with this strict secrecy in the preparations had to be borne.

In the light of the above factors, the plan of an offensive in the West was conceived along the following lines: The element of surprise will be maintained; a rapid breakthrough at a weak frontal sector and a deep thrust into the enemy area of operations will be attempted and carried out in weather conditions unfavorable to air activity. Considerable risks will be taken in order to destroy strong elements of the enemy forces with the objective of stabilizing the situation in the West for some time to come.

After careful consideration of all the advantages and disadvantages involved, the Führer informed his military collaborators at the end of Sep 44 (25 Sep 44), that he had decided to make the attempt. Hitler recorded his conception of the location, execution, allocation and commitment of forces, and timing of the offensive as follows:

a) Location

He considered the sector between Monschau and Echternach to be most suitable for breaking through the enemy lines because it was so thinly occupied by enemy forces. First US Army which had been committed on this front, had – according to available information – eight infantry and three armored divisions at its disposal. Its point of main effort was in the area on both sides of Aachen. Four infantry and one armored divisions had been committed in the Monschau–Echternach sector which extended over about 100 kilometers. Here was therefore the most suitable sector for a rapid breakthrough by the German forces, because of the relative weakness of the forces holding this front. In addition, the wooded area of the Eifel, which was in the rear of the German line, would make it possible to camouflage the assembly of the German troops from enemy air observation.

After the completion of the breakthrough, the thrust was to continue in a northwestern direction across the Ardennes, and then cross the Maas between Liège and Namur. Its objective was Antwerp.

b) Execution

It was to be attempted:

(1) To force a breakthrough as rapidly as possible in order to give the German panzer units the necessary freedom of movement;

(2) To obtain, by a rapid thrust, bridgeheads across the Maas between Liège and Namur;

(3) To reach Antwerp by thrusting further to the northeast and by-passing Brussels from the east.

The success of such an offensive depended on cutting off the rear lines of communication and supply of First US Army after the crossing of the Maas. These lines were assumed to extend along the Maas valley toward Liège. As soon as the Brussels–Antwerp area had been reached, all the rear communications of 21 A Gp would also be severed. If Antwerp fell into German hands, the Allies would lose the only port which could be used to full capacity and which they had so far been able to capture. If this thrust reached its objective, the prerequisites for a battle for the annihilation of the enemy forces, which were cut off from their supply lines, would have been established. The bulk of at least 20 to 30 Allied divisions would be destroyed.

c) Allocation of Forces

The first orders of the Führer were issued by way of general instructions to the various branches of the service. A detailed discussion on the requirements of forces was to take place only after an outline of the plan of operations had actually been presented. The first, preliminary calculation by the Führer himself, showed a minimum requirement of forces amounting to 30 divisions, at least ten of which were panzer divisions. From the beginning he had decided to strip all other sectors of the Western Front of all units suitable for feeding the attack, and above all for covering the extended flanks. He was prepared to take this risk because he believed that, with the beginning of the offensive, the enemy would immediately relinquish any intended attacks of his own, and would take up the defensive on all sectors of the front in order to assemble the forces needed for commitment in the breakthrough area. An unprecedented concentration of artillery, supported by rocket artillery units such as the Russians had used so successfully on the Eastern Front, was envisaged in order to force a rapid breakthrough. Blocking units, suitable for the protection of the flanks – particularly heavy *panzerjäger* (antitank) battalions – were to be brought up to build the most effective defence by fully utilizing favourable terrain features. The Führer paid particular attention to flank protection which was to be built up immediately after the Maas had been crossed because of the decisive importance of the crossing points. It was his wish that motorized flak be brought up for this purpose. He requested that orders be given to prepare sufficient quantities of POL and ammunition as well as transportation space, and that the execution of these preparations be strictly supervised. Orders were to be issued to the Luftwaffe to ascertain maximum fighter support over the zone of operations by reequipping and reorganizing all fighter formations in the Zone of the Interior.

d) Commitment of Forces

Adolf Hitler had in mind to use two panzer armies as spearheads of the offensive. One of these was Sixth Pz Army which was to command all SS panzer divisions. The two armies were to advance abreast and force the breakthrough across the Maas in the direction of Antwerp. Two other armies – consisting mainly of infantry and blocking units – were to be responsible for the protection of the flanks, one on the northern, the other on the southern flank. By the organization of a group of reserve divisions, the Supreme Command was to be given the opportunity of intervening at certain points and of building up points of main effort according to the developments in the situation.

The basic principles guiding the leadership down to the lowest echelons were to be the following: supported by a short but powerful concentration of artillery fire, the infantry units were to break through the front by surprise and pave the way for a rapid fanning out of the panzer divisions. Taking advantage of the element of surprise and the state of general confusion the enemy presumably would be in, it should be possible to form bridgeheads across the Maas already by the second day. After bringing up the second wave of panzer units and replenishing supplies, the advance in the direction of Antwerp would be resumed on a broad front. Infantry and blocking units were to follow as rapidly as possible in order to occupy favorable defensive sectors, particularly along the northern flank, because it was to be expected that the first countermeasures in strength would come from this direction.

The prerequisite for the success of such a plan was the maintenance of the element of surprise which could only be achieved by unusually strict measures of secrecy. If these measures succeeded, the leadership and the troops were to be guided by the single principle of both thrusting deeply into the enemy zone of operations and refusing to be diverted from their original objective by counterattacks against their flanks. Only then could the offensive be completely successful. Any tendency of prematurely turning off – for example against the flank of the enemy forces around Aachen – had to be strictly opposed from the outset, because the German forces would thereby only run into the enemy strength and could never obtain a complete success.

It was not considered as particularly alarming that flanks of great length would be formed during such an operation and that extended sectors would at first have only weak protection because the covering forces could arrive only after a certain delay and would have to occupy their positions. The same tactics had already been applied in 1939 in the Polish campaign and definite proof of their soundness seemed to have been given by the successes obtained in the campaign in the West in 1940. These tactics had also been one of the main reasons for the German victories in the East and were now being applied by the Russians. The preceding months had shown that the Allies now also considered their previous tactics as antiquated, which had originated in the position warfare of World War I, and which therefore had still been considered standard procedure by the Allies in 1940. These tactics consisted of first securing the flanks each time an initial success had been obtained. Experience had shown that the uncovered flanks resulting from such thrusts were similar to those which also appeared in the front line of the enemy, who was under attack, with the difference that the attacking forces had the advantage of being able to discount their effect from the beginning of the operation. These tactics were therefore no longer subject to dispute. A debate arose only over the question of the operational stage at which the risks of insufficient cover on the flanks would become too great because of the countermeasures, which could not only be anticipated, but could even be calculated beforehand with some accuracy. This question was therefore being discussed continually right up to the beginning of the offensive.

The question of the continuation of the operation, after Antwerp had been reached, was only touched upon by the Führer. He assumed that there would be a certain time-lag before the Allies would be able to take countermeasures on a large scale. First, they would have to realize the extent of the offensive. Then, they would have to consider the question of stopping their own attacks which were under way – for example in the Aachen sector. Finally, they would have to begin withdrawing their forces and would have to transport them to the breakthrough area. The Führer anticipated that additional delays would be caused by the fact that his opponents were allies of different nations, the military and political officials of which would probably need some time to come to an understanding with reference to the countermeasures which were to be applied. Furthermore, it was assumed that, because of the imminence of the danger, the enemy units transferred to the breakthrough area would probably be thrown into the battle immediately after their arrival. The threat of immediate concentrated counterattacks could therefore be discounted. Until the time when these counterattacks would start, sufficient German reserves would have to be brought up to reinforce the threatened flanks. The Führer did not consider it very likely that the enemy would – in order to avoid the danger of encirclement – abandon the whole area east of the Maas immediately after the Germans had succeeded in crossing the river. On the contrary, he believed that the forces to the north of the breakthrough wedge would attempt to reestablish contact with northern France along the west bank of the Maas by attacking in a southwestern direction. For this reason, the right flank was to be adequately protected by mobile units, which were to seek cover behind the Albert Canal as soon as they had crossed the Maas.

Depending both on the progress of the offensive and on the relief from pressure the adjacent sectors would derive from it, the second phase of the plan called for the transfer of the units, which would become available in these sectors, and of the divisions, which were meanwhile to be withdrawn from

Norway. These troops were to be employed to hold the breakthrough area. Small-scale holding attacks were to be carried out simultaneously all along the Western Front in order to prevent the enemy from uncovering too much of the rest of the front and bringing up all units capable of attack for the purpose of a counter-thrust.

The Führer also considered the possibility of turning southward after the breakthrough had succeeded, and attacking the rear of Third US Army while the right wing took cover behind the Maas. But, such an operation would lack a second pivot – a 'counterpole' – because it seemed probable that, by the time the offensive could begin, the German forces on the upper Moselle would be pushed back still further toward the West Wall. This operation could – in the best of cases – only lead to the destruction of a part of Third US Army. The result which could be obtained in case of success was therefore out of proportion with the expenditure of forces. Furthermore, the German right flank, which would – in spite of the possibility of seeking cover behind the Maas – be in great danger because of its exposure to the attacks by the reserve forces which could be brought up from the Aachen area without interference. For this reason, the project of covering such a thrust in a southern direction was rejected by the Führer, and was not taken up at any later date. Since it was to be expected that the enemy would start a number of large-scale attacks of his own before the beginning of the German offensive, all necessary dispositions had to be taken in order to reinforce the leadership, reserves, supplies, etc of those frontal sectors which were considered to be threatened, in a way which would guarantee that the preparations for the offensive could be carried out without consideration for the simultaneous conduct of a defensive battle.

(e) Timing of the Offensive
The Führer considered that six to eight weeks would be needed for the reorganization of the panzer units, the activation of the *volks grenadier* divisions, the *volks artillerie* corps, and the *volks werfer* (rocket projector) brigades, for procuring the necessary ammunition and POL, and for the assembly of the units. This calculation would put the date between 20 and 30 Nov 44, which also appeared to be the most suitable time from the point of view of the weather which could be expected to prevail at that time. Adolf Hitler requested maximum acceleration of all preparations in order to meet this deadline as nearly as possible.

At the conclusion of this meeting, which took place at the end of Sep 44, Genfldm Keitel and Genobst Jodl were given the following orders by the Führer:

a) Genobst Jodl was to prepare the first draft of an operations plan including accurate calculations on the forces required.

b) Genobst Jodl was to prepare a survey of all additional units – such as independent panzer battalions, *artillerie* corps, *werfer* brigades, etc – in cooperation with Gen Inf Buhle, who, as C-of-S of the *Heer*, was responsible for the activation of new units.

c) In connection with the order contained in paragraph a), Genobst Jodl was to prepare a draft of an order with regard to both security measures guaranteeing the maintenance of secrecy, and camouflage measures.

d) Genfldm Keitel was to present an overall estimate of ammunition and POL requirements.

e) An order for immediate withdrawal from the front of I and II SS Pz Corps with 1, 2, 9, and 12 SS Pz Divs as well as Pz Lehr Div, was to be given to OB West. These units were to move to the region east of the Rhine for reorganization and training.

The requested drafts were to be presented at the earliest opportunity.

3. THE ELABORATION OF THE FIRST DRAFT BY THE WEHRMACHT OPERATIONS STAFF AND THE *HEERES* STAFF UNDER THE DIRECTION OF GENOBST JODL (END OF SEP–BEGINNING OF OCT 44)

The area, which was under consideration for the intended offensive, had already played a part in the operations plan of the year 1940. Under a pretext, all relevant records were therefore requisitioned from the *Heeres* archives, which had meanwhile been moved to Liognitz. It was anticipated that the records of Fourth and Sixth Armies would contain terrain descriptions, troop assembly calculations and many other details which would facilitate the selection of an attack sector and would give some detailed information on the terrain difficulties which were to be encountered. However, the records, dispatched from Liegnitz on 5 Oct 44, did not contain a great deal of information which could have been of assistance in the planning. Nevertheless, the available records avoided duplication of work and assisted in obtaining a clear picture of the peculiar features of the attack area.

The other initial question was, what forces could be set aside by the end of Nov 44. The tabulation of divisions considered for the offensive and of all additional special units, which the C-of-S of the *Heer*, Gen Inf Buhle, had been charged with, was completed by 8 Oct 44. According to this calculation the following forces were to be available after 15 Nov 44:

a) **Panzer Divisions**
Six divisions subordinated to Fifth and Sixth Pz Armies, four of which had already been withdrawn from the front for reorganization. Furthermore, six additional divisions which were still employed on the Western Front and which had to be reorganized whenever this became possible. Two of the latter were panzer grenadier divisions.

b) Infantry and Assimilated Divisions

Two infantry or *Fallschirmjäger* divisions, consisting of three regiments each; ten *volks grenadier* divisions, consisting of three regiments with two battalions; three more *volks grenadier* divisions by 20 Nov 44, three additional ones by 30 Nov 44 and four by 10 Dec 44, for a total of ten additional *volks grenadier* divisions. Altogether, 15 divisions of this type would be available by 20 Nov 44, or 22 divisions by 10 Dec 44.

c) Artillery Brigades or *Volks Artillerie* Corps of 72 guns each, and *Werfer* (Rocket Projector) Brigades, etc

Four fully motorized and six partly motorized artillery brigades, as well as four fully and three partly motorized werfer brigades, would be ready by 15 Nov 44; two additional artillery and three *werfer* brigades by 15 Dec 44. There would therefore be a total of 12 artillery and ten *werfer* brigades available. In addition, 14 *Heeres* artillery battalions were to be ready for commitment by 15 Nov 44.

d) *Panzerjäger* (antitank) and *Sturmgeschütz* (Self-propelled Assault Gun) Battalions

Thirteen battalions were available, with three additional ones by 1 Dec 44, for a total of 16 battalions.

e) Engineer Units

Four battalions, six to ten bridge columns, one bridge train battalion, and one assault boat company.

In order to make these forces available it was necessary to withdraw two *volks grenadier* divisions from Holland, one from Denmark, two from Slovakia, and five from the Zone of the Interior itself. Furthermore, one infantry division had to be withdrawn from Norway. Five of these divisions had to be replaced by newly activated units. Three additional infantry divisions and three mobile units could be obtained by their withdrawal from the front, and by turning over their sectors to the adjacent divisions or by inserting other divisions in their place. Four *Fallschirmjäger* divisions were in the process of being activated, two of which could be assigned to participate in the offensive. The three panzer divisions which were committed in the A Gp G area, were not under consideration, because it was obviously inadvisable to strip the southern wing of the Western Front of their support. However, the prerequisite for the accuracy of these calculations was that the situation on the other fronts would not necessitate any transfers from the units reserved for the offensive, and that the Western Front would not prematurely absorb the forces which were being reorganized in its rear area. As a precautionary measure, it was therefore decided to base further calculations on the premise that one third of the forces reserved for the offensive would in the meantime be pinned down elsewhere. On 9 Oct 44, a map was completed on which were marked all the offensive possibilities the Western Front could offer. Attached to the map was an annex, which dealt with each possibility separately and classified each one according to its prospects as well as its disadvantages. The purpose of this method was to determine by systematic examination whether the prospective area of operations actually was the most favorable one. The following five operations were under consideration:

a) Holland
A thrust toward Antwerp, starting from the Venlo area and proceeding in a western direction.

b) Liège–Aachen
A main thrust from the northern corner of Luxembourg at first toward the northwest, then turning to the north. A simultaneous minor thrust from the area northwest of Aachen would work in conjunction with the main thrust, to bring about the collapse of the Anglo-American offensive front.

c) Luxembourg
Two thrusts from central Luxembourg and from Metz, which would join up behind the enemy front at Longwy. This attack would aim at recapturing the Minotte area, essential to the Saar industry.

d) Lorraine
Two thrusts from Metz and out of the Baccarat area (west of the Vosges), which would join up in a pincer movement behind the enemy front at Nancy.

e) Alsace
Two thrusts from the area east of Epinal and from the Montbéliard area, which would join up in a pincer movement behind the enemy front at Vesoul.

In weighing the pros and cons, the attached estimate concluded that the operations c), d) and e) should be rejected. Operation a) was considered very tempting, but entailing considerable risks. On the other hand, operation Liège–Aachen was considered worth while and it was suggested that the records of the year 1940 be consulted in elaborating it. Thus, systematic re-examination confirmed that the area selected by the Führer actually was the most promising on the whole Western Front. Nevertheless, the plan of attack was not established along the lines suggested by this survey.

Genobst Jodl – who had been entrusted with this task – presented the first draft of the operations plan on 11 Oct 44. This plan included points which had already been determined beforehand, and others which had been settled during the last few days. Its contents were the following:

a) The Distribution of Forces (forces assumed to be available)
12 panzer and 17 to 18 infantry divisions, for a total strength of 29–30 full divisions:

Right wing: Sixth Pz Army with four SS panzer divisions as shock troops, and approximately four infantry divisions to cover the right flank up to the Maas; one additional infantry division for the same purpose beyond the Maas. Total requirements: four panzer and five infantry divisions or nine full divisions.

Center: Fifth Pz Army with four panzer divisions as shock troops, and three infantry divisions to cover the left flank, particularly beyond the Maas. Total requirements: four panzer and three infantry divisions or seven full divisions.

Left Wing: Seventh Army with six infantry divisions for the protection of the left flank of Fifth Pz Army up to the Maas, and one panzer division as potential reserve for the front which was expected to extend over a long distance. Total requirement: one panzer and six infantry divisions or seven full divisions.

Reserves at the disposal of the Supreme Command: approximately three panzer and three to four infantry divisions for a total of six to seven full divisions.

The grand total therefore amounted to 29–30 full divisions.

b) The Launching of the Attack Forces

Sixth Pz Army was to be committed to the right wing with Fifteenth Army, which was pinned down by the Anglo-American attack at Aachen–Düren, adjacent to the right. Sixth Pz Army was to be responsible for the protection of its right flank up to the crossing of the Maas, while its left wing was adjacent to Fifth Pz Army which was attacking simultaneously. Its right boundary was to extend via Schleiden–Monschau (Montjoie)–Hohes Venn–Verviers–Liège–Tongres–Hasselt–Albert Canal, its left via Prüm–Vielsalm–Huy (excluding the town).

The boundary along the sector Hohes Venn–Verviers–Liège on the right flank was to be established in such a way, that the most favorable defensive positions were included in the Army sector. The establishment of the right boundary east of the Maas was to take in all other favorable terrain features. Beyond the Maas, the boundary was to remain open on the right, while on the left it was purposely not determined, because the developments in the situation were to be decisive on this side of the sector.

Fifth Pz Army, which was to be employed in the center between Sixth Pz Army and Seventh Army, was to have Prüm–Vielsalm–Huy (see above) as right boundary, and Neuerburg–Wiltz–south of Bastogne–St Hubert–Rochefort–Namur–east of Brussels as left boundary.

Seventh Army, on the left wing, was to be employed between Fifth Pz Army and First Army which was part of A Gp G. Its right boundary was to be the same as Fifth Pz Army's left one (see above), while its left one – depending on enemy resistance, terrain conditions, and the forces available – was to reach as far to the south, south-west and west as possible, with the line Diekirch–Neufchâteau–Givet considered a minimum requirement.

As to the topographical character of the attack area, it should be noted that it was divided into approximately equal halves by the Maas. This river represented a considerable barrier because of its width and depth, as well as its steep banks. Bridging such a river in the face of the enemy had to be considered a doubtful undertaking; therefore, the available bridges were of quite particular importance – all the more so since their number was very limited. In the event the attack sector was being extended via Namur to the south, the forces crossing the river upstream would, in addition, also have to bridge the Sambre which flows into the Maas at Namur. On the other hand, the Maas could also afford considerable protection once the attack had reached its banks and the enemy began to counterattack.

The area between the front and the Maas was more or less undulated, with elevations up to more than 700 meters. In parts it had mountainous character. The area was characterized by many forests and deep incisions cut by numerous small rivers and streams. The most important of these is the Ourthe which flows into the Maas at Liège after forming an S-curve from the south, thus cutting the attack sector almost perpendicularly, and forming a serious obstacle, should the enemy succeed in holding the opposite bank. Of the remaining tributaries of the Maas, the most important was the Semois, flowing in between Givet and Charleville. This river could offer good supporting cover toward the south. The Sauer, however, which also flows in the general direction west to east, but in the opposite direction of the Semois, was an unfavorable terrain feature, because it cut diagonally through the terrain of advance of Seventh Army. The Our, a tributary of the Sauer, flows into that river at Wallendorf. Both the German–Luxembourg border and the front extended along the Our, from Dasburg at Wallendorf. After passing Wallendorf, the Sauer forms a salient jutting out toward the east. At this point, the river is forced to by-pass the hilly terrain south of Echternach, after which it flows into the Moselle at Wasserbillig. As the enemy had occupied this salient, he was at this point on the flank of the jump-off position. The Our, which had cut a deep gulley into the land, and which could only be reached by roads studded with hairpin bends, had to be crossed by both Fifth Pz Army and Seventh Army immediately after the start of the offensive. Not one of its bridges was still intact and attacking forces would be further handicapped by very sudden changes in its water level from the autumn season on. Its width can increase quite appreciably from one day to the next. The left wing of the attack sector, no matter where or how the attack was launched, would be confronted with serious natural obstacles.

On the right wing, the Hohes Venn presented a natural obstacle to an attack. It had the characteristics of a closely wooded high moor and was therefore a hindrance to any attack in general, and particularly to a panzer attack. But, on the other hand it had the advantage of requiring only weak covering forces once this sector had been taken. However, in order to occupy the Venn, it was necessary first to occupy the dominating heights as far as Elsenborn (south of Monschau). In the center, the mountain range of the Schnee-Eifel obstructed the attack. The enemy was occupying one half of this mountain range and it would be extremely difficult to dislodge him by a frontal attack.

A comparison between the respective sectors assigned to the two attack armies shows that Sixth Pz Army had to cross a shorter distance before reaching the Maas than the other army. However, Sixth Pz Army would have to contend with the problems of Elsenborn and the Hohes Venn immediately after the beginning of the attack. During this phase of the fighting, Fifth Pz Army was in a more favorable position, provided it succeeded in a smooth crossing of the Our. But its difficulties would commence in the second phase, during which Sixth Pz Army would already have the advantage of an improvement in the terrain. During this phase, Fifth Pz Army would have to cross the Ardennes which ran straight across its line of advance.

The German Supreme Command was well acquainted with the terrain, since the 1940 offensive as well as the retreat in the autumn of 1944 had crossed this territory. It was therefore aware of the difficulties, if not dangers, which the mostly narrow and winding roads constituted to an offensive, particularly if this offensive was undertaken in the winter and bad weather was to be its pre-requisite. If he was not completely taken by surprise, the enemy would be in a position to cause considerable delay in an advance by the demolition of bridges; this delay would be due to the lengthy preparations required for river-crossings at other points, should such crossings be at all possible in view of the steep river-banks. Thus, the condition of these bridges had to be continuously reconnoitered, although, in this case, the attention of the enemy might be attracted by repeated reconnaissance flights.

Although the network of asphalt roads was not heavy, a dearth of roads actually existed only in a very few places. The larger road junctions such as Marche, St Hubert, and Bastogne were of great, but not of vital importance, because they could all be by-passed, if necessary. The fact that the enemy did not expect any large-scale German operations in the Eifel section because of the nature of the terrain, was obvious from the weakness of the forces he had committed to this sector.

In summarizing the situation, it is therefore correct to say that the area selected for the attack had great strategic advantages, but that considerable difficulties were inherent in its terrain conditions. These difficulties would particularly affect the panzer forces, and might affect them in such a way – particularly during the winter – that the success of the operation might he jeopardized. It was certain, that the demands made on the troops would be unusually high.

c) The Execution of the Breakthrough

It was planned that the breakthrough would be executed by the divisions employed along the entire attack front. It was their mission to occupy all the tactically favorable positions which were of importance for the launching of further operations. For this purpose they were to form battlegroups or *Kampfgruppen* which – reinforced by self-propelled assault guns and supported by the firepower of all their guns and rocket launchers – were to rip the enemy front, and thus make way for the panzer units by clearing a passage for them. They were then to turn against the enemy forces which were still resisting and completely annihilate them by thrusts against their flanks and rear in order to finally clean up the entire defensive front.

The selection of suitable breakthrough points was to be left to the armies concerned. The same applied to the points at which Fifth Pz Army was to force the crossing of the Our. Nevertheless, a breakthrough was mandatory in some of the sectors, either because of the prevailing terrain and road conditions or because of tactical considerations. One of these sectors was the mountainous terrain near Elsenborn, the possession of which was indispensable as cover to the north and protection for the approach routes of Sixth Pz Army. As to the Schnee-Eifel, it was intended that the local enemy position be by-passed on both sides, and then be taken from the rear. Corresponding to this method of securing the northern wing of the attacking forces, it was to be attempted in the southern sector, to obtain flank support by seeking cover behind the Sauer and building up bridgeheads across the river. For this purpose the initial attack was to take place in the Diekirch area.

d) The Launching of the Panzer Units

According to this plan of attack, Sixth Pz Army was to be given the following mission: One corps with two divisions was to start the attack up front, while another corps with two divisions was to constitute the second wave; the first wave was to advance through the gaps torn by the infantry, thrust to the Maas as rapidly as possible, and occupy bridgeheads in the sector of Liège–Huy (excluding the town): after consolidating the bridgeheads, bringing up the second wave, and replenishing supplies, both corps were to be committed abreast and start the attack on Antwerp. Army was to cover its own right flank simultaneously and was to build up a defensive front for this purpose along the general line Monschau–Verviers–Liège. The corps on the left wing of Fifteenth Army was therefore to be subordinated to its command; in the event the operation proved successful, this corps should be able to press forward its left wing, which was given the mission of neutralizing the mountainous terrain of Elsenborn – the northern pivot of the line of attack. Furthermore, Sixth Pz Army also had the mission of extending its defensive front toward the west by rapidly bringing up the infantry divisions it had been assigned. They were to build a defensive line in the tactically most favorable sectors, which was all the more necessary since strong forces were available to the enemy in the Eupen–Verviers area and it could be assumed that a counterattack from this area would soon be forthcoming. It was contemplated to ease the mission of Sixth Pz Army after the crossing of the Maas by again subordinating the corps on its right wing to Fifteenth Army. Only one infantry division could be spared for the flank cover beyond the river. If stronger forces were needed, Army would have to use some of its own. Engaged in fluid fighting, Army was supposed to take advantage of the protection the Albert Canal could offer to its flank. Fifth Pz Army was to be given a corresponding mission: Again, one corps with two divisions was to stand ready for the attack up front, while another corps with two divisions was to constitute the second wave; the first wave was to advance through the gaps torn by the infantry, thrust to the Maas and form bridgeheads in the Huy–Namur sector; this was also to be followed by bringing up the second wave, replenishing supplies, and the continuation of the attack in the direction of Antwerp. In the course of this movement, Army was to form east of Brussels a defensive front facing west which was to serve as cover for both itself and Sixth Pz Army. An effort was to be made not to employ the infantry divisions assigned to Army up to this phase of the operation, and to avoid that they should be expended by being pinned down prematurely while serving as covering forces east of the river. It was essential for both panzer armies that they should not be delayed in their thrust toward the Maas. They were therefore to by-pass strongly defended villages and positions which could not be captured by their first attack. They were not to allow themselves to be delayed by any efforts to cover their flanks. This mission – as well as the defense against counterattacks which were to be expected – was to be left to the infantry divisions in their wake in order to enable the panzer armies to reach the Maas with minimum losses and maximum speed. In order to take possession of the bridges across the river before they were demolished by the enemy, each corps was to form advance detachments commanded by men who were specially qualified to lead such *coup de main* operations.

e) The Commitment of Seventh Army and the Reserves
According to this operation plan, Seventh Army was to be given the following mission: To overcome the obstacles of the Our sector, turn to the Southwest, then force the crossing of the Sauer and build up a defensive front in a general direction toward south in order to cover Fifth Pz Army. The actual course of this line was to depend on the enemy reaction encountered and on the terrain conditions. One panzer division was to be allocated to Army in the event that a critical situation should develop.

Some of the reserves were to be at the disposal of A Gp B, while others were to be subordinated to OB West. The commitment of a third portion was to be the prerogative of OKW. If possible, panzer reserve divisions were to be committed only beyond the Maas and then, depending on the developments in the situation, either with Sixth or Fifth Pz Army. Only in the event of an emergency were they to be committed defensively against enemy counter-measures, or for overcoming resistance at critical points. If the operation developed according to plan, the forces, which at first had stopped along the breakthrough front − above all the *volks artillerie* corps and *werfer* brigades − were to be brought up to reinforce the flanks at points which were threatened by the enemy.Whether it would then be possible to withdraw additional divisions from other sectors of the Western Front on which the enemy pressure had meanwhile diminished, and whether these divisions could be brought up to the breakthrough area, would depend on the course of operations.

f) The Assembly of Forces

According to the plan, the area of Rheydt (northwest of Cologne) and the area north of Trier were designated as assembly areas for the divisions constituting the first wave. Thus, these areas were to extend so much farther to the north and south of the front selected for the attack, that they would give no indication of a pending offensive. One panzer division was to be reorganized near Cologne, another one in the vicinity of Bonn. The area south of the Moselle was assigned to two additional divisions. The divisions of the second wave were to be assigned assembly areas of adequate size further to the east. The moving into assembly positions between Gemünd and Bitburg in the attack sector itself, was to take place two days before the start of the attack. This plan of assembly was the basis for suggestions referring to relieving units, which had to be under-taken before the offensive, in order to reorganize the participating units and place them in their jump-off positions in time for the offensive.

g) The Timing and Speed of the Offensive under the most Favorable Conditions

In the event that the plan outlined on paper could be entirely transposed into reality, the entire British Army Group as well as the American units fighting in the vicinity of Aachen–Düren would be cut off from the rest of the Allied forces. A situation would then develop which was somewhat similar to that of the France–British Army after the German breakthrough at Abbeville. It was calculated that, under the most favorable conditions, Antwerp − the objective of the offensive − could be reached within seven days. A sketch drawn by the Wehrmacht Operations Staff to show how the situation could have developed under favorable conditions by the end of the first day of the attack, arrived at the conclusion that the attack on the Eupen-Verviers sector and on Liège would already have started, and that two bridgeheads would have been formed between Liège and Namur. It was assumed that the enemy would already at this time have considerable forces available on the northern flank, but that, in the south, the reserves which were to be brought up would have only reached the line Charleville–Chimay.

h) The Prerequisites for the Success of the Offensive

The German Supreme Command knew that the complete realization of its plan depended on very many factors, which could only be specified in advance, but not be predicted with accuracy. It was assumed that the thrust from the Maas to Antwerp could only be carried out if at least five divisions of the strategic enemy reserves could be annihilated, because these divisions would otherwise be able to strike at the extended German forces at any point and push them back. The danger, which would threaten the German flanks to the east of the Maas, had already been taken into consideration in the allocation of forces. Only practical experience could show whether these forces were sufficient.

The most urgent problem was whether developments during the weeks preceding the offensive would alter the assumptions on which the plan had been based. The Wehrmacht Operations Staff enumerated the following pre-requisites in its original draft: A stabilization of the Western Front, with Holland remaining in German hands and continued blockade of the Wester-schelde; a situation in the East which would not absorb more forces of the Commander of the *Ersatzheer* (replacement training army) than originally scheduled; the continuation of the personnel and material reinforcement program in the West, the execution of which, however, was being hampered by damages to the lines of communication and industrial plants; a rapid destruction of the enemy on the attack front which would have to compensate for the disadvantage that the German attack could not be adequately supplied from the Zone of the Interior; and, above all, the setting-in of a bad weather period lasting ten to 14 days, which would compensate for the enemy advantage in the air.

These were the outlines of the draft of the plan of operations which the Chief of the Wehrmacht Operations Staff had elaborated on the basis of the instructions he had received at the end of Sep 44. On 11 Oct 44, Genobst Jodl presented his plan, together with the data and sketches which had been prepared, to the Führer.

4. THE FÜHRER'S OPINION ON GENOBST JODL'S DRAFT
(11 OCT 44)

Adolf Hitler was in general agreement with the suggestions of Genobst Jodl. Nevertheless, he issued additional instructions on certain details which in his opinion would be of particular importance for the offensive.

First of all, he was of the opinion that the width of the attack front from Monschau to the confluence of the Our and Sauer, a distance of approximately 60 km, was still too narrow. He pointed out, that the broader the selected attack sector, the smaller the immediate threat to the flanks of the initial break-through area would be, in particular the threat to such vital sites as the starting points of the approach tracks. Therefore, he requested an extension of the attack front to the south in order to eliminate by the first attack the enemy salient in the Sauer sector in the vicinity of Echternach–Wasserbillig. He considered this area to be seriously endangered since at this point the enemy would have an opportunity to cross the Sauer and then to delay the advance of Seventh Army by means of a thrust into its rear. Actually, Genobst Jodl was of the same opinion, but he doubted whether Seventh Army would be able to carry out this additional attack with the relatively weak infantry forces at its disposal. The Führer ordered that this question was to be re-examined at a later date by OB West.

On the question of artillery preparations, the Führer declared that the assembly and commitment of the artillery and rocket launcher units was to be carefully organized and closely supervised, in order to concentrate for once the whole tremendous firepower which was to be produced by the commitment of the *volks artillerie* corps. Both the panzer armies were to be assigned experienced senior artillery commanders, who were to coordinate all the artillery forces, flak units, and rocket launchers for the purpose of a sudden concentration. In addition, it was to be their responsibility to elaborate a precise plan of fire and commit their units accordingly. All enemy targets within effective range of the German artillery were to be put out of action by the shock of this sudden concentration in order to clear the way for the shock troops forming the spearhead of the initial attack. The artillery and rocket launchers were to receive adequate supplies of ammunition for this purpose. Furthermore, the Führer requested that special attention be given to the selection of the troops which were to take part in the initial attack. He also emphasized the importance of adequate engineering equipment – particularly mine clearing equipment – as well as the allocation of self-propelled assault guns and mortars to reduce enemy pockets of resistance.

As to the actual operation plan, Adolf Hitler expressed the following views: He attached particular importance to the rapid creation of a defensive front in the Sixth Pz Army area because he, too, was of the opinion that the first enemy reaction would be, to throw in reserves from the major area of Aachen. Because of the high caliber of the enemy divisions employed in this sector, only the best German divisions were to be committed in this area. Therefore, the Führer ordered that the two *Fallschirmjäger* divisions were under all circumstances to be employed along this sector of the defensive front. He also expressed the wish, that OB West should employ 12 Volks Gren Div, which had already distinguished itself in the defense of Aachen, in the same sector. In order to strengthen these divisions in their power of resistance against tanks, Sixth Pz Army was to be given preference in being provided with self-propelled assault guns and antitank battalions; these battalions were to be given the primary mission of blocking the few roads leading across the Hohes Venn. With regard to the commitment of the panzer corps of Sixth Pz Army, the Führer stated that under no circumstances were they to allow themselves to be diverted by or involved in fighting on their right flank, which might well develop very early in the operation. Within the Army attack sector, the approach routes were to be chosen as far to the south as possible, in order to be protected from these flank attacks. As Liège was expected to be a strongly defended junction, it was under no circumstances to be an objective for the panzer units. The Führer was of the opinion that it would be impossible to take this town with forces of the approximate strength of one panzer division without sacrificing the entire combat efficiency of the division in the house-to-house fighting which was to be expected. A covering force was to be left facing Liège, but the city was not to be attacked. Army was therefore to be instructed that its northern most approach roads were to cross the Maas west of Liège. With regard to the commitment of Army beyond the Maas, Adolf Hitler pointed out the importance of covering the right flank. He wanted that cover to be obtained by committing armored combat teams in fluid fighting behind the Albert Canal, but in such a way that the main body of the panzer divisions would thereby not be diverted from Antwerp, their objective.

The Führer made no special remarks on the commitment of Fifth Pz Army. He pointed out that this army should not rigidly remain within its boundaries in establishing bridgeheads. In the event the situation should develop more favorably farther to the south, there would be no objection against Army crossing the Maas south of Namur. Although Army would in this case also have to cross the Sambre sector, it would not have to contend with strong resistance in the area west of Namur.

The Führer had requested an extension of the Seventh Army attack sector by shifting the left wing of the attack farther to the south. If it was possible to extend the attack front as far as Wasserbillig, a corresponding attempt should be made to build up the defensive front as far to the south as possible, and – if the occasion arose – connect with the Moselle along the line: Wasserbillig–north of Luxembourg–Arlon–course of the Semois–Maas to the south of Givet. He requested that the infantry divisions committed on the defensive front of this army also be reinforced by blocking units of all types, as well as engineer, antitank, and self-propelled assault gun battalions. However, the Führer was opposed to the immediate allotment of a panzer division to Seventh Army. He wanted to concentrate all panzer units for the frontal attack alone, and not use any panzer unit for defensive purposes. But he agreed to the commitment of one panzer unit from OKW reserves after the offensive had started, in the event that the situation along the defensive front of Seventh Army rendered such a commitment indispensable.

Using general terms, Adolf Hitler again underlined the basic concepts from which the operations plan had been evolved and which have already been mentioned. The question, whether parachute units should be air dropped in order to take possession of the Maas bridges in an undamaged condition and keep them open, was answered in the negative. He did not believe that the Luftwaffe would be able to carry out such a mission with any hope of success. Furthermore, the bad weather which was a prerequisite for the success of the attack, would, of course, render the execution of an airborne operation practically impossible. Instead, an attempt was to be made to take bridges across the Maas before they had been destroyed, as had originally been planned. Speedy advance detachments of the panzer divisions were to take advantage of the element of surprise. As a result of these considerations, the Führer ordered that the Luftwaffe was to immediately send forward all heavy and light motorized antiaircraft battalions, which were available, since, under somewhat favorable weather conditions it could be anticipated that the enemy would attack the bridges with all his air power. The commitment of the antiaircraft units for ground fighting or even for the protection of targets in the rear was to be of secondary importance and take place only in case of emergency.

The Führer was in complete agreement with the suggestion that A Gp B, commanded by Genfldm Model, should be put in charge of Fifth and Sixth Pz Armies, as well as Seventh Army, and be given the mission of carrying out the Offensive. Genfldm Keitel then informed the Führer that it would be possible to assemble the necessary quantities of POL and ammunitions by the end of Nov 44, and that he would request that this matter be thoroughly discussed with the OQU (*Oberquartiermeister* – chief supply officer) of OB West.

The 25 Nov 44 was considered the earliest possible date for the start of the attack. This day would be favorable because of the phase of the moon, which at that time would be new, and in consequence the assembly movements of the German troops would have the additional protection of the absence of moonlight to cover them, above all, from night air reconnaissance. All persons initiated in the plan were to work with speed and fervor to complete their preparations for this date since it could be anticipated that the flying weather would improve in the month of December. The concealment and maintenance of secrecy were of vital importance during the preparations for the Offensive. Since its success would mainly depend on the element of surprise, every possible precaution would have to be taken to prevent the enemy from becoming suspicious before the start of the Offensive, let alone that he be given some advance information. The Führer was in agreement with the suggestion that all preparations should be carried out under a completely different 'Motto', and that even the C-in-C West himself should be subject to this concealment until the time when the Führer decided that he be initiated into the real objective.

The basic plan was to direct the assembly of units and the beginning of supply deliveries in such a manner, that the arriving reinforcements be taken for strategic reserves against a possible enemy breakthrough toward the Rhine, which might be attempted from the Aachen area. A suitable motivation would thereby be given to the arrival of these reinforcements. The Führer then approved the issuance of a corresponding order to OB West. Additional details of the concealment of the assembly phase were now being worked out. At first, all arriving units – Sixth Pz Army, *volks grenadier* divisions, *volks artillerie* corps and *werfer* brigades – were to be assembled behind the Western Front, with two points of main effort, so that they might be utilized at any critical point of the front, also for defensive purposes. Their disposition was to be the following:

a) The main body of the immediate reserves was to be assembled in the area left of the Rhine, behind the inner wings of First Fs (*Fallschirmjäger*) and Fifteenth Armies.

b) One panzer corps, with from two to three tank units from A Gp G, was to be assembled in the area Traben–Trabach–Trier–St. Wendel–Kaiserslautern. Two new *volks grenadier* divisions were also to be assigned to this group. It was to be borne in mind, however, that these were only to be prematurely committed in case of extreme emergency, in order to maintain their combat strength for the Offensive. For this reason, all units which were not employed on the front were to remain OKW reserves. They could only be committed with the approval of OKW and then only for concentrated counterattacks in extremely critical situations, after which they had to be immediately withdrawn. For the same reasons, the delivery of supplies, such as ammunitions, POL, signal and engineers equipment etc, to the sectors of the front which were in immediate danger, was also carried out in a way which guaranteed that the preparations for these defensive measures were to be elaborated only within a very restricted circle. They were given the code '*Die Wacht Am Rhein*' ('Watch on the Rhine').

5. BEGINNING OF THE EXECUTION OF THE PLAN

On 11 Oct 44, the same day on which the Führer gave his consent to the draft of the plan, it was established who within the Wehrmacht Operations Staff was to be initiated in the plan, and how it was to be elaborated in the future. The number of officers and secretaries, who were to be initiated, was restricted to a minimum, and moreover, each person was required to give an oath of secrecy in writing.

In order to provide outward concealment, an order was dispatched, on 12 Oct 44, over the signature of the Chief of OKW; it was the order which had already been agreed upon during the discussions with the Führer. Keitel informed the Command Authorities on the Western Front, that it was not possible to stage a German offensive at this time, and thereby thwart the rumors of an early victory which the enemy was spreading among his troops. It was therefore all the more important that the reserves should be assembled in a way which guaranteed complete success for the imminent defensive battle. The current expenditures of the front were to be compensated by makeshift measures. Beyond that, the strategic reserves which were becoming available for commitment within the near future, were to be assembled behind the northern sector of the Western Front and were to be considered as OKW reserves. The order contained the necessary directives, which were to regulate the movements behind the front, the simultaneous withdrawal of units, which were to be reorganized, and the building up of supplies. The true significance of this order which was confined to general terms, and of the fragmentary orders subsequently issued by OKW, which pertained to the regrouping, reorganization and building up of forces in the A Gp B area, was concealed from all agencies.

During the following days, Genobst Jodl elaborated suggestions for the assembly of the reserves and submitted them to the Führer for his approval. The basic plan for the distribution of the divisions was the following:

a) Their disposition had to be arranged in a way that would correspond to the objective OKW was pretending the reserves were to be used for, namely a counterattack against an enemy breakthrough at Aachen.

b) During the long period of preparation, the reserves had to be distributed in a way which would make them immediately available in case of an extreme emergency on one of the frontal sectors.

c) On no account was the enemy to draw the conclusion from the disposition of the reserves that an offensive might be contemplated.

A linear disposition of the divisions behind the entire A Gp B front corresponded best to the three above mentioned points. The plan of concentration, therefore, envisaged that the divisions of the first wave would be assembled in the Rheydt area up to the north of Trier, while one panzer division would be concentrated in the vicinity of Cologne and another near Bonn, with two additional ones south of the Moselle. The divisions forming the second wave were to be assembled farther to the rear. This disposition was to be carried out according to an exact relief plan devised by OKW, and the concentration in the assembly areas behind the attack front was finally to take place two days before the beginning of the attack. This plan provided – especially for the panzer units – the exact march routes, objectives and billeting areas, in order to make certain that the concentration of the panzer divisions would be delayed until the last moment, but that the divisions would still arrive on time in the assembly area. This order was issued on 21 Oct 44, after its approval by the Führer.

A special section is devoted to the details of the plan of distribution. However, two measures should be mentioned already in this part which had an important bearing on the future strategic decisions. In view of the fact that 25 Nov 44 was envisaged as dead-line for the start of the Offensive, the *Heeres*

General Staff, which was in charge of the replacement training army, was informed on 25 Oct 44, that 12 *volks grenadier* divisions, which were to take part in the Offensive, were to be assembled in the West by 20 Nov 44. For the time being, five *volks grenadier* divisions were being held in reserve for the Eastern Front, but their number was further reduced later on.

The other measure pertained to the chain of command. The newly activated Sixth Pz Army had been transferred to Westphalia for reorganization. The staff of Fifth Pz Army, which was to occupy the attack sector to the left of the Sixth, was withdrawn from A Gp G on 15 Oct 44, and committed in the Aachen area between Seventh Army and First Pz Army on 22 Oct 44.

This change necessitated a reorganization of the army groups. In order to relieve A Gp B, which up till then had had control over the front from the mouth of the Schelde to Trier, and to enable Army Group to concentrate on the attack which it was to lead, the sector of the front which extended from the sea up to Roermond, west of München-Gladbach, was removed from its command. A new army group – A Gp H – was activated under the command of Genobst Student, and Fifteenth Army in Holland, First Fs Army along the German section of the lower Rhine, as well as the WB NDL (*Wehrmachtbefehlshaber Niederlande* – District Commander Netherlands) were to be subordinated to A Gp H. Thus, A Gp B only retained command over Fifth Pz Army, in the sector München-Gladbach–Düren, and Seventh Army, in the sector Düren–Trier. It was attempted to conceal these changes by camouflage designations and other measures.

The assumption of command by the new army group took place on 10 Nov 44. Supply preparations were made simultaneously with the strategic ones. It was estimated that about 17,000 cubic meters (4.49 million gallons) of gasoline and 50 ammunition trains would be required, and it was established that supplies of gasoline could be built up by the end of Nov 44. Thus, from the point of view of supplies it also seemed possible to meet the deadline for the start of the Offensive, which had been set for 25 Nov 44. In addition, the amount of information which was to be given one of these days to the OQu of OB West, was determined on 21 Oct 44. The draft of an order regarding the concealment of the plan – the order was to be given to OB West after his initiation – had already been prepared by 12 Oct 44.

Thus, the preparations of the Supreme Command had reached a stage, which allowed for the initiation of the immediately subordinate command staffs, which were to participate in the execution of the plan.

6. THE PREPARATIONS FOR OPERATION 'GREIF' BY OSTBF SKORZENY

A special operation, which was being prepared by itself, was given the code name 'Greif'. From the time of the earliest discussions, the question, as to whether it would be feasible to seize the bridges over the Maas while they were still intact, had been considered of vital importance. The Führer himself pondered over all imaginable solutions of this problem. As already mentioned, he had refused to commit airborne troops because he was convinced that their employment would not be successful [no doubt mindful of the problems his enemy had faced with a similar mission the month before at Arnhem]. Finally, he thought of calling upon Ostbf Skorzeny, who had proved himself to be the man for unusual, dare-devil operations by carrying out the adventurous abduction of Benito Mussolini from the Gran Sasso d'Italia. It was believed that Skorzeny would be capable of rushing far ahead of the regular troops and seizing one or more bridges with some picked men of his unit before the enemy had taken any countermeasures. On 22 Oct 44, the Führer, in person, acquainted him with his mission. Since it had been established during attacks in the East, that Russian soldiers had dressed up in German uniforms, and since – according to reports received – the same thing had also happened in the Aachen area, Skorzeny received simultaneous orders to activate a special commando unit and to equip its men with captured uniforms, weapons, and vehicles. All details were left to his own judgement and the *Heer* was to participate in the operation only insofar as to comply with Skorzeny's requests. He planned the activation of a panzer company, three panzer reconnaissance companies, two motorized infantry battalions as well as flak, antitank, artillery, and signal platoons; he visualized an overall strength of about 2,700 men. Skorzeny first tried to obtain volunteers, but since this medium proved insufficient, the *Ersatzheer* was called upon to provide additional men, some of whom, however, turned out to be unsuitable. The training of the others could not be carried out in the manner called for by the purpose of the operations, since the procurement of the equipment took more time than had been estimated. The available forces were organized to form 150 Pz Brig and the *Sonderkommandos* (special commando units), which were trained for three different types of missions, such as:

a) *Sprengkommandos* (demolition squads), formed by five or six men, with the mission of blowing up bridges, POL and ammunition dumps.

b) *Aufklärungskommandos* (reconnaissance patrols) of three to four men, if possible equipped with radio sets; their mission was to uncover the enemy movements and measures on both sides of the Maas, and simultaneously mislead the enemy by transmitting false orders, by changing traffic signs, by removing warning notices from mine fields, and by simulating mine fields with white tape markers.

c) *Führungskommandos* (signal detachments), which were to get into the enemy radio and telephone communications net, and by this method issue false orders to the enemy.

After the capture of the Hohes Venn, which, according to schedule, was to come off already on the first day of the Offensive, Skorzeny planned to bring up during the following night his so-called panzer brigade, which in reality had no claim to this designation because of its low strength and deficient organization. The brigade was to pass through gaps in the front, and then start its attack in three columns advancing on parallel lines toward the three Maas bridges at Amay, Huy, and Andenne. The prerequisite for the success of this operation was, that the movement of the columns be carried out without any fighting, so that the enemy would not be aware of their existence. In order to conceal the brigade, it was not brought up to the Münstereifel area until the night of 14 Dec 44; its panzers were hidden deep in the woods, in order to prevent even the German troops from noticing anything. For the same reason, all orientation in the terrain had to be dispensed with.

As to the actual mission, Skorzeny only initiated his closest collaborators. His men were told that their mission was to create confusion in the enemy ranks in case the enemy succeeded in breaking through near Aachen and was advancing toward the Rhine. Since the existence of this unit could – despite all efforts – not be kept a secret, and since all kinds of rumors about Skorzeny's mission were spreading, it was decided to deliberately encourage and even multiply the rumors. This is how it was rumored that he was to take Antwerp by a *coup de main* or even rescue the German troops in the Dunkirk pocket. This may also have been the origin of the rumor that Skorzeny's men were supposed to capture General Eisenhower, since in such times of tension even the most fantastic stories will be only too readily believed. The staffs and troops of the attacking forces were informed of the operation only on the day preceding the start of the attack. That the Offensive could not be won by underhand tricks and that the brunt would still have to be borne by the attack units themselves, seemed to be obvious to everyone. The skeptics proved to be right: since the gap torn into the front at the prescribed point was not sufficiently wide to let Skorzeny's panzers slip through unobserved, the surprise raids on the bridges had to be abandoned. Thus, only the special commando units saw any action, but even these not to the extent Skorzeny had anticipated. It was only in one single instance that an enemy unit was misled by false orders. As to the information obtained by Skorzeny's men, it can be said that some details proved to be valuable, but that it contained no fundamental observations. On the whole, the operation therefore came to an end just after it had really begun.

II. The Operations Plan after the Initiation of OB West, A Gp B and Army Commanders (end of Oct 44–mid Nov 44)

1. THE INITIATION

On 28 Oct 44, that is one month after the conception of the plan, the preparations for the Offensive entered their fourth phase. On this day OB West and A Gp B were initiated into the plan, which until then had been concealed also from them. They were to take part in the future preparations. For this purpose, the two Chiefs of Staff, Gen Kav Westphal and Gen Inf Krebe, were requested to report to the Führer's headquarters, and the Führer personally initiated them into the plan for the Offensive. During the discussions he emphasized, that the primary objective of the Offensive was the destruction of enemy forces and not the acquisition of territory. The thrust toward Antwerp seemed the best method to attain this objective because it would cut off not only the Americans in the Aachen area, but also the British who were deployed along the Dutch front. Genobst Jodl was in charge of the detailed discussions.

Both the generals were in favor of the Offensive; it was not up to them to venture any opinion, whether and how it was actually to be put into effect, but they were both agreed, that the date which had been suggested for the start of the Offensive – 25 Nov 44 – seemed too early to them. The plan for the Offensive was put in writing and sent to OB West and A Gp B with a covering letter from Genobst Jodl, dated 1 Nov 44.

According to this communication, the basic plan, which was left unchanged from the first draft, called for the destruction of the enemy forces north of the line Antwerp–Brussels–Bastogne by an attack in which Fifth and Sixth Pz Armies as well as Seventh Army were to be led by A Gp B. Their missions corresponded to those which had already been outlined in the first draft, but now they had been elaborated in greater detail:

a) Sixth Pz Army was to consider the Maas crossings on both sides of Liège. During the next stage, Army was to reach the Albert Canal between Maastricht and Antwerp, and finally the area north of Antwerp.

b) Fifth Pz Army was to cross the Maas between Amay and Namur, and hold the line Antwerp–Brussels–Namur–Dinant in order to prevent enemy reserves advancing from the west from penetrating into the rear area of Sixth Pz Army.

c) Seventh Army was to provide flank protection to the south and southwest. Its first objective was to reach the Maas and the Semois, and to succeed in linking up with the Moselle front in the area east of Luxembourg. It was to gain time by demolitions and build up a solid defensive front farther to the rear. For this purpose, Army was to receive numerous *pionier* (engineer) units for the construction of obstacles and was to be amply equipped with explosives, pak (antitank guns), and close-combat weapons against panzers (this part of the plan was at variance with the draft, but corresponded to the ideas of the Führer who wanted to extend the front toward the south; however, no definite line for the defensive front had been predetermined).

Thus, the attack area had been widened both to the north and to the south. The first draft had been enlarged by the project of carrying out a secondary attack, which would advance from the opposite direction toward the main attack. A Gp H, which, at this time, was still in command of the sector from the

Maas salient near Roermond up to the vicinity of Geilenkirchen, was to carry out the secondary thrust as soon as the enemy began to throw stronger forces against the switch position which Sixth Pz Army was to build up on its flank. This potential threat to its flank was to be expected by Army as soon as it passed through the area between Roer and Maas, and later on along the Albert Canal. Two possibilities were under consideration for this secondary thrust: either it could be carried out east of the Juliana Canal to the south, or from the Venlo bridgehead – which was subsequently taken by the enemy – to the south or southwest.

Genobst Jodl stated in the covering letter, that OB West would have to consider the following points of the plan as unalterable: the far-reaching objective, the general distribution of forces, and the width of the attack sector which had been decided upon to prevent the enemy from concentrating all his countermeasures on a narrow front. Choosing Antwerp as the objective was risky, he explained, and, considered from a purely technical point of view, it would seem in disproportion with the available forces. Nevertheless, the German Supreme Command was determined to stake everything on one card.

With regard to the commitment of the divisions, OB West was to act upon his own authority, with the exception of the *fallschirm* divisions and 12 Volks Gren Div, which – according to the Führer's request – were to be employed as flank protection of Sixth Pz Army between Roer and Maas. OB West was to decide upon the distribution of the other divisions, the artillery as well as the *Heeres* troops, and he was to select the points for the breakthrough. The question, whether the left boundary of the attack sector could be shifted further to the south, was deliberately left undecided. The distribution of the American divisions permitting, the Führer was in favor of including the Echternach–Wasserbillig sector, west of Trier, and of integrating the city of Luxembourg into the defensive front which was to be built up in that area.

A map attached to these documents explained the distribution of forces which was being visualized for the event of a successful outcome of the Offensive: the north and northwest flanks of the wedge pointing toward Antwerp were to be defended by making use of the Albert Canal and the Maas. The four SS panzer divisions and one infantry division, along with 12 Volks Gren Div, 3 and 6 Fs Divs and 89 Inf Div were to be committed in this sector, while Fifth Pz Army with four mobile and three infantry divisions was to hold the western and southwestern front, and Seventh Army with one panzer and six infantry divisions the southern front. Thus, the same 23 divisions were assigned to the three attacking armies which had already been considered in the first draft.

OB West now also received the order, which had already been prepared in advance, and which pertained to the maintenance of strictest secrecy and contained directives for its observance. It was not deemed advisable to immediately issue to OB West and A Gp B a comprehensive order covering the whole Offensive, in order to give them first an opportunity to express their opinion and submit the result of the deliberations of their staffs. Genfldm Model was to first present his comments and ideas to OB West, after which the latter was to give his opinion. As to the lower echelons, only the Commanding Officers of the three armies were to be initiated for the time being.

2. OB WEST, A GP G AND THE THREE ARMY COMMANDERS: THEIR CHARACTERISTICS AND THEIR COMMENTS ON THE OPERATIONS PLAN

By the initiation of the immediately subordinate commands, two military leaders were introduced to the plan, both of whom enjoyed the highest esteem within the German *Heer*, but who were as different from one another as is humanly possible. The C-in-C West, Genfldm von Rundstedt, had been appointed to this position in 1942, after distinguishing himself as an army group commander first in Poland, then in the West, and finally also in the East. He was looked upon as one of the most brilliant strategists in the *Heer*, and, according to some evaluations, he was rated superior to Genfldms von Manstein and von Kluge. However that may be, he was in any case the personification of that tradition which the German General Staff had inherited from Moltke and Schlieffen. Its significance – apart from inborn gifts which can never really be replaced by education and training – was methodical cultivation of the power of thinking and, by that means, a special faculty of seeing and judging which maintains a distinct ratio between imagination and sobriety. The general trend toward the development of a specialized type of 'working-bee', which had also made its inroads upon the German General Staff, and which had led to the type of general staff officer, who was telephoning from early morning to past midnight, who was up to his neck in calculations, and who was dictating letter after letter, was not personified by Genfldm von Rundstedt. On the contrary, he was the symbolization of the 'Great General', just like his famous predecessors: he left all detail work to his collaborators, and reserved his mental faculties for momentous decisions and for the missions ahead of him. Thus, he commanded by ruling, and thanks to his experience and his judgment, the machine ran smoothly, even though he did not try to crank each wheel himself and did not supervise its revolutions. His experience served as a substitute for the close relationship with the troops, which other army group commanders maintained by continual trips to the front, while the C-in-C West only paid an occasional visit to the coast. Von Rundstedt unquestionably was the dominating personality among his staff, venerated above all as a nobleman of the old school. He was a junker in the best sense of this word, although – as the son of an officer – he had already lost touch with the family. The distinction of his bearing, which never failed to impress those who came in contact with him, was more than an outer mask, it was the reflection of his inner life. The universal esteem enjoyed by von Rundstedt was based at least as much upon the confidence inspired by his upright and sincere personality, as upon his superior military qualifications. He never made any secret of his opinions, and it was common knowledge that he was accustomed to expressing himself very freely – both within an intimate and a wider circle – on the subject of the political and military leadership. However, this did not preclude him from executing orders with precision – whenever his counter-propositions had been unsuccessful. He was too much of a soldier to act differently: for the same reason for which he would not have tolerated any opposition to his command authority, he also did not consider it to be his own right to oppose orders from his superiors. It was only when a rapid decision was needed, but could not be obtained, that he took upon himself the responsibility for independent action. In such cases, he would fully defend the measures taken by him against any criticism from his ranking command.

Von Rundstedt had no definite interests besides his profession; however, he had a keen sense of humor and enjoyed company. There had been critical moments in his relationship with the Führer, and his transfer to the Western Front signified a partial loss of favor. But his ability and his personality were so outstanding, that the Führer, despite the fundamental differences which existed between these two men, did not want to dispense with his services, and the threat of invasion in the West had automatically made him once more one of the decisive figures. At this time it became evident that von Rundstedt, who by now had reached the age of 69, had meanwhile grown older, and that he no longer radiated the vitality which, in view of the imminent threat, ought to have emanated from the C-in-C West. He had become quite reconciled to the fact that Genfldm Rommel, in his capacity of Commander of A Gp B, had increasingly taken over the preparations for the coastal defense. After the Normandy landings had taken place, it was felt that a man of equal ability but of greater vigor was required for the position of OB West. For this reason Genfldm von Rundstedt was – in July 44 – replaced by Genfldm von Kluge. Nevertheless, he was reinstated in his old position by 1 Sep 44, because von Kluge's successor, Genfldm Model, was to be relieved of the duty of improving the West Wall.

Gen Kav Westphal was assigned as C-of-S of OB West; Westphal had occupied the same position in Italy under Genfldm Kesselring, but had been transferred owing to an illness from which, however, he had in the meantime fully recovered, thus being available for duty. By this choice the deficiencies of Genfldm von Rundstedt, which were due to his age, were to be compensated by his assistant. The new Chief of Staff, who had reached the rank of general at an unusually early age, distinguished himself by his vigor, clear vision, and energy. After this reshuffle, Genfldm Model was able to concentrate on the command functions of A Gp B, a task which now required all his energy.

A comparison of Genfldm Model – who from now on was to be of even greater importance for the plan of the Offensive than the C-in-C West – with Genfldm von Rundstedt would show few similarities. To begin with, they widely differed with regard to origin and age. Model, the son of a Silesian school teacher, was in his early fifties and was physically extremely vigorous. He was never tired and always on the move, in order to obtain on-the-spot information and to personally intervene everywhere. At the same time, he was completely indifferent to danger. By his extraordinary devotion he had succeeded in preventing, first the collapse of A Gp Nord, then that of A Gp Mitte on the Eastern Front. This had won him the unlimited confidence of the Führer, and had led to his appointment as Commander of the West *Heer*, when the same developments were threatening on the Western Front. And for the third time something happened which even the optimists had only dared to hope for: the West *Heer*, also, made a stand. It is difficult to say, how much of this success was to be attributed to the new commander, and how much was due to other factors. In any event the front was holding, and Model was the man in command.

It can be understood that such results could not be obtained by the patrician mannerisms of Genfldm von Rundstedt, but only by vigorous actions. Many stories were circulating, how Genfldm Model had intervened down to company level, and how he had put the intermediate and lower commands 'on the ball'. But actions which might be considered brusque or even brutal by some people, were in reality dictated by the feeling of heavy responsibility which compelled Model to set an even higher standard for himself. Furthermore, his inner conviction told him that, by demanding the impossible, he could inspire his subordinates to extreme efforts which were needed to avert the impending fate. Even in the heart of this strong-willed man, who had always considered will power and faith as important factors in his estimates, the faith in still being able to force a change for the better, had now begun to waver.

Model combined this unusual energy with practical wisdom and penetrating logic. While he could not compare with Genfldm von Rundstedt as a strategist – his boundless energy showed a tendency degenerating into stubbornness – he was still far more than merely a good tactician. Above all, he had brilliant ideas even in the most critical situations. Genfldm Model constantly kept his staff on the move, since he was a very fast worker himself and had no consideration for others. He was interested only in military matters, and did not radiate kindness or warmth. But the respect for his ability, energy, and courage was widely acknowledged. This was also true with the lower echelons, because he maintained close contact with them, fulfilled their wishes whenever he could, and always took care that clear-cut decisions be taken. Genfldm Model, also, was a product of the General Staff School. But he was the representative of a type which had emerged only during World War II. Despite the extreme demands which Genfldm Model made, Gen Inf Krebs, who had at one time been attached to the embassy in Moscow, had been his chief of staff and collaborator for the past two years. This was not only a proof of his ability but also of his adaptability. Since Krebs had always held general staff assignments, he lacked the contact with the troops which his superior possessed. Taking charge of a command of his own would probably not have been his forte; but as assistant to a strong personality, who delegated all administrative details to somebody else, he could perhaps best develop his abilities. Sanguine by nature, he was inclined to make optimistic evaluations of the situation, which did not fail to influence the leadership of Army Group. While Model made such high, even unrealizable demands, in order to confer upon his subordinates some of his own energy, and thereby obtain more from them, his chief of staff turned out to be of no help in upholding his principle, the application of which – though dangerous – had become practically unavoidable after five years of war.

Besides these four men, who differed so widely from one another, the three Army Commanders were also participating in the further preparations; there again, deep contrasts were to be found among the three, and also by their comparison with those already mentioned. The Commander of Sixth Panzer Army, Obstgrf Sepp Dietrich, was in a category by himself. He had risen step by step from the rank of Technical Sergeant in times of inner-political upheavals, due to the political developments and his personal audacity, and he enjoyed popularity with the general public, who scarcely knew anything about the other army commanders. This popularity was based upon his rise from the bottom, his relations to the leading personalities, and his unrestrained joviality. He had had a good opportunity to develop his abilities in the lower command echelons. However, already as a division commander, he had to rely heavily upon the assistance of others, although nobody could deny his cunning. Nevertheless, his rise continued, since he was a favorite with the Führer, and because the SS were anxious to place their own men in the limelight. But, Sepp Dietrich was sensible enough to realize that by now more was being expected from him than he was capable of doing. For this reason, he relied completely upon his chief of staff in matters pertaining to higher command functions. In order to compensate his obvious deficiencies, he was assigned one of the best qualified general staff officers, Brigf Krämer. But, this assignment did not do away with his deficiencies. In addition, although 'Sepp', who continued to enjoy noisy parties with plenty of drinks, could count on the devotion of his companions, he had meanwhile lost his enthusiasm for self-sacrifice. Now, he first considered himself and his family. He was therefore also no longer capable of inspiring his divisions with the enthusiasm which had formerly emanated from him.

Sepp Dietrich was quite popular with the other generals, although they were fully aware of his weaknesses. They liked his bluntness, his comrade-like ways, and his straightforwardness, and they knew that he occasionally – and at the right time – put in a good word with someone at the top. A greater contrast than the one between the Commanders of Sixth Pz Army and Seventh Army could hardly be imagined. The only similarity between Sepp Dietrich and Gen Art Brandenberger was their Bavarian origin, but its effect on Brandenberger was quite different. There was no trace of Bavarian joviality in his make-up. On the contrary, he was the typical general staff officer, thoroughly trained and used to obeying orders; his features were somewhat similar to a scientist's, and he corresponded to the type of the 'working-bee', mentioned in the preceding pages. His method of leadership was in a certain way a confirmation of the judgment frequently uttered by the general staff officers hailing from northern Germany, who asserted that their Bavarian comrades were inclined to get lost in details, and were liable of failing to see the wood for the trees, because they were too deeply engrossed in their work. But, this judgment can, in the case of Gen Art Brandenberger, only be applied in a qualified sense. He maintained continuous contact with the troops, had a good understanding of their worries and plight, and was recognized for his personal courage. His staff held him in high esteem as a man; on the other hand, he was no spellbinder since he was unable to rid himself of his inhibitions. He knew his job of military leader inside out; he made deliberate decisions, and critical situations never surprised him because he was used to carefully considering all unfavorable possibilities in advance. Gen Art Brandenberger indubitably was fully capable of commanding an army; but it is equally unquestionable, that it was a mistake to place him directly under Genfldm Model. Their way of thinking showed such fundamental differences, that they talked over one another's head. This chasm was already evident during the preparations for the Offensive. After its start, it widened so much, that Genfldm Model finally obtained the transfer of Gen Art Brandenberger.

Thus, the request, which Adolf Hitler had made on 11 Oct 44, that the most suitable leaders were to be employed for the planned offensive, had not been complied with in two decisive positions. In the case of Sepp Dietrich, political reasons had led to entrusting him with the command of one of the attack armies in spite of his military deficiencies. As to Gen Art Brandenberger, the *Heeres* personnel office has to be blamed for its lack of vision, since it could have foreseen that he would not be able to collaborate with Genfldm Model, and he should therefore have been employed on some other front.

For this reason, only the Commander of Fifth Pz Army played an important part in the preparations for the Offensive.

Gen Pz von Manteuffel, who was slightly younger than the other two Army Leaders – he had not reach reached the fifties – had received his training in the cavalry. Manteuffel was the personified proof of an old saying that, whenever the cavalry produces a qualified leader, he always possesses many qualities which the training in this branch promotes particularly, such as for example a mind averse to petty details, a quick grasp of any situation, and an ability to make rapid decisions. Furthermore, he also proved that one might become a good tactician and an expert writer without passing through the General Staff School. He, too, spent much of his time with the troops (during the Ardennes Offensive his staff car was shot to pieces three times in succession). His manner of first listening quietly to everything and then stating clearly and definitely, how it was to be done, ensured him of the strong effect of his decisions. In addition, he was a leader by birth, being the descendant of a family of long-standing soldierly traditions, and this natural gift found its expression in the manners of a gentleman. His bearing was particularly taut, a fact which can often be observed with persons below average height. During his youth he had taken part in horse races, and was to remain a devoted equestrian. But as a general, he fully believed in armored weapons. The great successes, which he had obtained as commander of an armored division in the East, had been the reason for his rapid promotion to the position of army commander. One might say that Gen Pz von Manteuffel, also, differed greatly from Genfldm Model. But Model respected him as a man and as a soldier, and they therefore collaborated well.

What were these seven men's comments on the directives for the attack, which had been given to the chiefs of staff in the Führer's headquarters, and then – on 1 Nov 44 – had been sent to OB West?

As a result of the general situation and the peculiarities of the personalities involved, it was obvious, that Genfldm Model would have the main say, and that he in turn would rely most upon Gen Pz von Manteuffel's opinion. Besides, the contribution of the C-in-C West was not to be underestimated, but since Genfldm Model was to lead the attack, Genfldm von Rundstedt left it to him to make alternative proposals. Whenever he agreed with Model's suggestions, he lent them the weight of his authority in order to obtain their approval in the Führer's headquarters.

The first step taken by OB West was to arrange for a conference on 2 Nov 44, in the A Gp B headquarters, east of Krefeld. The following persons took part in this conference: the C-of-S, OB West, Gen Kav Westphal, Genfldm Model and his C-of-S, Gen Inf Krebs, the Army Commanders, and the Commander of Fifteenth Army, Gen Inf von Zangen, whose army was in charge of the Maas sector, and who had to be initiated because of the secondary thrust which was being planned in the bend of the Maas. During their detailed discussion, the main questions under consideration were the strength of the available forces and the objectives which could be attained with those forces. Model and von Manteuffel were of the opinion that the objective (Antwerp) was out of proportion with the forces which were to be made available. To the question of the C-in-C West – who shared their opinion – whether Gen Pz von Manteuffel considered it feasible to reach the Maas, von Manteuffel replied that he believed his army would be able to reach it, provided certain prerequisites would be fulfilled.

On 3 Nov 44, Genfldm Model, Gen Pz von Manteuffel and Gen Inf Krebs met for another discussion of the plan for the Offensive. The outcome of their conversations was the following:

a) Considering the limited strength of the available forces, it would be better not to thrust forward beyond the Maas, but rather to fan out to the northwest and north with both panzer armies, after they had succeeded in breaking through and reaching open terrain. They were to pivot to the right in such a manner that the left wing of Fifth Pz Army would be covered by the Maas. This main thrust, which was to be covered by Seventh Army to the south, was to be supported by a secondary thrust by Fifteenth Army from the Sittard area. The two limbs of the pincers would meet in the vicinity of Tongres, northwest of Liège, and form a pocket in which the British and American troops – about twenty to twenty-five divisions – fighting between Sittard and Monschau, would be trapped. In case of success, the Maas could then be used as a covering line, affording both security and economy of manpower. The question of what was to happen once it had been reached, was to be left open until later. If the situation continued to develop favorably, the planned attack on Antwerp could still be carried out.

b) If the plan of the Führer was to be enforced, it was suggested that Fifteenth Army not be committed. Instead, the forces, which were to be allocated to Army, were to be distributed among Fifth and Sixth Pz Armies in order to reinforce their thrusts.

c) It was considered of vital importance that the reinforcements of personnel and equipment, which were to be provided for the operation, would not be reduced. Above all, this was to apply to both Fifth Pz and Seventh Armies.

Numerous requests and suggestions were expressed by Army Group in conjunction with the Armies as a result of this and subsequent discussions. Of these, the following should be mentioned:

(1) The allocated stocks of POL and ammunition would have to be supplied to the troops already before the start of the Offensive.

(2) The panzer divisions and *volks artillerie* corps, in the Aachen area would have to be reorganized and reinforced in view of the threat of an enemy breakthrough in that area.

(3) The mission of the Luftwaffe would consist not only of fighting the enemy air forces, but also of supporting the ground forces by reconnaissance and by combat against ground targets.

(4) In order to enable the engineer troops – there was a general shortage of

troops in this branch – to carry out their proper mission, forces of the *Organization Todt* (labor battalions) would have to be employed.

(5) The repairs of equipment and the reorganization of the motorised forces would have to be vigorously pushed; the same applied to the signal units.

3. THE 'LITTLE' AND 'GRAND' PLAN: THE POSITION TAKEN BY OB WEST (3 NOV 44) AND ITS INTERPRETATION BY THE FÜHRER

The suggestions made by both Genfldm Model and Gen Pz von Manteuffel were not merely modifications of the original plan transmitted by the Wehrmacht Operations Staff, but, with all their apparent similarity, they actually provided for a second solution to the problem of annihilating the greatest possible number of enemy divisions by an offensive from the Eifel area. It was being asserted, that this solution was more appropriate considering the forces available, and for this reason offered more chances of success than aiming at Antwerp, a far too distant objective. It was obvious to those who participated in the preparations of the plan that the alternative propositions were more than a mere variation of the first plan. Thus, they immediately adopted the expression '*kleine Lösung*' (little plan) for the new suggestions, and correspondingly used the expression '*Grosse Lösung*' (grand plan) for the plan of the Supreme Command (the general staff slang terms used were 'Little Slam' and 'Grand Slam', expressions taken from the game of Bridge). The basic concepts of the 'little' plan had already been under consideration as solution b) at the time when the offensive possibilities were being computed by the Wehrmacht Operations Staff on 9 Oct 44. But, it had not been followed up at that time because the Führer had already made up his mind in favor of the 'grand' plan. Now, the identical concepts were once more being brought up for discussion by A Gp B, thereby obliging everybody involved to reconsider this possibility.

To characterize the difference between the two plans by the contrast between little and grand would be an understatement. Genfldm Model actually had an unadulterated battle of encirclement in mind, which was to take advantage of the fact, that both enemy flanks were all the more threatened, the farther the enemy extended the Aachen salient. Thus, one third of the ring existed already, in the event that an encirclement was to succeed. Although the plan of the Supreme Command also aimed at the encirclement of strong enemy forces, it combined some other projects with this primary objective. In addition, the enemy was to be deprived of his only port in serviceable condition and the entire front between the line of departure and Antwerp was to be rolled up. While this plan was to enable the Germans to immediately regain the initiative, Genfldm Model intended to pave the way for it by carrying out the battle of encirclement. However, the Supreme Command had approached the concept of a battle of encirclement by the subsequent addition of the secondary thrust from the north. Considered from this point of view, was the 'little' plan a consistent step further in the direction which had been taken when that alteration had been made?

This point of view would blur the fundamental issues. If the 'little' plan was being used as basis, without consideration of the 'grand' one, the same breakthrough area as for the 'grand' plan could be used; however, a different attack sector and a different distribution of forces would have to be chosen. In that event, Sixth Pz Army would not only have to carry out the main thrust, but also provide the main defense. This added responsibility would call for additional reinforcements for Army, which could only be obtained by weakening the two other armies, or by depleting the reserves, or, alternatively, by narrowing the attack sector. If the left wing was to extend less far to the south, other considerations would have to be taken into account. Thus, the distinction between the 'little' and the 'grand' plan consisted not only in a difference in the choice of objectives, but also in the manner by which they were to be attained. In summarizing, it can be stated, that Genfldm Model first of all wanted to obtain a decisive military success, and then, if the situation was favorable, he wanted to exploit this success dynamically. The plan of the Führer not only aspired to both simultaneously, but also to a geographic gain which was to be obtained by the same thrust. Already on 3 Nov 44, OB West dispatched his answer to the documents which had been forwarded to him on 1 Nov 44. This reply was based on the discussions of the previous day and entered into the views of Genfldm Model, insofar as they had been expressed by him. Attached to the letter was a draft of the troop concentrations and the first attack objectives, as well as a plan for the withdrawal of troops. This was to be carried out along the front before the Offensive, in order to reorganize and make ready the divisions which were to take part in the attack. The reply was based on the notion that the choice of Antwerp as objective of the offensive was one of the points which were to be considered as unalterable by OB West. Genfldm von Rundstedt therefore did not contest this point, but declared that on the whole he was of the same opinion as the Supreme Command. The suggestions, which he had been asked to submit, differed – according to his explanations – only slightly from the concepts of the Führer. And yet, under close scrutiny these suggestions were quite similar to the 'little' plan. He declared that it was necessary that the secondary push out of the Maas salient (from the Süsteren–Geilenkirchen area) be carried out from the start. Furthermore, he wanted to strengthen the right wing of this attack group. Thus, he intended not only to carry out the secondary thrust, which up to the present had only been considered as a supporting action, simultaneously with the main effort, but also with increased forces. If these suggestions were adopted, the operation would consist of a pincer movement with one main and one secondary limb, which would both link up behind the American and British forces fighting in the Aachen salient. OB West explicitly stressed, that the objective of his suggestions was to annihilate the enemy forces within the triangle of Sittard–Liège–Monschau.

Whereas the plan of the Supreme Command foresaw two phases, each evaluated as equally important and organically connected, namely the capture of the Maas crossing points and the thrust on Antwerp, this plan not only stressed the first phase in particular, but also gave it the characteristics of a complete operation in itself. Whether, how and when the second phase was to follow, remained a question.

Since this inclination towards the 'little' plan necessitated the shifting of the southern boundary of the attack sector farther to the north, OB West simultaneously requested this move. He suggested that Seventh Army provide cover along the line Givet–Libramont–Diekirch, that is behind the line Givet–Neufchâteau–Diekirch, which had been considered a minimum requirement in the draft of Genobst Jodl. This was still farther behind the line Maas (south of Givet)–course of the Semois–Arlon–north of Luxembourg–Wasserbillig, which had been selected by the Führer. With regard to the question of the forces available, OB West pointed out that, under unfavorable circumstances, the deficiency of three to four panzer divisions would have to be taken into consideration by the time the attack was due to start. He asserted that the starting day visualized for the attack – 25 Nov 44 – would be the earliest possible date. Should the enemy attack before then, all plans would have to be considered as momentarily void.

In concluding, OB West pointed out that the forces, which were destined for the operation, were extremely weak compared with those at the disposal of the enemy, and considering the territory they were to gain. In addition, he declared that it would be very difficult to hold any territory unless the enemy had been completely destroyed by that time. He therefore requested that the possibility should again be explored, whether additional units could not be brought up, and whether some more units could not be withdrawn from the front and replaced by forces which would have to be brought up from the Zone of the Interior. Apart from these suggestions, OB West declared that the cooperation of very strong forces of the Luftwaffe would be decisive.

The Führer made the following observations with regard to the alternative suggestions of OB West:

The destruction of the enemy forces in the Aachen–Maastricht–Liège area was all the more feasible, the deeper the German attack thrust into the enemy rear communications, supply lines, and supply centers. If the Germans turned toward the area in which the bulk of the enemy forces was concentrated, immediately after the breakthrough had been achieved, then the conditions would everywhere be the same as those governing a frontal attack. In that event, the enemy would be in a position to use strong forces for his immediate defense or counterattack without being forced to carry out extensive troop movements.

Thus, the Führer rejected the 'little' plan and insisted on the 'grand' one. The Führer also gave a negative answer to the question whether the German offensive was to be delayed in view of a premature start of new large-scale attacks by the Allies. He was of the opinion that, should the enemy start a large-scale attack in the Aachen area, this would mean the pinning down and using of strong units as well as a large-scale consumption of all types of supplies and equipment. Should the enemy tie down his reserves and material in a large-scale battle, a thrust deep into the rear of his armies would therefore seem even more profitable than an offensive at a time when he had not yet started to attack, and therefore still had all his reserves available for immediate countermeasures. In accordance with this fundamental concept, the Führer therefore also refused to grant the secondary thrust a greater significance than the one contained in his plan. The question of the advisability of launching a containing attack in order to prevent the withdrawal of enemy forces, was left open by the Führer. He inclined toward the point of view of Genfldm Model and Gen Pz von Manteuffel, that it was preferable – once the Offensive was progressing successfully – to bring up all available reserves behind the attack divisions in order to take advantage of the breakthrough, instead of unnecessarily using them up for unsuccessful containing attacks on other sectors of the front. After discussion of the changes suggested by OB West, the original plan of operations was therefore being maintained. In addition to preparing the Offensive, OB West was now being given the mission to take all necessary measures to successfully withstand an Allied large-scale attack without having recourse to the forces destined for the Offensive. However, the 'little' plan had thereby not been definitely abandoned. Genfldm Model continued to elaborate his plans and waited for an opportune moment to submit his suggestions once more for another discussion.

4. THE BASIC DIFFERENCE IN OPINION BETWEEN THE SUPREME COMMAND AND THE COMMAND AUTHORITIES IN THE WEST

The difference in opinion between the Führer, OB West and A Gp B had a significance which went far beyond its cause. The most obvious explanation would be to consider this difference of opinion as the result of a conflict between the experts and the leader, who was an autodidact in all spheres of life and therefore also in military matters, even though some of his ideas were good. That some of his strategic concepts were original, could not be denied by even those men who otherwise strongly criticized Adolf Hitler's military leadership. But this explanation would be an over-simplification. Thanks to his unusual memory and due to extensive reading as well as continuous discussions with experts, the Führer had acquired a specialized knowledge, which was superior to that of the majority of his senior staff officers. Besides, he was assisted by an operations staff, composed of Genobst Jodl and his subordinate officers, which could make up for his deficiencies insofar as they consisted of lack of military training. The objection is not valid, that the Chief of the Wehrmacht Operations Staff and his officers were only puppets of the Führer, who were carrying out his instructions blindly. Genobst Jodl had the opportunity of expressing his own opinions and objections, and constantly made use of this opportunity. Also, Adolf Hitler needed such an opposing counterpart, since it was his way, never to make important military decisions on the spur of the moment, but on the contrary to clarify and develop them during the long, and often too long discussions, which were drawn out for days by endless talking and arguing. It would be closer to reality, if one attributed the now obvious difference of opinion to the Supreme Command's *'Frontfremdheit'* (failure of keeping touch with the front) which had been accentuated in the course of the war. Every staff organization, from division level on up, is subject to this danger. It can be remedied by interchanging members of such staffs at regular intervals with officers from the front who can understand the evolution in the technique of warfare, the front line situation, and the condition of the troops. Moreover, this danger can be reduced by frequent visits to the front and by conversations with officers and men who have taken part in heavy fighting. All these remedies had been used by the German Supreme Command; but the centralization of all executive powers in the hands of the Führer made it practically impossible for him to leave his headquarters, be it only for two or three days. Due to his method of exercising his command functions, the same also applied to Genobst Jodl. For this reason an expedient was adopted according to which general staff officers, who were members of the Wehrmacht Operations Staff, were sent to the front from time to time, particularly in times of crisis. Upon their return, they made written and oral reports on the impressions and experiences they had been submitted to. Then again, the Führer availed himself of the opportunities offered by different ceremonies, such as the conferring of decorations on officers and men, to question them in detail on their experiences. Some of them might not have had a chance to say much, while others in the festive frame of mind engendered by such an honor, might have made the mistake of painting too rosy a picture. On the other hand, there still were plenty of those who used the opportunity to speak freely of the difficulties and worries in the front lines. Thus, everything, that could possibly be done under prevailing circumstances, was being attempted in order to counteract the Supreme Command's lack of keeping in touch with the front. But all these measures were only expedients which did not change the facts. There always remained the insurmountable contrast between those who had had practical experience at the front and who, in many cases, had to pay for it with their own lives, and those others who acquired their knowledge from hearsay, or from reports and statistics. And this contrast was further enlarged as a result of the constant deterioration of the situation in the air, above and behind the Western Front, so that the countermeasures advocated by the Führer's headquarters were very often based on a situation which in reality no longer existed.

But this was still not the decisive point. Supposing, Adolf Hitler himself, or just Genobst Jodl, would have been able to take time off for on-the-spot studies of the characteristics of warfare in the West. Supposing also, that they would have realized, exactly as the troop and army commanders in the West had before them, that the divisions, despite their unshaken morale and despite the amazing performance in make-shift defense, no longer corresponded to those units which formerly had been victorious. The front line units had been decimated by death and injuries. Imagine also, that they have been convinced that despite the statistically astounding performance of the supply services, gaps in equipment still existed everywhere. What if they further realized that behind the front the chaotic condition of communications was extending farther all the time, with the result that only by night and in rainy weather a few isolated trains could be dispatched, and that even the motor vehicle traffic threatened to come to a standstill? Would these facts have altered the decision of the Supreme Command? Would the Führer in that case have changed his mind and adopted the 'little' plan instead of the 'grand'?

Let us, for the moment, completely ignore the political side of the question, which undoubtedly played a great part, since a complete change of fortune now hardly seemed conceivable, and let us confine ourselves to the initial hypothesis. In that case, the question has to be answered by a decisive 'No'. And this 'No' leads to the real difference in opinion between the concepts of the Führer and the command authorities in the West. If one wants to express it in abstract form, it is the conflict between the General Staff and the Revolutionary. In this connection, the term 'General Staff' is not being applied in its strictest sense; what is really meant, is the manner of thinking which is inherent to the highest levels of command. This manner of thinking is a very distinctive method of forming judgment and making decisions, which in the end also requires some inspiration and therefore justifies its claim to the title '*Kriegskunst*' (art of war), but which, in the course of time, had been more and more assimilated to a science. The strong point of the German General Staff, from which Genfldms von Rundstedt and Model as well as their chiefs of staff had risen, consisted in the fact that its technique had made as much methodical progress as the military profession would permit. Once the plan of an offensive had been conceived, the General Staff would therefore first of all subject it to a systematic counterproof, the object of which was to ascertain whether there were any other possibilities, and if so, whether these were any better or worse than the plan which was under scrutiny. Then the General Staff would study the plans of the enemy and consider his future actions, and evaluate its own prospects accordingly. If, after these considerations, it was established that the initial plan actually was the best, then one began to manipulate countless factors, most of which were anything but precise from the outset, the exactitude of which, however, could – as a result of long experience – be more or less exactly evaluated. This speculation extended over the following fields: with maps on hand, all conceivable displacements of forces were considered; the reports on the condition of all the units, which were available or destined for the offensive, were being interpreted in the most realistic manner; very sober calculations expressed in kilometers, in altitudes from the ground, in depths of river beds, in tonnages and cubic meters, and in railroad and motor vehicle capacity. Exact calculations were made on the effect of the artillery, the mortars and the Luftwaffe, as well as on enemy countermeasures and the supplementary forces required to make them ineffective. Finally, careful weighing of all the beneficial and hampering factors which had to be taken into consideration. Imagination and inspiration were not part of this process of work, and the faith and the will power of the leadership or the troops were just two factors among many others when considered from so completely realistic a point of view. The final task in such calculations consisted of reducing all these facts and drawing the logical conclusion, that so much of the objective could most probably be attained with so many troops, so much supplies, and so strong a support by artillery and Luftwaffe.

This was the work which had been done by OB West, A Gp B and the three army staffs. Their conclusion was as follows: The area chosen for the attack was the right one, and a breakthrough will be possible. But the objective has been set at too great a distance. Only half this distance can be covered with the forces available, but it will be worthwhile attempting the offensive. Should it succeed, then one could look further ahead, make a new evaluation, and if its result was positive, one could still start on the second half of the plan.

But, Adolf Hitler reached his decisions by quite different methods and evaluated situations according to different standards. As a former acting corporal he had a pronounced understanding for the underdog, the 'armer Wurm' (poor worm), and thanks to his vivid power of imagination he fully visualized the difficulties of combat conditions, although they had undergone such drastic changes since the days when he himself had been at the front. As a result of his experiences in World War I, he, above all, adhered to the fundamental notion that the troops should never be made to feel uncertain by being given the possibility of a withdrawal. Hence, his resistance to granting permission for any evacuation or withdrawal to a new line whenever such a move was suggested to him. He was convinced that, if only the will to resist was inflexible, most requests for withdrawal would be superfluous. This will to resist also became a dominating factor in his positive planning The experiences he had acquired during the days of his revolutionary ascent are reflected in his manner of thinking. Had his thinking been schooled according to general staff standards, he would have estimated at each step he had climbed, that reaching the next one was an impossibility. Then, he would never have undertaken any attempt to seize power since, according to sound calculations, it seemed hopeless from the beginning. He had remained a revolutionary in his way of thinking even after he had seized power, and he therefore considered it as a natural process that initial successes created openings for further successes because they encouraged one's own forces and paralyzed the enemy. The Führer applied to his military leadership exactly the same notions which had proved their value in his political career: from the first, he set his objectives so high, that dispassionate observers were of the opinion they could not possibly be reached. He, on the contrary, believed that the further developments would immediately jump the rails of premeditated calculations, as soon as the first success had been obtained, and that then the impossible could still be reached with the help of the energies generated on one's own side and the general paralysis on the enemy's. This was what he meant when he used his favorite expression 'Fanaticism', and this was what he constantly demanded from the Wehrmacht. After all, a considerable number of successes he had obtained during the first years of the war, had been won against the predictions of the General Staff, and he considered these successes a justification for constantly believing that fanaticism, this unknown quantity, would always be a decisive factor. Had he believed in the Bible, the passage, which speaks of 'faith that moveth mountains', would surely have been the one nearest to his heart.

The most critical problem of the German General Staff in World War II might actually have been that based on his initial successes, Adolf Hitler could say, he was the genuine realist, and not the General Staff which had always set its objectives less far. He, the realist, had foreseen the actual developments much clearer, just because he had included the incalculable in his estimates. However, the circumstances had changed and once again the General Staff was making the correct evaluations. The explanations, that intentionally juggled figures were being submitted to the Führer or that he ignored unfavorable facts, are an over-simplification. On the contrary, Adolf Hitler nourished a never-dying suspicion of the data which were being submitted to him; due to his astounding memory, he was able to detect mistakes even where so many experts had failed to discern any. He was therefore always being informed in the most extensive manner. The justification of the second explanation, however, cannot be denied. But, Hitler did not simply brush aside inconvenient facts; on the contrary, he tried to interpret them and to find reasons, why they could not be exact, or he thought of countermeasures which he believed could change negative facts into positive ones. Had events continued favorably, this trait of his character would not have become so obvious. But, since the situation developed unfavorably, the former 'Realist' turned out to be an arithmetician whose calculations were no longer coming out right. It would be wrong to consider Hitler a man living in an illusionary world, because, now as ever, he stayed with his feet on the ground. He merely underestimated the enemy strength, which he did not wish to admit, and he overestimated his own forces, which he wanted to see in their entireness, but under present circumstances, were no longer available. Thus, he always arrived at wrong results. Separated from his troops, he especially failed to take into account how exhausted they really were, and that all their fanaticism could not make up for their lack of physical strength and equipment. There can be no doubt, that this method was effective in obtaining much better results from the German Wehrmacht, than even the most optimistic observers would have believed. But, there were limits to the Wehrmacht's strength, and Adolf Hitler failed to fully realize them during the preparations for the Ardennes Offensive, just as he had on previous occasions. The course of the Offensive proved that the estimates of the commanding officers in the field were more realistic.

The reason why the conflict between 'grand' and 'little' plan did not lead to a crisis in the leadership, was to be found in the fact that the question of adhering to Antwerp as objective could be shelved for the time being. In any event, the Maas had to be reached. If the Germans did not succeed in capturing any river crossing, and if they were therefore held up on its bank or even before they had reached it, then the protagonists of the little plan could expect that their suggestions would forcibly have to be adopted. If, on the other hand, the enemy was driven back beyond the Maas, and it was possible to gain better understanding of his countermeasures, then only would the moment have arrived to thrash out the difference of opinion. By that time it would be possible to ascertain – instead of merely guessing – what German forces still were available to drive a wedge as far as Antwerp, and what American and British forces could be expected to counteract this move.

Besides, insofar as Genfldm Model himself was concerned, he approached the Führer's point of view by his inclination of always demanding the impossible in order to obtain the utmost. Thus, even if he was not in favor of Antwerp as immediate objective, it must have been to his liking as a password. Now, what about the protagonists of the 'grand' plan?

There can be no doubt that Adolf Hitler stood for Antwerp as objective, not only in order to inspire his generals and troops, but that he actually believed in his innermost that its realization would be possible. Whether Genobst Jodl was equally convinced or whether he only accepted the Führer's plan because he thought it advisable to set a distant objective in order to keep the three armies in line and prevent them from delaying their advance by secondary gains of territory, has not been revealed even to his closest collaborators, far less has it been put down in writing. If his opinion was at variance with the Führer's, then he, more than anyone else, was obliged to keep it a secret in order to preserve the unity of the Supreme Command and prevent any uncertainty in the designation of the objective.

Thus, the Supreme Command insisted on the 'grand' plan. But, it did not obstinately insist on the execution of its plan. On the contrary, as related in the following pages, the Führer thought of another method of exploiting the Offensive, should the situation require it. This is the explanation of the fact, that the Supreme Command, once it had realized that the attack had already bogged down before reaching the Maas, immediately forgot about both the 'grand' and the 'little' plan, and changed to a different method of taking the initiative: local attacks were to be carried out on the frontal sectors, which the enemy had meanwhile been obliged to uncover, first on the northern Alsatian front, then on the Saar front, and so on. The objective was to dissipate the strategic reserves of the enemy, and to thereby render him incapable of mounting new large-scale counteroffensives.

This served to smooth over the fundamental differences between the Führer and the top commanders. This also explains, why the difference of opinion on the 'grand' and the 'little' plans which was constantly being brought up during the following weeks by Genfldm Model with the consent of OB West, did not cause any lasting friction.

The student of strategic matters will certainly be interested to know, how Army Group intended to realize its plan of fighting a battle of encirclement in the Aachen area from the initial stage of the 'grand' plan. But the two men concerned with this suggested change in the direction of the attack, Genfldm Model and his C-of-S, Gen Inf Krebs, are no longer alive to tell their story.

5. THE ORDERS FOR THE ASSEMBLY, FOR THE ATTACK AND FOR THE ATTACK PROCEDURE ISSUED BETWEEN 5–16 NOV 44

We have paused in order to clarify the conflict of principles between the Supreme Command and the leadership of the West, and to consider the concepts which brought them together again. We now turn our attention to the course of the preparations during the last few weeks.

An order issued by the Führer on 5 Nov 44, originated in the above-mentioned concepts of the Supreme Command. It was sent to OB West and regulated the regrouping and assembly of forces for the Offensive – insofar as this had not been done before. The real significance of these measures had, by this time, become known to the Army Commanders and their immediate assistants. As to the other headquarters, which were to take part in the Offensive, camouflaged instructions were issued, informing them that these measures were being taken in anticipation of possible, large-scale enemy attacks in the direction of Mülheim–Cologne or Cologne–Bonn, and on both sides of Metz in the direction of Saarbrücken. The contents of these orders were as follows:

a) OB West was to make arrangements for the organization of the chain of command on the Western Front and for its division into sectors, which were to correspond to the disposition envisaged for the Offensive. For this reason, Sixth Pz Army, which was still being reorganized in Westphalia and which was to be ready for commitment by 6 Nov 44, was to be subordinated to OB West after 10 Nov 44. (A special order was issued on 6 Dec 44.) The staff of the other attack army, Fifth Pz Army, which was in charge of the Aachen sector since 22 Oct 44, was to be replaced by the staff of Fifteenth Army, which up to that time had been in control of the Dutch front. WB Ndl was to take over the latter sector. First Fs (*Fallschirmjäger*) Army was assigned the sector Nijmegen–Roermond. All these measures were to be camouflaged by all possible means. The reorganization of the front was to be concealed from the enemy by the following camouflage designations: Fifteenth Army was to be called Fifth Pz Army, WB Ndl was to be Fifteenth Army, Fifth Pz Army was designed as *Feldjägerkommando zbV* (Special Field Police Command Staff), and the name of Sixth Pz Army was to be Sixteenth *Auffrischungestab* (Reorganization Staff). In addition, the staff of a fictitious Twenty-Fifth Army was organized for the purpose of further deception. Its appearance in the area west and northwest of Cologne was to simulate the arrival of reinforcements in that area. The disposition of units, which was determined on 5 Nov 44, and which was not changed up to the start of the Offensive, was therefore as follows:

A Gp H

(1) *From the Dutch coast–north of Nijmegen:*
    WB Ndl (allegedly Fifteenth Army)
(2) *Nijmegen–Roermond:*
    First Fs Army

A Gp B

(3) *North of Roermond–Düren:*
    Fifteenth Army (allegedly Fifth Pz Army)
(4) *South of Düren–Trier:*
    Seventh Army
In addition, in the assembly stage: Sixth Pz Army (allegedly
                                      Sixteenth *Auffrischungestab*)
                                        Fifth Pz Army (allegedly
                                        Feldjägerkommando zbV)
furthermore, allegedly: Twenty-Fifth Army.

A Gp G

(5) *South of Trier–west of Hagenau:*
    First Army
(6) *Hagenau–Swiss border:*
    A Gp Oberrhein   (directly subordinate to OKW)
    (RF-SS)

b) In addition, OB West was ordered to repel enemy attacks with the troops already committed. The divisions destined for the Offensive could only be employed in the sectors assigned to them: The remaining divisions, belonging to the OKW reserve, could only be committed with the Führer's approval. The only exception to this order was to be made in the case of an enemy airborne landing, in which case OB West was authorized to immediately commit all forces available in the vicinity.

c) Finally, the order issued on 5 Nov 44, contained the following details:

(1) A GPs H and G, which forcibly had to stand behind A Gp B, were to receive all newly activated fortress troops, that is to say, forces which were not capable of taking part in the Offensive; in addition, A Gp H also was assigned 5 Fs Div, which was strong in numbers but poorly equipped, so that it could be considered as being only semi-mobile.

(2) The *volks werfer* brigades were at first not to be committed, because they were short of ammunition.

(3) The *volks artillerie* corps, the firepower of which was to be of great importance in the Offensive, were – only in an emergency – to be committed in the A Gp H and G sectors.

On the same day – 5 Nov 44 – the Führer also issued the order, which was being held in readiness, and which announced the camouflage operation 'Watch on the Rhine' and gave directives for the maintenance of secrecy. The draft of the basic plans for the attack procedure was being prepared simultaneously, followed by the directives for the commitment of engineer troops on the next day. In the course of the further preparations, the most important question, which was also being emphasized by OB West, was whether the forces originally destined for the Offensive, could not be increased. In the draft prepared on 11 Oct 44, the strength of the three attack armies had been evaluated at nine, plus seven, plus seven divisions, for a total of 23 full divisions, the reserves at six to seven additional divisions. The grand total had been estimated at 29 to 30 divisions. On 7 Nov 44, the Wehrmacht Operations Staff evaluated the forces which were now available. According to these calculations the three attack armies had 15 panzer and panzer grenadier divisions, as well as 23 *volks grenadier* and infantry divisions at their disposal. The grand total therefore was 38 divisions, or eight to nine more than anticipated. However, four panzer and panzer grenadier as well as one *volks grenadier* division (11 and 21 Pz Divs, 17 SS Pz Div, 25 Pz Gren Div and 36 Volks Gren Div) were pinned down by the defensive battle southeast of Metz. Only about one or two of these divisions could, in time, be transferred to A Gp B. Thus, the actual additional strength consisted only of five to six divisions. The Wehrmacht Operations Staff therefore made a number of suggestions for obtaining additional forces which were to be put in effect.

Thus, their planning and the preparations were now completed. On 10 Nov

44, the Führer signed the order for the forward displacement and assembly for the attack in the Ardennes along the following lines.

a) The objective of the operations was to bring about a turn for the better in the campaign in the West, and thereby perhaps the entire war, by the annihilation of the enemy forces north of the line Antwerp–Brussels–Luxembourg. 'I am,' declared the Führer, 'resolved to adhere to the execution of the operation and to accept the greatest risks, even if the enemy attacks on both sides of the Metz and the imminent thrust into the Ruhr area should lead to great territorial and strategic losses.' The other points of the attack order dealt with:

b) and c) The missions of the three attack armies (as mentioned above).

d) Disposition of forces (as mentioned above).

e) Completion of concentration and assembly by 27 Nov 44.

f) Instructions for the final assembly before the attack.

g) Distribution of the artillery forces.

h) Commitment of the engineer troops.

i) Commitment of the Luftwaffe.

Completion of the assembly by 27 Nov 44, signified that the attack would presumably begin on 1 Dec 44, that is one week later than had been anticipated as late as 1 Nov 44. But even this new date could not be adhered to, because the preparations took longer than expected. One important reason for this was that the German railroads had been so badly damaged by enemy air attacks, that the trains loaded with new equipment were either brought to a stop or had to be re-routed over long distances. The late arrival of tanks, weapons and equipment delayed the training of the troops, while the late arrival of the vehicles, harnesses, etc, caused delay in the assembly. Every possible effort was being made to keep open the vital railroad lines and the most important through stations, and astounding achievements were being accomplished; but all these efforts could not prevent the wheels of the German war machine from grinding and turning more slowly than had hitherto been the case.

There were three different reasons why the task of the railroad lines could not be alleviated by the large-scale employment of truck convoys: First of all, all road traffic was endangered during the daytime or on moonlit nights; then, there was a shortage of POL which made it compulsory to save every possible gallon; and finally, the shortage of transport space, and the extensive wear and tear of most vehicles which might have been employed.

The dilemma of the Supreme Command, which resulted from this situation, was as follows: while it was undeniable, that the German forces grew stronger and improved every day, the enemy did not remain idle either: he was also reorganizing his forces and was increasing them simultaneously by transferring additional divisions to France. Above all, there was reason for apprehension in the fact that the secret could not be kept indefinitely, and that the element of surprise, which was of decisive importance, would be lost by further delay.

In view of the incompleteness of the preparations, Gen Pz von Manteuffel suggested that the date of the attack be postponed from 1 Dec 44 to 10 Dec 44. Although Genfldm Model agreed with the motivation of this suggestion, he preferred, for the present, to adhere to 1 Dec 44, presumably because of his fundamental principle of demanding more than what was feasible in order to obtain the utmost.

On 12 Nov 44, that is two days after the Supreme Command had issued the attack order, some special instructions for radio deception were given. A number of questions, which still remained undecided, were discussed during a trip to the Western Front, which Genlt August Winter, the Deputy Chief of the Wehrmacht Operations Staff, made between 11–13 Nov 44. His talks were held with OB West and A Gp B, and his visit also served the purpose of familiarizing him with the situation, since he had only recently been appointed to this position.

On 18 Nov 44, the directives for the attack were issued after the Führer himself had signed them. The success in achieving the strategic and tactical surprise was considered of vital importance. The start of the attack was to depend on the setting-in of a bad-weather period. Adjustment fire was prohibited. The fire preparation was limited to about one hour, but was to be carried out with ample expenditure of ammunition. Artillery reconnaissance was to start at once. The composition of the attack groups was to take into account that a number of divisions were still without combat experience. It was indispensable that the breakthrough succeeded and at a rapid pace. On the other hand, all precautions were to be taken to preserve the combat strength of the armored units. For this reason, the first wave was to be mainly composed of infantry divisions, supported by self-propelled assault guns. Once the breakthrough had been achieved, individual instructions for which had been issued in detail, the watchword was to be: 'Thrust on and across the Maas!' Separate instructions followed on the advance, on the collaboration with the Luftwaffe, on the flak artillery, and on the supply services.

On 18 Nov 44, OB West was issued additional instructions on betrayals by deserters, and on the capture of reconnaissance patrols and combat outposts. Any sign that the enemy was growing suspicious, was to be reported, in order to avoid a repetition of the situation in 1918, when the troops at the front, but not the leadership, were aware of the fact that the enemy had advance information on the impending German attack. Would it be possible to carry out the preparations according to plan?

III. The Operations Plan during the last Weeks before the Start of the Offensive

1. THE PLAN FOR THE OFFENSIVE UNDER CRITICAL PRESSURE

In the new phase, after issuance of the fundamental orders, the main task of the Supreme Command was to harmonize the defensive battles along the front with the preparations for the Offensive. Its success depended, above all, on the extent to which it would be possible to hold back the reserves, which were being assembled for the Offensive, and which were subject to being employed in critical situations on sectors under attack. The additional mission of exactly observing all simultaneous enemy measures was to obtain information, which would enable the Supreme Command to make a good guess on the withdrawals and reinforcements the enemy intended to carry out in the prospective sector of operations. The other missions of the Supreme Command – such as the maintenance of secrecy and of the punctual accomplishment of the personnel and materiel preparations, as well as the issuance of additional orders, were less important. The Führer controlled this phase of the preparations as he had in the past. He discussed everything in great detail with the competent collaborators and personally requested the issuance of all the necessary instructions. In order to ascertain that the secrecy of the plan was not broken by a slip of the tongue or in any other way, the Führer made the following arrangements: during the daily discussion on the situation, the plans for the Offensive were not mentioned, but after its conclusion he detained all those officers who had been initiated into the plan of the Offensive, and who had made a special written promise to maintain its secrecy. Only then did he open discussions on all questions which had to be settled. Above all, Adolf Hitler's personal co-operation meant, that he reserved for himself the decision, to which extent the frontal sectors under attack were to receive help, or whether the yielding of territory was to be considered preferable in order not to endanger the execution of the Offensive by premature use of the accumulated reserves. For this reason, he flatly refused the request OB West made on 8 Nov 44, that the OKW reserves should be made available for employment in critical situations on the Western Front. OB West justified his request by explaining that, in case of emergency, he must be able to make rapid dispositions of troops. This point of view was only admitted insofar as airborne landings were being excepted from the prohibition to touch the reserves. Apart from this exception, OB West had to obtain permission from the Führer for the commitment of any reserve unit down to *volks artillerie* corps level. In order to further clarify this principle, OB West and the Commander of the Luftwaffe were instructed on 9 Nov 44, that the guiding principle was, not to touch the attack forces. If some ground was lost, and all available means had been exhausted, the loss had to be taken into account.

How strong was the enemy and what were his intentions? These were the initial questions which were to determine all transfers of German forces. In an evaluation, submitted by OB West on 2 Nov 44, he estimated the enemy forces employed along the front at about 17 armored and 40 infantry and airborne divisions, as well as 14 armored brigades. In addition, three armored and five infantry divisions were being held as reserves, and two or three units had not yet been identified. Out of approximately 80 units, only one quarter were at this time engaged in fighting. Thus, the main body was still assembling for action, and – according to the opinion of OB West – all available forces were being brought up to the concentration areas. The most important increase had been ascertained in the Metz area. In comparison, the increase in enemy forces in the vicinity of Aachen was smaller, but here they were concentrated in a narrower area. OB West therefore anticipated in the lower Rhine area an American offensive, which was to be supported by British forces. However, he believed that most of the British forces were not yet ready for an attack. He assumed, that the British, after having completed the assembly of their forces, would not continue their attacks in a northern direction, but that they would attack in an eastern and subsequently in a southeastern direction, in order to join up with the Americans along the German Sector of the Lower Rhine. In conjunction with these actions, he also considered the possibility of an airborne landing to the west of the line Duisburg–Düsseldorf, or even for the purpose of forcing the Maas crossing, because – according to his calculations – the enemy still had, for this purpose, three or four units at his disposal. OB West expected the attacks to start in the first half of Nov 44, and it seemed probable that those in the vicinity of Metz would precede the attacks near Aachen. But he considered it feasible that the enemy might attack simultaneously at all three points of main effort – Metz, Aachen and center of the Maas. It will be observed that this estimate omitted to mention the Schelde delta, although the final battle for Walcheren and Beveland had not yet finished. It was to be anticipated that this battle would soon come to an end. Then, all hope of blocking the harbor at Antwerp would disappear, and then, also, the adjoining area of Bergen op Zoom–Breda–Hertogenbosch, which was being stubbornly defended, would lose its significance to the Germans. Beyond this area was the river Maas, which, immediately before entering its estuary, constitutes a tremendous obstacle, and which therefore formed a safe line which at the same time also was sparing manpower. The troops fighting here were, step by step, withdrawn beyond the river, and on 9 Nov 44, the bridgehead near Moerdijk, which had been held up to that time, was abandoned. Since it was not to be assumed that the enemy, after having succeeded in taking an objective, which was of considerable importance to him, would continue his attacks in an area presenting so many natural obstacles, the Führer agreed on 17 Nov 44, that the forces on the Dutch front be spread out thinly in order to build up reserves and obtain forces for the other fronts.

The offensive, which was being prepared on the Aachen front, and which had been mentioned by OB West in his report, seemed to be materializing already on 2 Nov 44. But for the time being, it was confined to local, though very tough fighting, which resulted in heavy losses to both sides to the southeast of the city. Here, the Americans attempted to widen the gap in the West Wall, which they had sometime ago succeeded in opening at Vossenack. Their objective was to penetrate as far as the two Roer dams. If these dams were opened, the water level farther down the valley would rise so high, that the crossing of the Roer would become extremely difficult. German counterattacks succeeded in reducing the gap, which the Americans had previously widened at this critical point. A new line was being established in the Hürtgen forest, which, for the time being, barred the access to the Americans' objective, because it appeared to be certain that the enemy would renew his attempts at the same point.

The main attack started on 16 Nov 44, and by 19 Nov 44, it was spreading to the entire Geilenkirchen–Eschweiler–Stolberg Sector. On 22 Nov 44, Eschweiler was lost, but the continuity of the front was maintained, and the German Supreme Command observed very closely to see if the strategic reserves of the enemy were being drawn into the battle. It was a struggle for every foot of ground; every slope, every hill was bitterly contested. The Americans pushed on from one village to the next. By the evening of 28 Nov 44, after twelve days of fighting, they had advanced 15 km at the deepest point of penetration. Jülich and Düren now lay within range of their light artillery, and the German troops were relentlessly being pushed back toward the Roer. On the twentieth day of battle, on 5 Dec 44, the fierceness of the fighting seemed to abate somewhat in this sector. However, the fighting continued on the left wing, against which the enemy was launching a secondary thrust from the vicinity of Vossenack, the point where he had previously penetrated. By 8 Dec 44, the battle in the main sector erupted with renewed violence. On 11 Dec 44, the Roer line was being occupied between Jülich and Düren; to the west of Düren, there still was a German bridgehead, and on the left wing near Vossenack, the situation was as tense as ever. By the middle of Dec 44, the result of the battle, which by now had been lasting for one month, was the following:

The territorial gains, which the Americans had obtained since 16 Nov 44, were sizable, when considered from a local point of view, since the enemy had succeeded in advancing his front line into the lower plains of the Rhine valley, and was approaching Cologne. Considered from an over-all standpoint, however, the course of the battle could be regarded as a German success, because the Americans had not attained their main objective, a breakthrough. For the time being, the Roer constituted an obstacle which could not be lightly surmounted. This was all the more so, inasmuch as frequent rains had transformed the battle area into a muddy quagmire, which favored the defense and prevented the attack forces from fully exploiting their superiority in the air and in armored weapons. As a result of these unfavorable conditions, the enemy had been obliged to employ a higher percentage than usual of his other units, and the losses he suffered were correspondingly high. That these battles were absorbing strong enemy forces, was confirmed by information stating that one new enemy unit after another had been recognized on or behind the front, and that his strategic reserves were being reduced correspondingly.

This was the most favorable development possible in connection with the offensive which was being planned. As long as the enemy command authorities could be presumed to have strong reserves at their disposal, it was to be anticipated that they would carry out rapid and strong counterthrusts, the direction of which would be incalculable. By now, the battle along the Roer, together with the fighting in the southern sector of the Western Front, which might as well be mentioned right here, had already pinned down so many forces, that the unknown quantity of enemy reserves, which had, at first, been estimated at a high figure by the German Command, had now shrunk to a much smaller one. Accordingly, complete and overwhelming surprises no longer had to be expected from reserves which might be brought up from the rear.

On 3 Dec 44, it was estimated that the Allies had approximately 76 divisions in the West (after converting the brigades and counting them for nine divisions). According to the available information, these were distributed along the front from Holland to Switzerland in the following way:

21 A Gp (First Can and Second Br Armies)	23 full divisions
12 A Gp (Ninth, First, and Third US Armies)	$28\frac{1}{2}$ full divisions
6 A Gp (Seventh US and First Fr Armies)	$20\frac{1}{2}$ full divisions
Committed at and behind the front	72 full divisions

In view of the fact that additional divisions from the United States were being transferred to the European Theater, the strategic reserves were estimated at approximately three to six full divisions.

A further advantage in the present development was, that the Americans were committing several divisions, which had been exhausted by the battle on the Roer (the 2, 4 and 28 Inf Divs (US)), in the very sector which was under consideration for the attack. This was another factor improving the chances of success. Furthermore, it was another indication of the scarcity of forces which was prevailing on the enemy side. This favorable development, however, was being obtained by an extreme strain on the German forces.

By 21 Nov 44, OB West had already been obliged to announce that the defensive battle in the Aachen area was consuming considerable forces of A Gp B. Two, perhaps even three, *volks grenadier* divisions (the 47, 340, as well as 352) were being involved in the battle, and 12 Volks Gren Div, which had been selected to cover the right flank of Sixth Pz Army in the coming Offensive, could not be withdrawn. As long as the battle continued, four mobile divisions (9 and 116 Pz Divs, as well as 3 and 15 Pz Gren Divs), which had all been destined for the Offensive, would be pinned down. It seemed probable that, in addition, 10 SS Pz Div would also have to be employed in the battle. Since a similar situation was developing on the A Gp G front, OB West estimated on 21 Nov 44, that, for the immediate future, four of the *volks grenadier* and nine of the mobile divisions would have to be deducted from the total available reserves. But, in these figures OB West had included some divisions which had not been destined for the Offensive. In the event that the divisions could be withdrawn, they would first have to be reorganized. OB West drew the conclusion that the remaining forces would be insufficient to assure the success of the planned attack. The picture painted by OB West turned out to be too gloomy since, after all, three of the *volks grenadier* and four of the mobile divisions, consequently the majority of the divisions included in the above estimate, took part in the Offensive. On the other hand, it has to be considered a very important factor that these divisions were given little or no time at all for their reorganization and restoration, and that they therefore participated in the Ardennes battle with diminished combat strength.

The above mentioned estimate was made on 21 Nov 44, immediately after the beginning of the Roer Battle. With every additional day the ranks of the defenders grew thinner and the risks of a breakthrough increased. But, the guiding principle was nevertheless being maintained: to bear the brunt of the battle while committing as few forces as possible, but which would just about suffice to prevent a breakthrough and leave the reserves for the Offensive untouched. This meant that tremendous sacrifices were being demanded from the fighting forces, and that the nerves of the intermediate command, which was being involved in one critical situation after another, were being strained to breaking point. If one considered the Roer defense in connection with the preparations for the Ardennes Offensive, it will be seen that this battle was by far its most arduous part. Thus, the outcome of the Roer Battle was, that the German forces were reduced in number, that some divisions were no longer available for the attack, and that others could not be sufficiently reorganized, and that therefore the original proportion of strength could not be maintained. On the other hand, the strategic reserves of the enemy, which, as recently as the end of Sep 44, had seemed so formidable, were very considerably reduced, and the forces he was committing on and behind the front could be assumed to be as weakened as the German ones.

The material effect of this battle on the planned Offensive is of particular importance. During its course, it had proved impossible to avoid diverting stocks of ammunition and POL destined for the Offensive. OKW agreed to these expedients only under the extreme pressure of critical situations, and then saw to it that the stocks were quickly replenished. Thus, the Roer Battle had no influence on the Ardennes Offensive in that connection. On the other hand, the allocations of weapons and equipment to the attack units were in direct relation with the high consumption necessitated by the battle which lasted for weeks. The German Command found no explanation for the fact that the British, during all this time, did not start the expected major attacks in their sector. Instead, they were content with first driving back the Germans behind the canal in the vicinity of Meijel toward the Maas, and then eliminating the Maas bridgehead, which up to then was still being held in front of Venlo. Thus, by 3 Dec 44, the Maas line, which economized forces and offered relative security, was being occupied also in the Nijmegen–south of Roermond sector. Had the British attempted any major operations, additional German forces would have been absorbed; this would have led to the commitment of more divisions, and would have upset the German plans even more than the attack against the Roer line.

In connection with the plan for the Offensive, the withdrawal beyond the Maas was of importance insofar as the secondary thrust from the north, which had been under consideration in Nov 44, was supposed to be launched from the Venlo bridgehead. Instead, only the other project which had been considered at the same time, could be planned, namely a thrust to the east of the Maas which was to be carried out from the salient in the front, which had now been formed south of Roermond, and which was first being defended by Fifth Pz Army and now by Fifteenth Army. The immediate objectives, which now were in front of the sector considered for the secondary thrust, were Sittard on the right and Geilenkirchen on the left. A further consequence of this withdrawal was, that the sector Arnhem–Nijmegen had again acquired a greater importance. This sector had been the center of attention in Sep 44, but had meanwhile lost its importance. At this point, the British held excellent jump-off positions both for a thrust to the north toward the Zuider See, which would cut off Holland, and for a push eastward toward Kleve which would unhinge the Maas front.

The developments in the A Gp G area were different from those in the A Gp B sector. Here, too, relative quiet prevailed at the end of Oct/beginning of Nov 44. In Lorraine, First Army, which was in command up to the Nancy–Strasbourg boundary, was still in front of the West Wall. Further to the south, Nineteenth Army was holding the hastily prepared positions west of the Vosges. In thrusts, which at some points led to fierce fighting in the foot-hills of the mountains, the Americans and French were attempting to obtain favorable jump-off positions for further attacks.

The Metz area was considered the main danger spot where the Germans were still holding a bridgehead on the west bank of the Moselle, which was supported by the former fortress. The expected major attack began on 7 Nov 44; by the next day, it extended from Pont-à-Mousson up to the Rhine–Marne Canal, which passes through the Saverne Gap. On 9 Nov 44, the enemy started to attack also north of Metz, and achieved notable successes from the beginning. To the southeast of Metz, the hills of Delm and the Nieth sector had to be yielded, and in the northern sector, the enemy pincer advanced so far that the encirclement of Metz seemed imminent. All possible measures were hurriedly taken to build up food supplies in the city and to restore its old fortifications. But these measures had scarcely been initiated when the enemy was already drawing closer to the city from the north and from the south. In order to avoid a gap in its front, First Army had to disengage its forces from Metz and take up a shortened position in the direction northwest to southeast. Since the forces left in the city, which were now without outside assistance, were insufficient for a defense of all the installations, one fortress after another was captured by the enemy. By 21 Nov 44, all practical resistance ceased, even though some of the fortresses held out a little longer.

The resistance offered in the Metz sector was to serve the purpose of pinning down enemy forces, and was thereby to afford sufficient time to First Army to occupy another position and regroup its forces. But the sudden collapse of the Metz defenses brought no significant alleviation from this direction although the Army was given a short breathing spell.

On 14 Nov 44, OB West reported that the combat strength of First Army had considerably diminished. He had therefore requested replacements and new materiel, and added that no forces could be withdrawn from Nineteenth Army. According to his evaluation, it would be impossible – even though one infantry division was being brought up – to withdraw within conceivable time the four mobile divisions committed to the A Gp G area, which were supposed to be reorganized (11 and 21 Pz Divs, 25 Pz Gren Div, and 17 SS Pz Gren Div). Since some of these units had been destined for the Ardennes Offensive, the developments in the First Army sector were also interfering with the plans for that Offensive.

Another threat to the German plans appeared on the front which was adjacent to the south. Here, the enemy exerted pressure against both the Sarrebourg depression and the Belfort Pass. On 21 Nov 44, the enemy reached Pfalzburg after having advanced beyond Sarrebourg. Armored points, thrusting to the south of the Saverne Gap, were already reaching the advance area of Strasbourg. Hoping that the first enemy forces would only be weak and could still be stopped by a flanking thrust, the Supreme Command agreed to release Pz Lehr Div, which was one of those units that had, already in Sep 44, been withdrawn from the front in order to serve as backbone of the coming

Offensive. This élite division, which was still being reorganized, began its attack on 23 Nov 44, the day on which enemy tanks entered Strasbourg.

On the same evening, OB West reported that the thrust via the Saverne Gap was being followed up by other attacks. Thus, the West Wall and the Palatinate were also said to be in danger. According to OB West, the reason for the enemy successes was the weakening of the divisions employed in this frontal sector; their value had never been high, but they had been submitted to many weeks of incessant fighting without receiving reinforcements, and were exhausted. He continued by reporting, that there was a lack of reserves and that the counterattack by Pz Lehr Div would not achieve its objective. Whatever forces, at present being transferred from Holland, had been promised to Army Group, would arrive too late. The loss of Alsace could only be prevented by the immediate transfer of one infantry and two panzer divisions. These additional units could not be obtained from the forces subordinate to OB West. This request, however, could only be granted, if some of the Sixth Pz Army units, which had been reserved for the Offensive by OKW, or some of the reserves, which had been accumulated, were to be used for this purpose. The Führer refused to authorize this, and OB West on 24 Nov 44 was informed accordingly. In spite of the increasing danger in Alsace–Lorraine, he wanted to maintain his present operations plan and therefore became reconciled to additional territorial losses. Thus, A Gp G was compelled to continue the fighting on its own resources. This decision was all the harder for Gen Pz Hermann Balck, the commander of A Gp G, inasmuch as another change was just occuring in southern Alsace. On 21 Nov 44, the enemy had entered Belfort, thereby forcing the Belfort Pass, and, similar to the events near the Saverne Gap, armored points simultaneously succeeded in thrusting far to the east. They penetrated into Mulhouse, but – contrary to what happened in the north – they were cut off from their rear communications. This situation, however, only lasted for a few days, after which the French managed to reestablish communications along the Swiss border, and thus Lower Alsace was also considered lost. Besides, this new enemy success endangered Nineteenth Army: the Vosges position might unhinge from its two open flanks, and the Army might see its withdrawal cut off. All attempts to release forces by a withdrawal from the Vosges *Vorstellung* (Advance Position) to the *Kammstellung* (Ridge Position) and to thereby restore the situation in the south, were in vain. It was to be considered a success that new defensive positions were established south of Strasbourg and north of Mulhouse. These lines averted the worst disaster and made it possible to hold on to the ridges of the Vosges. The risk had to be taken, that Nineteenth Army might be caught in a pincer movement by flank attacks and be cut off from the Rhine. But, this risk had to be taken, since it was a question of preventing the enemy from reaching the Rhine line which would release a number of his divisions for other purposes. Whereas the situation on the southern wing of A Gp G was stabilized after the beginning of Dec 44, the central sector of its front continued to remain unstable.

First Army still had the support of the West Wall, which had been hastily repaired, and which was provisionally occupied by forces of the Home Army. But, attempts were being made to hold on to as much advance territory as possible. On 28 Nov 44, Pz Lehr Div, which, in spite of all efforts, had not succeeded in obtaining any decisive results, was withdrawn in order to serve as 'Feuerwehr' (fire department) at any threatened point in the Army sector. The 21 Pz Div was tied down by enemy thrusts in the vicinity of Merzig and Saarlautern, which could be stopped only at a short distance from the Saar. Small, but steady advances by the enemy would not be prevented, nor was it possible to save Kaiserlautern, which was captured on 5 Dec 44.

According to the plans at that time, the offensive of A Gp B was due to start within the next few days. The Pz Lehr Div was therefore instructed to proceed to the entraining points. The Führer Begleit Brig, which had temporarily been made available to Army Group as supporting unit, was also taken back into the OKW reserves. On 5 Dec 44, 11 Pz Div was to follow, and on 6 and 7 Dec 44, the *volks artillerie* corps which had been loaned to Army Group. But, A Gp G was forced to report that it could not carry out these instructions, because the enemy was now exerting pressure on the First Army front with a force consisting of ten infantry and three panzer divisions at full strength. There were indications for an impending encirclement of Saarbrücken, and, in addition, a thrust near Weissenberg appeared to be threatening. The real strength of the eight exhausted infantry divisions of A Gp G was only that of three, while the four mobile units could only be counted as one and one half. While the Germans had 90 tanks and self-propelled assault guns available for commitment, the enemy strength was estimated at 700 to 800 tanks. OB West added, that he had already transferred to Army Group all the forces he had at his disposal, namely three divisions from Holland, and that he therefore felt compelled to leave – until further notice – 11 Pz Div and one Volks Art Corps with A Gp G, thus assisting Army Group at the expense of the planned Offensive.

By 7 Dec 44, the critical situation on the Saar front had developed so far, that the fighting had extended to Völklinger, a town in the immediate vicinity of Saarbrücken, and that a gap in the West Wall near Dillingen was widening. It was possible to prevent a complete breakthrough at this point, but now Saargemünd, into which the enemy had penetrated on 10 Dec 44, became a new danger spot. Hagenau was also imperiled. Once again, it was 11 Pz Div which prevented a breakthrough near Saargemünd on 11 Dec 44. Then, the enemy tested the West Wall defenses near Saarlautern, near Weissenburg, and in the vicinity of Bitsche. The danger, that one of the points, which had been softened up, would give way, increased by the hour. Thus A Gp G was, by mid-

Dec 44, in a more than critical position. Both on the Rhine and the Vosges fronts as well as along the West Wall, disaster seemed to be impending at any moment, should the enemy continue to commit his forces as he had hitherto. During all these weeks, Army Group had been requesting with increasing urgency that it be allocated additional forces, weapons and equipment. But, Army Group only received the barest necessities and could therefore only patch up its front by extending its divisions to the utmost. Some of these divisions had been submitted to continuous fighting since the Mediterranean coast had been abandoned and had covered gigantic distances on foot. The replacements Army Group had received were not used to fighting and extreme hardships; but those, who had withstood the last few weeks, had by now been assimilated by the regular troops. But then, the demands made on the replacements were truly extraordinary. On 18 Nov 44, OB West reported that the morale of the A Gp G units was excellent, but that they had reached the end of their strength. Detailed reports gave the Supreme Command exact information on the hardships suffered by the individual soldier, as well as on the performance of the lower command, and on what had been accomplished by this combination of battle-tested and untrained soldiers. These reports also described how – despite their efforts – the troops were forced to give ground because they lacked everything, particularly heavy weapons, and because of their great numerical inferiority.

Thus, the Supreme Command was aware of the situation in the Army Group sector and knew its needs. Nevertheless, the Supreme Command continued to keep the left wing of the Western Front at a disadvantage by only ever granting a fraction of the requests. It was reconciled to the fact that the enemy had penetrated into Metz, Strasbourg, Belfort, and Mulhouse, that nearly all of Alsace–Lorraine had been lost, and that the Saar, the Palatinate and Baden were now in the danger zone. All these sacrifices to keep the accumulated reserves intact! Thus, the Supreme Command paid, already before the beginning of the Offensive, an extremely high price for its execution.

In addition, the plan for the assembly of forces was – in spite of the meagre allocations – hampered by the happenings in this sector just as by the Roer Battle. Two units had to be temporarily released from the OKW reserves, and the conditions of these had been obviously reduced. The 11 Pz Div, which at first had been included in the attack forces, was now completely excluded from participation in the Offensive, and the same or a similar fate befell several other units. This disadvantage was, however, offset by the fact, that the enemy was now employing strong forces opposite A Gp G, and that his units were undergoing strenuous combat. It has already been mentioned in the description of the events on the A Gp B front, where similar incidents had occurred, how the strategic reserves of the enemy were reduced by the fighting, and how, for that reason, the prospects for the Ardennes Offensive had improved. This fact, together with the conviction that the situation of A Gp G could only be alleviated by an attack in the adjacent sector, were the main factors which determined the Supreme Command to maintain its course.

2. THE FURTHER ELABORATION OF THE PLAN

Genfldm Model had – after his meeting with the Commander of the Fifth Pz Army, Gen Pz von Manteuffel, on 3 Nov 44 – become even more firmly convinced than he had been on the previous day at the conference of the C-in-C West, that the 'little' plan was better than the one elaborated by the Führer's headquarters. But, that conviction had not found its expression, since the C-in-C West had already on the same day transmitted his reply to the directives issued by Genobst Jodl. Although he had also adopted the 'little' plan in this reply, he did not stress it with the same emphasis which Genfldm Model presumably would have applied. Since the Führer had maintained his preference for the 'grand' plan after having studied that reply, the question seemed to have been settled once and for all.

But, Genfldm Model was not the type of man to content himself with a decision which he was opposed to. On the contrary, he merely waited for a suitable moment in order to bring up his plan for reconsideration.

Even though he considered the question of whether the offensive should be undertaken one way or the other as still being open, the mere fact that he would have to lead an offensive spurred his energy to the utmost. Bound by the obligation not to do anything, which would excite attention, he made unobtrusive inspections of the terrain and the assembly area in order to obtain detailed personal impressions of everything. At the same time he maintained the closest contact with the staffs which had been initiated into the plan. Weekly meetings with the Army Commanders were instituted in order to synchronize all preparations. The first meeting took place at Fifteenth Army headquarters on 16 Nov 44; the following officers attended: the Commanding Officers of Fifth and Sixth Pz Armies, as well as those of Seventh and Fifteenth Armies. The second one was held at Sixth Pz Army headquarters on 22 Nov 44; the same officers were present with the exception of the Commander of Fifteenth Army. A third meeting was held on 5 Dec 44, at Seventh Army headquarters, with the Commanding Officers of Fifth Pz and Seventh Armies in attendance. The over-all picture of the plan was, however, scarcely being mentioned, since – for the purpose of maintaining secrecy – Model confined his explanations to absolutely essential matters, even in the presence of his Army Commanders. In addition, Genfldm Model took part in map exercises, which the Army Commanders carried out with their subordinate generals after they had been initiated on the plan. These exercises were held in Seventh Army headquarters on 29 Nov 44, and in Sixth and Fifth Pz Army headquarters on several occasions.

The plans, which Genfldm Model submitted to the C-in-C West on the basis of the attack order issued on 10 Nov 44, were in turn transmitted by him to the Führer's headquarters on 18 Nov 44. The C-in-C West enclosed a map and several documents, and added an endorsement to the effect that he agreed with the opinion of Army Group. The Supreme Command gave, on 22 Nov 44, a temporary reply to all questions which were yet unanswered, and on 25 Nov 44, it made definite decisions.

The report of Army Group B contained the following points:

a) Provided that the element of surprise was maintained and the attack constantly fed with new forces, the planned operation could be carried out with the forces suggested and in the manner prescribed. The best prospects of success existed, if the attack was directed against the exhausted enemy in the Aachen area. The Commander of A Gp G – and consequently also the C-in-C West – requested freedom of action for the necessary preparations and for an early start of the attack. (The Supreme Command [Hitler] decided: The weather conditions were to be the determining factor. The Führer would fix the date for the start of the attack. Improvised decisions were out of the question.)

b) The decisive factor for the success of the attack and the retention of an area extending over almost 300 km in depth would be the continuous reinforcement of the attack armies and the assembly of strategic OB West reserves. Once the battle had been joined, the enemy would certainly commit not only his strategic reserves, but also all units near the front. Four infantry and five to six armored divisions would probably be brought up from the south and southwest, and two infantry and four to five armored divisions from the north. It was therefore of decisive importance that the panzer units reach the Maas between Liège and Namur on the first day, and form bridgeheads. No let up in the advance was to occur. Speedy maneuvering was to prevent the build up of an enemy defense line along the Maas. (The decision was: Agreement with the conclusions. It was to be anticipated that the enemy, also, was using up his reserves in the current defensive battle.)

c) The further the two panzer armies advanced, the more their flanks would be extended. For their protection an OB West reserve force of at least three *volks grenadier* and two or three panzer divisions would be required. The C-in-C West requested the transfer of:

(1) Two panzer or panzer grenadier divisions, as well as one panzer corps headquarters staff with corps troops;

(2) One *volks grenadier* division and two panzer or panzer grenadier divisions; all these units were needed as strategic reserves;

(3) Furthermore, four or five additional *volks grenadier* divisions would be needed in Dec 44 in order to relieve mobile divisions.

(The Supreme Command decided: OKW was providing strategic reserves within the limits of possibilities. This problem had nothing to do with the preparations for the attack. Sizable contingents would have to be obtained in the manner described below.)

d) Later on, it was intended to withdraw mobile units and *Heeres* troops from other sectors of the front and transfer them into the area of the Offensive. (Decision: Agreed.)

e) The start of the operation would depend on the outcome of the battle near Aachen and on the reorganization of the panzer divisions as well as on the transfer of *Heeres* troops. The launching of the attack before the beginning of Dec 44 did not seem feasible. (Decision: Agreement.)

With regard to the plan of distribution OB West had sent to the Supreme Command, he was instructed to concentrate the forces in a smaller area during the first phase of the attack. The combat sectors were at first to be narrow, and become wider, in order to give the combat teams a choice of several objectives once they had reached the banks of the Maas, where a decision would have to be made. With regard to the timetable, which had been submitted, OB West was instructed to wait for subsequent orders.

The Supreme Command had – on its own account – already gathered for the Offensive all the forces, which could be withdrawn in the West, in the Zone of the Interior and in other theaters of war. It was therefore impossible to completely satisfy the new request for additional forces. This must have been obvious also to Genfldm Model. It can be assumed that he submitted his request in order to make his principal ideas even more plausible. These were once again focussed on the 'little' plan, that is to say, a suggestion, which had not only met with the renewed approval of the C-in-C West, but which was also being supported by the Commanding Officers of the two panzer armies. It would have been against regulations, if Army Group or OB West had declared their intention to change the fundamental principles of this order. That they actually had the 'little' plan in mind, was demonstrated by another suggestion, which the C-in-C West made on 21 Nov 44. To a report on the extent to which his forces were being pinned down and worn out by the enemy attacks, he added the suggestion to quickly exploit the temporary weakening of the enemy forces, and to use the special reserves, which had been left untouched, for launching an enveloping attack against First US Army opposite Seventh Army and the wings of Ninth US and Second Br Armies in the Roermund-Gei-lenkirchen area. By a defensive battle of this type, which would at first only have a limited local objective, a strong enemy group of forces could certainly be annihilated. In that way, a sound basis for the Offensive could be obtained, quite apart from its strong psychological effect.

Thus, the C-in-C West attempted to make the 'little' plan more palatable to the Supreme Command by presenting it as the operation's initial phase, which was to improve the starting position for the plan adopted by the Führer, and which was to produce a more favorable ratio of forces for the main attack. But even this method did not have the desired effect, because what he was actually suggesting would have turned into a battle of attrition, which presumably would have spared so few of the reserve units, that the initial phase could not possibly be followed by a second one. For this reason, the Supreme Command refused to be diverted from its intentions.

The temporary decision of 22 Nov 44 was followed by a definite one on 25 Nov 44, both of which were in reply to the suggestions transmitted on 21 Nov 44. In this final decision the Führer informed the C-in-C West as follows: Since the beginning of the defensive battle the enemy actions had substantiated the prerequisites for the attack. The attrition of the enemy forces was considerable. The bulk of the enemy reserves were pinned down near the front or had already suffered casualties. The difficulties in the enemy supply system were growing. The front, which had been chosen for the breakthrough, was as sparsely occupied as ever. In spite of the undesirable fact that so many German attack forces had been pinned down elsewhere, the Führer was still unswervingly resolved to adhere to the objective and the scope of the original plan. He flatly rejected the 'little' plan with all its implications, such as turning off already east of the Maas. The Führer completely agreed to the suggestion that bridgeheads be formed across the Maas on the first day of the Offensive. Under favorable conditions resolute leaders of advance detachments might achieve this already at dawn; such leaders had to be found. The Führer particularly emphasized that the two attack armies should not in advance be tied down to one or two Maas crossings, but should be assured of freedom of movement within a wide sector. For this reason, the boundary was to be drawn in a manner which would guarantee the Maas crossing near Huy to Sixth Pz Army. The combat sector of Fifth Pz Army would accordingly have to be extended to the south as far as Givet. The Führer approved of the plan for the launching of the breakthrough, but he preferred an even stronger concentration of forces – especially of the artillery units – at the points of breakthrough, which were to remain as narrow as possible.

So far, no decision had been made on the southern boundary of the left attacking wing. The Führer had from the very start, considered the Our salient, which was projecting to the east between Echternach and Wasserbillig, a menace to his plans – just as the heights of Elsenborn constituted a threat in the north. At both these points, the enemy would be strongly tempted to thrust into the attack wedge at the most dangerous points, namely just above its base. Considering the limited forces available, OB West hesitated to overtax Seventh Army by too extensive a mission, all the more so, since Army also emphasized the difficulties of this task. OB West had explained that he did not believe a double envelopment of the Echternach–Grevenmacher salient was feasible. But, the Führer insisted on his point of view, that the enemy forces in this salient had to be wiped out, since this operation was the prerequisite for the thrust of the left Seventh Army wing, which was to be carried out from the line south of Vianden–Echternach in the direction of Luxembourg. But, since envelopment was not feasible, OB West now received orders to unhinge the army positions in the salient by a thrust from the north; only after this operation had succeeded, could the thrust toward Luxembourg be considered as promising.

The Führer's reply contained the following comments on the subject of the allocation of forces, which had been broached once more by OB West: The reduction in the forces destined for the attack was offset by the simultaneous expenditure of enemy forces. His immediate reserves had decreased correspondingly. Two *volks grenadier* divisions would be added to the German forces during the first half of Dec 44 – 560 Volks Gren Div by 6 Dec 44, and 167 Volks Gren Div by 13 Dec 44; in addition, one panzer division – 10 SS Pz Div – would also become available. However, these divisions would not arrive in time for the attack itself, which, during its development, was to receive the following reinforcements:

a) By the withdrawal of units from other sectors of the Western Front.

b) By the transfer of three additional *volks grenadier* divisions (the 79, 259, and 320), as well as one *gebirgs* (mountain) division (6 SS Geb Div), which was being transferred from Norway.

c) By the bringing up of well-armed *marsch* (replacement transfer battalions, with a total strength of 50,000 men; they were to be integrated into the fighting units at the rate of 20,000 by 1 Dec 44, 20,000 by 8 Dec 44, and 10,000 men by 15 Dec 44.

There was no question of launching the attack at an earlier moment in order to exploit a situation which momentarily seemed more favorable. The deciding factor was to be the weather which was to compensate for the enemy air superiority. The Führer maintained his authority to fix the date for the start of the attack. With regard to the timetable, he wished that units with tracked vehicles, which were parts of mobile divisions, be brought up one night later, in order to prevent premature detection of the plan. On the following day – 26 Nov 44 – Genobst Jodl had a conference with the C-in-C West at the latter's headquarters in Ziegenberg, near Frankfurt. He again confirmed that the distribution of forces and the attack plan – the 'grand' plan – were irrevocable. Furthermore, he availed himself of the opportunity to inspect the command and security facilities of the shelter and barracks camp *'Adlerhorst'* (Eagle's Eyrie) in the vicinity of Ziegenberg. This camp had been established for the campaign in the West in 1940, and was now being considered as a possible command post for the Führer, the Chief of OKW, and the Chief of the Wehrmacht Operations Staff during the coming Offensive.

Upon his return to Berlin, Genobst Jodl obtained from the Führer decisions on all matters which were still unresolved and then informed OB West:

a) The 10 Dec 44 was now being considered as zero day.

b) All withdrawals necessary for the attack were to be carried out accordingly.

c) The defensive front of Sixth Pz Army between Monschau and Liège was to be amply provided with heavy antitank weapons.

d) The starting time of the artillery preparation was fixed at 0530; the firing was at least 30 to 60 minutes; the infantry attack was to start between 0600 and 0630.

Thus, the decision had been taken. But was it the correct one? In conformity with the methods employed by the General Staff of examining all decisions, by comparing them with all other feasible plans to establish whether the best plan had really been chosen, the possibility of an attack to the south of the selected attack area was again considered. The impetus for this reconsideration came from the loss of Alsace and Lorraine. In connection with some discussions the Führer had a draft for an operation to retake Alsace and Lorraine submitted to him on 26 Nov 44. The advantages of this plan, which had already been included in the various plans discussed in Oct 44, were the regaining of the Minotte area and the coal and electrical power plants of St Avold, the possibility of decisively alleviating the pressure exerted on Nineteenth Army, and the prevention of the reconstruction of the French Army by the annihilation of its élite divisions. However, even more considerable disadvantages outweighed these advantages, and the plan was dropped. It was only after the beginning of the Offensive that the examination of this plan resumed.

The C-in-C West could not reconcile himself with the decision giving him the time for the start of the Offensive. This really was a subject which could be considered from different points of view. The Führer's concept had been, that the infantry should launch its attack already during the night, if possible before midnight, in order to enable the tanks to start off in the morning and give them the whole day. The C-in-C West had been of the opinion that the troops were not sufficiently trained for night combat with its high requirements, for orientation and other abilities. At the end of Nov 44, it was being considered whether the attack might not be carried out with the assistance of searchlights, but it was found out that they could not be moved up fast enough. A Gp B objected to the decision of 26 Nov 44, because it believed that there would still be thick fog by 0530, which would prevent the artillery fire from being fully effective. On 29 Nov 44, the C-in-C West therefore transmitted his request to delay the attack until 0800, and submitted another timetable with corresponding changes. This request, which would, above all, have had an adverse effect on the launching of the armored units, was not granted by the Supreme Command. Since by now the Commanding Generals had also been initiated in the plan, the time had come for the issuance of the attack order by A Gp B, the command, which was to be in charge of the attack. It was issued on

29 Nov 44, and – since the Supreme Command had persisted in its point of view – it was entirely based on the Supreme Command's attack order of 10 Nov 44. Except for some minor rectifications requested by the Führer on 9 Dec 44, this order remained valid for the Offensive, which was to start on 16 Dec 44.

The planned Offensive had – during its preparatory stages – always been known by the purposely misleading designation '*Wacht am Rhein*' (Watch on the Rhine); at this point Genfldm Model gave it the camouflage title of '*Herbstnebel*' (Autumn Fog).

3. THE BERLIN CONFERENCE OF 2 DEC 44

The rectifications of the attack order were the result of a conference, which took place in the Reichs Chancellery in Berlin on 2 Dec 44. The conference had been requested by Genfldm Model on the insistence of Gen Pz von Manteuffel; the Führer had granted his request. Besides these three, Genfldm Keitel, Genobst Jodl and Obstgrf Dietrich were also present. Genfldm von Rundstedt was represented by Genlt Westphal. The subjects of the discussions, which lasted for hours, were the following: The expansion of the attack, its execution, the commitment of the panzer divisions, the attack date, and other pertinent questions. With regard to the distribution of forces, the following decisions were taken:

a) The 10 SS Pz Div, which was still employed in the Jülich–Düren sector, was to be withdrawn and transferred to Sixth Pz Army.

b) The Führer Begleit Brig, which was part of the OKW reserves, was to take part in a later phase of the attack and be subordinated to Fifth Pz Army.

c) The reinforced Führer Gren Brig was to be transferred to A Gp B for commitment on the left wing in the Seventh Army sector.

d) Furthermore, an order was approved, which was to be issued by OB West; it stipulated that 11 Pz and Pz Lehr Divs, which at the time were still committed in the A Gp G sector, should be held ready for withdrawal by 4 Dec 44.

These were mostly units which had already been included in previous estimates, and which were now being given more definite assignments. Since these decisions were not fully enforced they proved to be quite ineffective. The Commanding Generals were still worrying that despite all these efforts, the available forces would not suffice. Genfldm Model emphatically stressed the anxieties, which he and his army Commanders were harboring on the general personnel and supply situation. The Supreme Command could only acknowledge their anxieties and refer them to the extreme efforts it had made to gather all the forces which could possibly be assembled, and to equip them as well as the present circumstances would permit.

This brought up another point which was of great importance to the Army Commanders. They all requested strongly that the starting date of the attack, which at present had been fixed for 10 Dec 44, be further delayed in order to allow them to complete the reorganization of their divisions, which – according to their opinion – had not been accomplished, and to wait for the arrival of the missing equipment. But, in view of the general situation and the threat that the secret might be prematurely discovered, the Führer declined this request. Naturally, one of the subjects, which came up for discussion, was that of the enemy air superiority. On this subject the Führer announced, that, after deduction of all the losses anticipated during the first days after the start of the attack, the Luftwaffe could be expected to accomplish 800 to 900 sorties a day, 60 of which would be made by the new jet planes (Messerschmitt 262 and Arado 234); this would mean a considerable relief for the ground forces.

Three of the special questions, which came up for discussion, ought to be mentioned:

a) Gen Pz von Manteuffel, basing his argument on his experience on the Eastern Front, suggested that the panzer forces be issued five VS (*Verbrauchssatz* – amount of POL required per 100 km*), which would give them an operating range of 250 km. Efforts were made to comply with this requirement, but it could not finally be met; the actual issue amounted to only one and one half VS for an operating range of 75 km, a fact which later on had very unfavorable effects.

b) The question of the time of the attack was once again under discussion. Contrary to the opinion expressed by the C-in-C West on 29 Nov 44, Gen Pz von Manteuffel was in favor of the time, which had originally been set, that is 0530; he was convinced that a breakthrough by the infantry could – due to the enemy air superiority and artillery strength – not be carried out by daylight, when the enemy would be ready for defense. If the attack were launched before dawn, the panzer forces, which would be brought up during the night, could already start off by the break of day, that is, at a time when the enemy could have brought up his local reserves, and when the German infantry could be expected to be brought to a stop. The Führer shared the same opinion; the starting time, therefore, remained fixed at 0530. However, Genfldm Model authorized the Army Commanders to take the local conditions into account, when elaborating detailed plans for their sectors. For example, along the German border, rivers had to be crossed on the left wing of Fifth Pz Army and in front of Seventh Army, and the distance between the front lines differed in the various sectors. For this reason, advance elements were authorized to silently creep up to the enemy positions under the protection of darkness even before the official starting time. But great care was to be taken that the attention of the enemy not be at any point aroused before the opening of fire,

---

* Amount per 100 km of level terrain; in the hilly Ardennes with its winding, muddy roads this amount cannot be reckoned to take the forces more than half that distance. Ed.

which was to simultaneously take place at 0530 in all three army sectors; this plan was to guarantee a simultaneous sweep across the entire, long attack front.

c) Army Group had suggested, that one regiment of each unit, which was to take part in the Offensive, should be inserted in the front line already before the attack in order to familiarize the units with the terrain and facilitate the attack itself. This suggestion was disapproved because of the necessity to maintain secrecy. They were only authorized to advance to a line where there was no danger of the Americans prematurely taking prisoners from divisions. The experiences made with searchlights were also brought up for discussion. Since most of them had been unfavorable, the idea to use searchlights was abandoned.

At the end of the conference, Genfldm Model made another attempt toward the adoption of the 'little' plan. Adolf Hitler disapproved, but added that it could still be carried out, should the attack fail to develop as expected. The preparations should therefore proceed according to the schedule of the 'grand' plan.

The results of the conference became a number of orders which were issued on 3 and 4 Dec 44, covering a wide range of subjects such as the allocation of horses and motor vehicles, the bringing up of security forces in order to relieve the fighting forces, etc. A summarizing order was also issued, in which the previously submitted distribution of forces was approved, except for minor alterations. The assembly areas for the OKW reserves were to be designed in a special order. The maintenance of secrecy was once again emphasized. In consideration of the varied attack conditions in different sectors, a unified regulation of firing preparations was not issued. It was also deemed important for the progress of the Offensive, that the attack as well as the advance continue during the night.

On 8 Dec 1944, a new operations draft was received; it had been prepared by OB West on 7 Dec 44, and was based on preceding discussions and on a report submitted on 6 Dec 44. In this draft, OB West reverted to the suggestion to carry out a secondary thrust from the north, which was to be launched from the salient south of Roermond. This plan had been abandoned in order to concentrate all forces in the attack sector. Genfldm Model had shared this opinion; but, he had meanwhile made a personal inspection of the attack sector, and he was now, after all, in favor of carrying out this thrust, which was one of the prerequisites of the 'little' plan he was sponsoring. The two mobile units and the two infantry divisions, already committed in this sector, were to carry out this attack. The staff of XII SS Inf Corps, which was also employed in this sector, was being considered for the command functions. Its Commanding Officer, Gen Inf Günther Blumentritt had, during the meetings near Ziegenberg on 10 and 11 Dec 44, an opportunity to convey the following outlines of this mission to the Führer:

a) The attack on the right was to be carried out by 9 Pz and 176 Inf Divs. They were to advance eastwards, by-pass Sittard, and thrust toward Maastricht, then encircle Sittard and secure a crossing over the Maas.

b) Simultaneously, 59 Inf and 15 Volks Gren Divs were to attack on the left in the direction of Heerlen. After the capture of Maastricht and Heerlen, the attack was to advance farther to the south. It was to be expected that elements of Sixth Pz Army advancing via Liège would be able to connect with XII SS Inf Corps.

In the opinion of the Supreme Command, the main function of such an attack would be to pin down enemy forces. But it could only be successful after the enemy had started to withdraw forces from the XII SS Corps sector. For this reason, there was no question of launching this attack simultaneously with the main assault. On 12 Dec 44, OB West therefore received a negative reply. The Supreme Command maintained this point of view when OB West resubmitted his suggestion on 16 Dec 44.

On 9 Dec 44 certain alterations in the attack order submitted by Army Group on 29 Nov 44, were finally made by request of the Führer, but these were minor. Thus, the 'grand' plan had prevailed in spite of all repeated efforts Genfldm Model had made for exactly one month – 2 Nov–2 Dec 44 – to obtain the adoption of the 'little' plan. He had not been successful, but, despite all rejections, his suggestion had not been simply filed away: the Führer himself kept the plan in mind in the event that operation 'Autumn Fog' did not succeed as expected.

4. THE OPERATIONS PLANS OF THE ARMIES

On 10 Dec 44, the Armies issued their final orders for the attack. These were merely a summary of all the detailed discussions, decisions and orders, which were the result of weeks of deliberations, first within the Army Staff organizations and later their subordinate commands.

We shall start in the north of the attack sector.

a) Sixth Pz Army

Army had suggested that both panzer armies launch their attacks from the farthest point south of the Hohes Venn and the Schnee Eifel, half of which was occupied by the enemy and which was difficult to attack from the front. The two armies would thereby be able to take advantage of the more favorable terrain southwest of Prüm. Army had planned the two armies be committed abreast, as close to each other as possible, in order to obtain a strong spearhead. These suggestions could not be complied with, because the Supreme Command considered a wide attack front as extremely important, and also believed the capture of the heights of Elsenborn, which constituted a threat to the flank, to be a prerequisite for the farther advance. Instead, Army received the following mission:

On X-Day, after intensive artillery preparation, Sixth Pz Army was to commit its subordinate infantry divisions to break through the enemy defense front in the Monschau–Krewinkel sector. Then, without considering their flanks, its panzer units were to thrust across the Maas south of Liège, and continue their advance toward Antwerp while covering their flank along the Albert Canal. Carefully selected advance detachments, commanded by particularly daring officers, were to quickly capture the Maas bridge south of Liège before their demolition by the enemy. In accordance with the wishes of the Führer, Liège itself was not to be attacked.

The LXVII Inf Corps, which was being employed on the left wing of Fifteenth Army, but which was to be subordinated to Sixth Pz Army for the attack, was to be committed along the general line Monschau–Verviers-Liège for the purpose of building up a strong defense front. After the Maas crossing had been accomplished, Corps was to be once more subordinated to Fifteenth Army. The boundary with the Fifth Pz Army along the line Prüm (exclusive)–St Vith (inclusive)–Huy (exclusive) was not to be compulsory in order to give to whichever army advanced the fastest every opportunity to exploit a favorable development. The terrain assigned to Army was extremely difficult for panzer units, and particularly unfavorable right at the beginning. Only after the Hohes Venn had been crossed, was there any open terrain in view. Until then, the tanks would, most of the time, not be able to leave the roads. The planning of the distribution of traffic on these roads presented special problems since only few of them could be used. Based on the experiences of the retreat and careful reconnaissance, five roads were selected, four of which – the ones farthest to the south – were designated as approach tracks. They were known to be unsatisfactory, but that could not be helped. On the northernmost road only an armored reconnaissance patrol was to advance, since it was to be exclusively available to the infantry divisions.

An additional difficulty in the launching of the Sixth Pz Army attack consisted in the fact that the bulk of Army was to thrust to the northwest, while its infantry forces were to simultaneously build up a defense front on the right flank. The Führer had repeatedly emphasized that the panzer divisions were to avoid being pinned down too early, and were not to prematurely turn off to the north. Once they had broken through the enemy front, the infantry divisions therefore had to be immediately regrouped for their next mission; then, their advance had to be speeded up in spite of the terrain difficulties, so that they could serve as flank protection. It was essential that, during that time, they should be allowed sufficient space for their deployment, and that their supply roads should not be blocked by tanks.

Since the two missions given to Army were contradictory in their contents,

Army had requested, that Fifteenth Army be given the flank protection mission. However, this request had been rejected, in order to ensure a unified command. For the same reason, even the left wing corps of Fifteenth Army was subordinated to Sixth Pz Army for the duration of the attack.

Since it was believed that three enemy divisions, namely forces for an attack against the Urft dam and replacement units, were in the Elsenborn heights, Army also wanted to employ three divisions in that sector. But, by order of Army Group, only two divisions were to be committed for this purpose, which, however, were to be picked for their excellence. The importance of using especially good divisions and reinforcing them by the allocation of heavy weapons for the purpose of right flank protection had repeatedly been stressed by the Führer.

When the launching of the panzer forces was being considered, a decision had to be made, whether the two corps were to be launched abreast or echeloned in depth. Army would have preferred to commit them abreast, because, this way, more tanks could be employed from the first. But, the terrain difficulties were such, that insurmountable traffic congestion would have been unavoidable. Furthermore, a commitment in depth also seemed preferable because Army would thus have some panzer reserves on hand, which could be committed in case of an early threat to its right flank or in case of stoppages during the advance of the infantry. In addition, this method had the advantage that fresh panzer forces could be employed at the front in the event that the first wave was rapidly exhausted. This decision, which had been taken after careful consideration of all the pros and cons, was approved by Army Group.

The second corps was to follow immediately behind the one in front so that it could thrust toward Antwerp as soon as it had crossed the Maas. The corps in front was to cover the right flank beyond that river. Advance detachments were to attempt to take the Maas bridges while they were intact. (It was not known to Army until the very last days that this was also one of the objectives of Operation 'Greif'; this fact did not influence its decisions.)

In accordance with the instructions received, the line Simmerath–Eupen–Limburg–Liège was being considered for flank cover. Three *volks grenadier* divisions (the 326, 246 and 12) as well as the 3 Fs Div were available for its protection.

The staff of Sixth Pz Army, which during the assembly had been transferred from Westphalia to the Cologne area, in a camouflage designation, took over – on 8 Dec 44 – the control of supplies in the front sector Monschau–Schnee Eifel (exclusive). On 11 Dec 44, Army assumed full command. For this purpose, Army moved its command post to Münstereifel on 10 Dec 44. On the same day, its attack order was issued and disseminated to its subordinate units.

During those days, Army was also informed that parachute troops would participate in the operation. One *Fallschirmjäger* battalion consisting of about

250 men, which was to be under the command of Obstlt von der Heydte, was to jump on the attack day ahead of the panzer advance points, with the objective of either opening the way for the tanks in the Hohes Venn area, or preventing American forces from penetrating southward between Eupen and Verviers before a defense front could be built up.

Army requested that the *Fallschirmjäger* troops be committed in the Monte Rigi area, because, according to the over-all evaluation, their commitment in this area seemed to be the most promising. The mission of the *Fallschirm* group was changed accordingly; it was to take along many 'dummies' in order to simulate a large-scale action. Army had requested that the attack be further postponed, since many gaps in its reorganization had still not been closed. It was greatly relieved, when the start of the attack was delayed. According to the evaluation of the Army Staff, all preparations had by now been carried out and brought to a point, which made the success of a breakthrough – at least as far as the Maas – seem feasible. But, Army did not believe that this would be an easy achievement. OKW expected that the Maas could be reached within two days from the start. Army calculated the following schedule: One day for the breakthrough across the enemy positions, one day for surmounting the Hohes Venn with the panzer divisions, and two days for the Maas crossings – thus, altogether four days.

b) Fifth Pz Army

During the preparations for the Offensive, the staff of Fifth Pz Army had been handicapped, because, from the end of Oct 44 onward, it had been in charge of the Aachen sector and thus, from 16 Oct 44 on, it had been preoccupied with command functions for the defense in front of the Roer. Its relief by Fifteenth Army had to be postponed several times and did not take place until the end of Nov 44. Similarly, XLVII Pz Corps, which was to be employed at the point of main effort of Fifth Pz Army, was withdrawn from the Aachen sector of the front only on 5 Dec 44. Army took charge of its attack sector on 10 Dec 44.

The mission of Army was to achieve a breakthrough in the Olzheim–Gemünd sector and to thrust across the Maas on both sides of Namur in the direction of Brussels, which was to be by-passed on the left. Those Army elements, which were to cross the Maas above Namur, would also have to cross the Sambre. In contrast to its adjacent armies, Fifth Pz Army was, at first, not concerned with its flank protection. Its first objective was to reach the Maas and to secure river crossings. For this reason, its spearheads were to thrust past any resistance and advance as rapidly as possible in a western direction.

Two mobile divisions – 116 and 2 Pz Divs – were to be in front, and two additional units, Pz Lehr Div and Führer Begleit Brig, were to constitute the Army reserves, with three and one half divisions. In addition, four infantry divisions were subordinated to Army at the time of the attack.

Fifth Pz Army was, at the time when the attack was being launched, weaker than Sixth Pz Army, which had four entire panzer and five infantry divisions. Besides, since the Sixth Pz Army sector was narrower, since each of the four SS panzer divisions had approximately 30 tanks more than the other mobile divisions, and since their reorganization had been more thorough, the point of main effort was on the right.* However, it had to be taken into account that, once the breakthrough had been achieved, four of the infantry divisions belonging to Sixth Pz Army would be pinned down while providing flank protection.

On the basis of its mission and the distribution of forces, Fifth Pz Army expressed the following requests:

a) That it should not be compelled to adhere to a rigid operations plan determining its roads and objectives, which would prevent Army from taking advantage of any opportunities which presented themselves, and from shifting its point of main effort. Above all, each army be allowed to cross the Maas wherever it succeeded in doing so.

b) Army would commit all three corps abreast on a wide front in order to penetrate the enemy positions as rapidly as possible.

c) The Army would by-pass Bastogne, if necessary, and only encircle the town to avoid any unnecessary loss of time on this side of the Maas.

Army suggested that no heavy barrage be laid down before the attack, in order to maintain the element of surprise. This suggestion was approved only for the Fifth Pz Army sector; however, the other suggestion, that the attack start at night, was rejected.

Furthermore, Army urged that the point of main effort be shifted to the center of Army Group, that is, to its combat sector, with the motivation that both the wing armies would certainly be attacked on their flanks, and might thereby be pinned down. Army therefore suggested, that the plan for a secondary thrust from the north be abandoned, so that the forces of the main wedge could be reinforced. These suggestions were not addressed up to the beginning of the attack. As the reader will remember, both Army Group and OB West were in favor of this secondary thrust; for this reason, the forces destined for the thrust remained southeast of Roermond. But, when the Offensive got under way, the two mobile divisions committed in the north were moved farther south and committed in the Fifth Pz Army sector. At a time when Sixth Pz Army had already been pinned down, the point of main effort of the attack group was shifted to Fifth Pz Army. But, this shift came too late to be effective.

---

* This count is not strictly accurate. 1 SS Pz Div had 107 tanks and 20 assault guns at the beginning of the attack and 12 SS Pz Div had 77 tanks and 59 assault guns and tank destroyers. In Fifth Pz Army, 2 Pz Div had 75 tanks and 45 assault guns and 116 Pz Div had 69 tanks and 13 tank destroyers. Ed.

The suggestion Army made with reference to Bastogne was not approved. The Führer decided that Bastogne had to be taken. The free choice of Maas crossing points and the commitment on a wide front were approved.

Thus, Army committed its forces as follows:

On the right wing: The LXVI Inf Corps, with 18 and 62 Volks Gren Divs. Its mission was to carry out an enveloping attack on the Schnee Eifel and take St Vith; then the Corps, echeloned in depth, was to continue its thrust toward and across the Maas in the Huy–Andenne sector, or be transferred to the left Army wing.

In the center: The LVIII Pz Corps, with 116 Pz Div and 560 Volks Gren Div, was to cross the Our river on both sides of Ouren, and then continue – via Houffalize and across the Maas – its thrust in the Andenne–Namur sector, and build up bridgeheads on the other side of the Maas.

On the left wing: The XLVII Pz Corps, with 2 Pz Div and 26 Volks Gren Div, was to cross the Our on a wide front in the Dasburg–Gemünd sector; then, Corps was to by-pass the Clerf sector, take Bastogne, and finally, echeloned in depth, thrust toward and across the Maas at and south of Namur.

The Army reserves: The Pz Lehr Div and Führer Begleit Brig were to be held in readiness, and were to be launched for a rapid penetration by assault toward the Maas as soon as one of the corps had succeeded in breaking through.

After Houffalize and Bastogne had been taken, all three corps were to cross the river Ourthe, which cut their attack sectors perpendicularly, and were to surmount the main ridge of the Ardennes before they reached the Maas.

In view of the difficult nature of the terrain, in which the breakthrough was to take place, a drastic limitation of baggage was ordered; furthermore, only vehicles which could be assumed to be capable of overcoming the terrain difficulties, were to be used for this operation. Selected assault detachments and handpicked assault companies were to be launched for the breakthrough; the main body of troops was to be held back as reserve or direct pressure detachments. For the Offensive, Army set the following schedule:

First day: Breakthrough across the enemy positions, conquest of the Our and Clerf sectors, construction of one bridge per corps.

Second day: The line St Vith–Houffalize–Bastogne was to be reached and bridgeheads across the Ourthe were to be obtained.

Third day: The units were to fan out, receive supplies, and continue their thrust toward the Maas.

Fourth Day: The Maas was to be reached.

Thus, Army assumed that the first important objective would be reached within the same delay of four days that had been estimated by its right neighbor, Sixth Pz Army.

c) Seventh Army

The mission of the left wing army was to protect the open flank of Fifth Pz Army as far as the Maas. For this purpose, Army was to pivot to the left, after the breakthrough had been achieved, and then advance its right wing far enough to link up with the left wing of Fifth Pz Army and maintain contact. Thus, Army was to execute a movement, which, even in flat terrain without the impediment of river crossings, is difficult to carry out. The movement can be demonstrated by a comparison with three bent fingers, which are to be stretched, the first one only a little, the second one half way, while the third one was to be fully opened. In this manner, Army was to obtain the right position for a front, which was to provide cover from northwest to southeast, and build up a line between the Maas and First Army, which was under A Gp G and was not taking part in the Offensive. Army was to conquer the necessary terrain as quickly as possible. It had to be considered a certainty that the enemy would counterattack the Army.

As already mentioned, the question of how far the covering position was to be advanced, and where the left attack boundary was to be established, had been discussed at length. The arguments in favor of a thrust to the Semois sector was, that it constituted a favorable defense position, above all against armored attacks. And, the inclusion of the Echternach salient up to Wasser-billig seemed recommendable, because the enemy would otherwise threaten the attack wedge at its base, in a situation which was similar to that near Elsenborn. But, it became evident that the forces available were insufficient for so distant a thrust. The sector Vianden–Echternach, which was finally assigned to Army, corresponded to its strength and to the space it would require for the execution of its movements. The line Gedinne (25 km southeast of Givet)–Libramont–Martelange–Mersch–Wasserbillig was to constitute the Army front, which meant a reduction in its objective.

Should Army be able to thrust across this line, it was to do so; in any case, it was to intercept enemy attacks along this line, and not any farther to the rear. Its right wing was to always keep abreast of the left wing of the Fifth Pz Army. Advance detachments were to take up positions beyond that and reach as far as the Semois sector.

In the draft, the strength of Army had been evaluated at one panzer and six infantry divisions. Army, itself, calculated its requirements as follows:

One panzer division, which was to keep up with the mobile divisions of Fifth Pz Army,

Six infantry divisions for the defense front,

Two to three divisions as Army reserves,

Altogether nine to ten divisions.

The Army Commander justified these requirements by asserting that the main effort of the counterattack would probably be directed against the most vulnerable point of the German operation, that is against the line Bastogne–Echternach. On the contrary, Army Group was assuming that the pressure against this front would be less strong, and would rather be directed against the points of the armored spearheads. For that reason, Army was assigned only part of the forces it had requested. As a replacement for the panzer division originally destined for Army, Führer Gren Brig was subordinated to Seventh Army only after the start of the attack (20 Dec 44). Furthermore, two of the infantry divisions originally destined for Army were eliminated during the preparatory stage, with the result, that Army received three formations less than originally planned. Army thus started off with only four divisions; it had no reserve units of its own since all the available ones had been set aside as OKW reservers.

With so few forces at its disposal, the commitment of the Army units had to be as follows:

On the right wing: The LXXXIV Inf Corps, which was already being employed, with 5 Fs Div to the right and 352 Volks Gren Div to the left.
On the left wing: The LXXX Inf Corps, which was inserted during the attack, with 276 Volks Gren Div on the right and 212 Volks Gren Div on the left.

The LXXX Inf Corps was given the special mission of forcing the strong enemy artillery group – which had been recognized in the Alttrier–Christnach area, and from which interference at the river crossings of the Our and Sauer, was to be expected – to change its gun emplacements as the result of a direct thrust it was to undertake from Wallendorf and Echternach on Alttrier. The *bewachrungs* (rehabilitation) battalion, which, together with one *festungs* (fortress) machine gun battalion, was defending the southern Army sector, and which was, at first, to remain stationary, was, later on, to join in the attack.* It was expected that, with the Offensive progressing, the front at Wasserbillig could be pushed forward.

Due to the great width of the sector assigned to Army, which was to farther expand in correspondence with the successes obtained by Fifth Pz Army, the divisions were, at first, to be distributed by groups so that they could quickly build up centers of gravity after the enemy started to counterattack.

The LIII Inf Corps was being held at the disposal of Army to command the units which were to be brought up during the Offensive. Behind the Army

---

* These were 44 *Festung* Machine Gun Battalion and XIII/999 *Festung* Battalion, a penal formation. Ed.

sector, 9 and 79 Volks Gren Div had been assembled as OKW reserves. Subordinate to each of the two attack corps were one *sturmgeschütz* (self-propelled assault gun) brigade, one *volks artillerie* corps, and one *volks werfer* (rocket projector) brigade. Some of the self-propelled assault gun battalions, which were part of the T/O strength of the *volks grenadier* divisions, only arrived during the first days of the attack. On the morning of 16 Dec 44, Army had at its disposal altogether about 60–80 self-propelled assault guns, which were ready for commitment.* But, due to the inadequacy of the bridges, the first guns could cross the Our only on 17 Dec 44.

Since, contrary to the original plan, no mobile division had been assigned to Seventh Army, its main preoccupation was the problem of keeping contact with the left wing of Fifth Pz Army. As an expedient, several mobile advance detachments [e.g. one regiment of 5 Fs Div], the equivalent of approximately one battalion, were loaded onto trucks, and were allotted self-propelled assault guns, pak, and engineer troops equipped with obstacle construction materiel and mines.

Army was to cross the Our and the Sauer, and it was to be assumed that, at the time of the attack, the rivers would have risen higher than usual; for this reason, the allocation of four engineer battalions, six to eight bridge columns, 100 large pneumatic pontoons, and other equipment was of decisive importance. It was intended to build military bridges across the river Our, to replace these later by emergency bridges, which had already been prepared, and then to use the same military bridges for crossing the Sauer. Although this Army request had, in general, been approved, the promises made in this connection were not kept. Army actually received only two engineer battalions and one bridge column; furthermore, these units arrived only in the last moment and were therefore not able to take part in the preparations. Because of transportation difficulties, all efforts to improve this inadequate allocation of engineer forces proved fruitless. It was only after the attack had begun, that construction units of the *Organization Todt* and two additional bridge columns arrived. Army, therefore, still insisted on 14 and 15 Dec 44, that one of the main prerequisites for its attack had not been fulfilled. However, its request, that the attacks be postponed, was refused by Army Group.

On 10 Dec 44, Seventh Army handed over the command of the sector assigned to the two attack armies to Fifth and Sixth Pz Armies respectively; Army itself, retained the sector Vianden–Nittel (on the Moselle), and correspondingly transferred its command post from Münstereifel to Wittlich.

---

* Actual number was only 33 in the 11th StuG Brigade. 276 VG Div and 212 VG Div in LXXX Corps began the attack with none. Ed.

5. THE FINAL DISTRIBUTION OF FORCES

The first draft of the plan for the Ardennes Offensive, which had been submitted to the Führer on 11 Oct 44, and which had been approved by him, had been based on the commitment of 29–30 full divisions. Of the divisions destined for the Offensive, a large number were at that time still in the front line; they needed thorough reorganization, all the more so since most of them had not had a rest since the Invasion, and because the West Wall units, assigned to them, had not yet been indoctrinated. Some of the other units had not finished their initial organization. There was therefore much to be done before the attack could be started. The two questions which dominated during the intervening period were:

a) To what extent would it be possible to withdraw from the front the divisions destined for the Offensive in time to afford them sufficient reorganization?

b) To what extent would it be necessary to support threatened fronts by the commitment of units, which had been destined for the Offensive, but which now remained pinned down by the fighting?

By the end of Oct 44, the preparations had reached the following stage:

a) Sixth Pz Army was being reorganized in Westphalia; the Pz Lehr Div had to be withdrawn from Army; its reorganization could not be completed, because Division had to be prematurely committed in the A Gp G sector.

b) OB West had so far only been able to withdraw 2 Pz Div from the front. Six more panzer units were to be reorganized: the 9, 11 and 116 Pz Divs, 10 SS Pz Div, and 3 and 15 Pz Gren Divs.

c) Three of the divisions, which were to be brought up, had so far arrived, but 269 Inf Div had been diverted to A Gp G, and 256 Volks Gren Div had been employed in the Fifteenth Army sector.

d) The assembly of *volks artillerie* corps and *volks werfer* brigades started on 28 Oct according to plan. OB West was authorized to employ the corps with the permission of OKW for the purpose of forming defensive centers of gravity. However, they were only to be committed as one unit and not perhaps by the battalion. On the other hand, the *werfer* brigades were not to be employed before the Offensive because they were short of ammunition.

Thus, the preparations of the forces destined for the Offensive had to be altered already in Oct 44. The description of the fighting during Nov 44 has already shown that even more changes had to be made during that month. The battle on the Roer started on 16 Nov 44; it continued up to the beginning of the Offensive, and during the second half of the month, critical situations developed in Alsace and Lorraine. Although the allocation of forces at the expense of the Offensive was being kept as low as the seriousness of the situation would permit, several of the units destined for the attack had to be considered as lost for that purpose or, at least, as prematurely exhausted. Also, the enemy pressure near Aachen and on the Moselle front had a very unfavorable effect on the reorganization which had been planned. This trend continued during Dec 44. The Commanding Officers pointed out, that the forces destined for the Offensive would be insufficient, and, for that reason, the 'little' plan would have to be adopted, if additional units did not become available from the Zone of the Interior or from other theaters of war. These objections were overruled by the Supreme Command, which pointed out that the enemy forces were also being exhausted, that, above all, his strategic reserves were being pinned down, and that thereby the enemy resistance against the Offensive would have diminished.

The forces, which were finally committed for the Ardennes Offensive, compared with the estimates of the first draft were as shown in Tables 1 and 2.

Table 1: Planned vs. Available Forces for the Ardennes Offensive

	Draft of 11 Oct 44	Employed on 16 Dec 44 & in reserve	Added During the Offensive	Not at all or not sufficiently reorganized
Panzer Divisions	10	7	1	3
Panzer Brigades	–	2	–	–
Panzer Grenadier Divisions	4	–	2	2
Infantry and *Volks Grenadier* Divisions	16	13	1	3
Fallschirmjäger Divisions	2	2	–	1
Full Divisions:	32 after deduction of deficiencies: 29–30	24 (two panzer brigades counted as full divisions)	4	9

Thus, the Ardennes Offensive, was carried out with 28 full divisions. Since both the panzer brigades represented only reinforced regiments, the total strength remained well below the figure estimated on 11 Oct 44. The reality was even further behind the estimate because three divisions arrived late, and almost a third of all divisions had not completed their reorganization. The distribution of the divisions among the Armies was as follows (the figures in parentheses represent mobile divisions):

Table 2: Planned and Actual Disposition of Forces for the Ardennes Offensive

	Draft of 11 Oct 44	Employed on 16 Dec 44 & in reserve	Added during the Offensive	Total
Sixth Pz Army	9 (4)	9 (4)	–	9 (4)
Fifth Pz Army	7 (4)	8 (4)	4 (3)	12 (7)
Seventh Army	7 (1)	4 (–)	–	7 (1)
Reserves	6–7 (3)	3 (1)	–	–
Total	29–30 (12)	24 (9) (two panzer brigades counted as full divisions)	4 (3)	28 (12)

The reorganization of the panzer divisions was accomplished in the following manner:

		Allocation of Panzers:
Reorganizations	1, 2, 9, and 12 SS Pz Divs	100%
Preferential reorganization	2 Pz Div, 116 Pz Div	80%
	Pz Lehr Div	70%
Limited reorganization	3 and 15 Pz Gren Divs, 10 SS Pz Div, 9 and 21 Pz Divs	60–70%

The motor vehicle transportation space available to the completely reorganized divisions amounted to 80% of the authorized strength, while the other divisions had only 50–70% of their basic allowance. There was an extreme scarcity of heavy vehicles, and an almost complete lack of prime movers and wreckers.

The 10 SS Pz Div and 21 Pz Div were not committed to the Offensive, while 11 Pz Div, 17 SS Pz Div, and 25 Pz Gren Div remained in the A Gp G sector. The three latter divisions had been included in the estimates of the first draft.

Altogether, A Gp B had, in mid-Dec 44, approximately 1,800 tanks and self-propelled assault guns.* Of these, a considerable number were tied down by the defensive battle of Fifteenth Army, at the time when the Offensive started. Furthermore, it must not be forgotten that many tanks and assault guns were not available for commitment because of the delay in their repairs. There was an absolute shortage of spare parts, because the production of new tanks had been

---

*Totals were actually 1,427 armored fighting vehicles (AFV) with 270 in short-term repair. Of these only 717 were directly available at the Ardennes front. Ed.

Adolf Hitler and Alfred Jodl seen just after the attempt on the German leader's life at his Rastenburg head-quarters on 20 July 1944. Hitler clutch-es his injured right hand and Jodl's head is bandaged. On the far left of the picture is Martin Bormann. *(U.S. National Archives, Hoffman Collection)*

Below left: Generalfeldmarschall Gerd von Rundstedt, who was in charge of forces on the Western Front (OB West) in late 1944. *(U.S. National Archives)*

Below right: Generalfeldmarschall Walter Model. *(Wenger Collection)*

Inspection of a German volksgrenadier unit during field training in the autumn of 1944. *(Gaul Collection)*

Two heavily armed Waffen SS panzergrenadiers move past a knocked-out American armored car of the 18th Cavalry Reconnaissance Squadron near the Belgian village of Poteau. (*U.S. National Archives*)

German soldiers search for gasoline and other supplies near the village of Roth on 17 December 1944. *(U.S. National Archives)*

German soldiers of the 3rd Fallschirmjäger Division remove the boots of Americans of the 612th Tank Destroyer Battalion, killed in the fighting for the village of Honsfeld on 17 December 1944. *(U.S. National Archives)*

A Mk V Panther of the Fifth Panzer Armee pauses to receive orders from a German command car. *(Bundesarchiv)*

A U.S. 105mm howitzer firing from the Ardennes heights near Manhay. The American artillery assembled during the fighting was a major impediment to the German advance. *(U.S. National Archives)*

Americans of the 83rd Infantry Division man a 57mm anti-tank gun covering a snowy road in the Ardennes. (U.S. National Archives)

A German Panther of 1. SS Kampfgruppe Peiper knocked out by Allied air strikes on 18 December 1944, just above the bridge at Cheneux on the Ambleve River.
(U.S. National Archives)

Infantry of the 3rd Armored Division run for cover during the fighting for Monte-le-Ban near Houffalize on 15 January 1945. *(U.S. National Archives)*

Graffiti left behind by members of the 12. SS Panzer Division in Binsfeld, Luxembourg: 'Ein Volk! Ein Reich! Ein Führer!' – 'One people! One nation! One leader!' In the foreground is Private Joseph Klem of the 357 Infantry Regiment, 90th Infantry Division, photographed here on 31 January 1945. *(U.S. National Archives)*

German soldiers suffering from exposure are taken captive near Bastogne by the 4th Armored Division, 10 January 1945. *(U.S. National Archives)*

given preference in the war economy. In some cases the shortage had reached such a degree that newly arrived tanks were being taken apart in order to procure spare parts. Sixth Pz Army was the best equipped since it had received approximately 250 new tanks during its reorganization period. Its four divisions therefore had 80–100 tanks each, and its two [sic] independent panzer *abteilungen* (tank battalions) had 40 and 50 tanks respectively. Thus, Army had approximately 450 tanks and self-propelled assault guns when it started its attack.*

The three panzer divisions of Fifth Pz Army each had approximately 60–70 tanks in serviceable condition. In addition, Führer Begleit Brig had 100 tanks, some of which, however, were not in serviceable condition.** Including assault guns, Army had approximately 350 heavy armored vehicles [396 in actual total]. Since Seventh Army had at first not been assigned any mobile unit and had only 60–80 assault guns of its own [33 assault guns were actually available], the Offensive therefore got under way with approximately 850–900 tanks and assault guns [717 in first wave – Ed]. 80% of these were to be considered as ready for immediate commitment.

In the period between 1 Nov and 15 Dec 44, replacement transfer battalions with a total strength of 77,000 men were transferred to OB West for the reorganization of its subordinate units. This was the equivalent of approximately six divisions. In order to attain this figure, the corresponding transfers to all other fronts had to be temporarily suspended.

Some explanatory comments must, of necessity, be devoted to the newly activated divisions, which were to take part in the Offensive.

a) The new *volks grenadier* divisions

These divisions can be divided into two categories: They either were infantry divisions, for which this designation was to represent a distinction and which, after their redesignation, were to be reorganized correspondingly – as for instance 12 Volks Gren Div. Or they were cadres of divisions, which had been shattered in the East or in the West, and which had been reorganized with convalescents, recruits, personnel from the Luftwaffe and the Navy, and other replacements. Their organization and equipment made them particularly suitable for attack. Although the numerical strength of their infantry units was lower than that of the former infantry divisions – three regiments with only two battalions each – they were, without exception, equipped with automatic weapons; also, their artillery was more mobile. Now, for the first time, these divisions were to be employed on a large scale during the Ardennes Offensive. Whether they would live up to the expectations, could only be answered by

---

* Actual totals including independent units & AFV in reserve in Sixth Pz Army was 642 on the eve of the offensive. Ed.

** Its actual tank strength (including StuG Brigade 200), reported on 17 December, was 23 MkIV tanks and 48 assault guns. Ed.

their performance in combat. The Führer had particularly great expectations, not only because of their equipment, but also because of their combat morale which he had sought to improve by a whole series of special measures. The disadvantage of these *volks grenadier* divisions, which was evident even before the beginning of the attack, was, that they had been incompletely equipped, and that most of them had never before been submitted to battle conditions.

b) The *volks artillerie* corps

They, too, were newly created units, which so far had, only in a few isolated cases, been tested in battle. They had really been organized as expedients, since considerable artillery elements were often saved from destruction when infantry divisions were shattered. Insofar as these elements were not being used for the organization of new units, they constituted independent units of 72 guns each which were designated *volks artillerie* corps. Their advantage was that they represented high fire power which could quite easily be transferred from one sector to another. Thus, the intermediate command had an opportunity, which so far had been limited by the requirements of its own units, to intervene in the first fight and build up points of main effort. Since the success of the Ardennes Offensive depended on the rapid accomplishment of the breakthrough, these corps were given a particularly important mission.

It had proved impossible to avoid that some of these corps were employed beforehand. However, on the whole, the combat strength of these corps was complete when the attack started. In the fully mobile corps, each gun had its own prime mover. The semi-mobile corps had so-called *Zugstaffeln* (prime mover detachments) which moved one battery after another up front. The Offensive proved that their mobility was insufficient. Of course, the terrain and the road conditions prevailing during the Offensive were particularly unfavorable. The same difficulties had to be contended with in the case of the *werfer* brigades. Their weakness was their short range. Also, their ammunition supplies were insufficient. For this reason, this new weapon, which besides its intrinsic effect also has a psychological one, was not fully effective.

In addition to these artillery reinforcements, considerable elements of *Heeres* troops were also being allocated to OB West. He was to receive the following forces during Nov 44: three heavy machine-gun battalions, five *volks artillerie* corps, one 21 cm *werfer* battalion, two self-propelled assault gun brigades, 16 *Heeres* and *festungs* artillery batteries with eight additional heavy caliber batteries, five heavy *Heeres* antitank battalions, three *volks werfer* brigades, and four *werfer* battalions, and, finally, some engineer units. Although part of the heavy *Heeres* artillery was destined for the Metz sector, the bulk of these transfers was to be employed in the Offensive, including 54 cm railway guns. In addition to these units, there were also antiaircraft and antitank battalions.

From the outset of the Offensive it was quite obvious that the engineer forces were insufficient; they were urgently needed in the hilly terrain, and particularly for the river crossings. The Army Commanders had repeatedly requested additional engineer forces but only part of the promised engineer battalions and bridge columns finally arrived, and a high percentage of those only arrived in the last moment because there was a general shortage of engineers and engineer equipment.

The transfer of these units as well as of all the others, which had to be transported by train, took place under worse conditions than had been assumed because of the increase in air attacks on railroad installations, especially on junctions and at large switching yards. In the area west of the Rhine only the hours of darkness and rainy days were suitable for movements by rail. That the movement was carried out successfully, was most of all due to the efforts of the railroad personnel and of the repair columns; it also was facilitated by the dense railroad net in the West.

However, this favorable situation applied only to troop movements. Considerable delays in the schedule of trains loaded with materiel could not be prevented, while some of them were completely side-tracked. Since both the training and the combat strength depended on the timely arrival of the materiel, the effect of these delays was doubly felt by all units which were to take part in the Offensive. In addition, one of the essential prerequisites of the first draft had been that the Supreme Command should have strong reserves, approximately six to seven divisions, at its disposal in order to employ them during the Offensive according to the developments in the situation. On 9 Dec 44, an order was issued with reference to the OKW reserves, which rescinded the preceding orders of 4 and 5 Dec 44, and gave the following instructions for the assembly of these reserves:

a) The 6 SS Geb Div, which was being transferred from Norway, was to be assembled west of Münstereifel (however, before its arrival in that area, Division was diverted to A Gp G).

b) The Führer Gren Brig was to assemble in the area south of Münstereifel–Blankenheim (it was subsequently committed in the Seventh Army sector).

c) The 3 Pz Gren Div was to be withdrawn from the Roer front after 10 Dec 44, was to be reorganized, and held as OKW reserve behind the left wing of Fifteenth Army (it was subsequently committed in the Fifth Pz Army sector).

d) and e) The 9 and 167 Volks Gren Divs were to be held in readiness west of Gerolstein (subsequently, only 9 Volks Gren Div was employed in the Seventh Army sector).

f) The Führer Begleit Brig, which had again been withdrawn from A Gp G, was to be assembled in the Kyllburg–Bitburg area (it was subsequently committed in the Fifth Pz Army sector).

g) The 11 Pz Div, which was to be withdrawn from A Gp G, and which had been destined for Fifth Pz Army, was to be transferred to the Army sector (in reality, its commitment in its present sector was temporarily prolonged by an order issued on 7 Dec 44; subsequently, it was not withdrawn and therefore could not be used for the Offensive*).

h) The 257 Volks Gren Div was to be held in readiness west of Wittlich and was destined for Seventh Army (it was transferred to A Gp G on 16 Dec 44, and was to relieve 11 Pz Div). The 10 SS Pz Div, which was employed on the Roer front, and the relief of which the Führer had again insisted upon on 6 Dec 44, could only be relieved at so late a time, that it could finally no longer take part in the Offensive.

Thus, on 9 Dec 44, four mobile units were still being considered as available OKW reserves, but only three of them, including two brigades, took part in the Offensive. In addition, the reserves consisted of four infantry divisions, only one of which was finally committed. The reserves available to the Supreme Command therefore actually consisted of only four units, including two brigades. During the course of the Offensive, this shortage of reserves was relieved by the transfer of the two mobile divisions, which had been assembled in the sector near Roermond for the purpose of carrying out the secondary thrust from the north. Those two units – 9 Pz Div and 15 Pz Gren Div – were, after 24 Dec 44, committed in the Fifth Pz Army sector.

This survey indicates that the plan of attack had been hampered and disrupted for a number of widely different causes, and that the Offensive had to be undertaken with an over-all strength which was inferior to that considered essential in the estimates.

Of the other factors, which had unfavorable effects on the Offensive, the following should be mentioned:

That it was possible, to procure the quantities of POL allocated for the Offensive, may be considered a considerable achievement by itself, considering the fact that, in addition to the limited crude oil production within the Reich, the production of southwestern Hungary was the only outside source. As to the coal distillation plants, all efforts at decentralization to smaller plants as well as other measures could not prevent a continuous drop in production. Nevertheless, it was possible to procure the 4.49 million gallons destined for the Offensive and to transport them to the West. However, it proved impossible to immediately bring sufficient POL up to the assembly areas to issue five VS to the mobile units, as requested by their commanders. The necessity of maintaining secrecy, the density of the traffic on all approach roads and routes, and the limited transportation space prevented the delivery of the POL. Thus, most of the tanks only had 1.5 VS when they started out, which, in the hilly terrain,

---

* In reality the commander of A Gp G, Gen Hermann Balck, held the division for several days when it might have been transferred; it then moved in fits and starts to the Bitburg area after Christmas, but was never committed. Ed.

corresponded to a radius of action of only 75 kilometers. To bring up POL, once the Offensive was under way, naturally was even more complicated.

Thus, the shortage of POL, about which everybody was complaining after the Offensive, was really more a transportation problem than a question of insufficient quantities.

According to calculations, the POL supplies on hand ought to have been sufficient to reach the Maas. Captured POL stocks, however desirable they would naturally be, therefore would not be counted upon.

The stocks of ammunition provided for the Offensive proved to be sufficient up to the time when it became necessary to switch to the defensive.* Ammunition was on hand for the first eight days, and was either being shipped, or was ready for shipment in the dumps, for the succeeding eight days. The food supplies presented no particular difficulties.

Thus, the only supply problem was the POL question which, before the start of the Offensive, had already been considered with anxiety. However, it should be mentioned that the obligation to save POL had hampered operations during the preparatory stage, and that many defects could have been overcome had there been more gasoline.

The concentration of the attacking forces was accomplished without special difficulties in spite of the disruption of the railroad traffic, the intricacies of the assembly area, the restriction to darkness, and the hampering camouflage. By 2400 on 15 Dec 44, the assembly was to be considered as generally accomplished according to plan.

Although all the top commanders were of the opinion that serious deficiencies still existed, and would therefore have preferred a further delay in the start of the attack, the attack armies estimated that their mission could be carried out successfully. Their optimistic point of view was partly based on the morale and spirit of the troops, which had received a new impulse due to the extensive preparations. However, these estimates were also based on the continuity of the flying conditions, predicted by the weather forecast, and on the actual realization of the assistance of the German Luftwaffe which had been promised. It was unavoidable that a reverse should occur, when it turned out that neither of these two hopes were to be fulfilled.

6. THE SUPREME COMMAND ISSUES THE FINAL ORDERS

By the end of Nov 44, the Führer had moved his headquarters from East Prussia to Berlin. Here, he had an abscess removed from his vocal cords, a minor operation which did not affect his general health. About 11 Dec 44, the Führer moved to the command post 'Adlerhorst', which had been prepared for him. It was situated near Ziegenberg, north of Frankfurt on the Main, and was an

---

* Ignores the lack of ammunition for an adequate initial barrage. Ed.

installation equipped with air raid shelters, barracks, etc. The Chief of OKW, the Chief of the Wehrmacht Operations Staff and their closest collaborators also moved there. The operations staff, which followed by echelon during the next few days, occupied permanent barracks near Friedberg.

Here, the danger from the air was not greater than in and around Berlin. On the other hand, the new Führer's headquarters in the field had the advantage of a very close connection with OB West, who was billeted at Castle Ziegenberg, only a few kilometers away. The other command authorities, also, could more easily be reached than from Berlin.

The Führer felt the need for once again establishing personal contact with the Army Group and Army commanders, a number of divisional commanders, and other officers who were to take over important functions during the Offensive. Thus, on 11 and 12 Dec 44, they were recalled from the front in two equal shifts and assembled at the OB West headquarters.

The discussion was preceded by a private conversation which the Führer had with the Commanders of two battle-tested divisions – 9 and 116 Pz Divs – Genmaj Freiherr von Elverfeldt (later killed in the fighting for Cologne) and Genmaj Siegfried von Waldenburg. They were to be decorated with the Ritterkreuz (Knight's Cross), but, at the same time, they had been called upon to give the Führer an opportunity of obtaining detailed information on the condition and morale of the troops. After the Führer had expressed his thanks and appreciation to the two generals, he initiated them into the plan of attack. He explained that he was fully aware of the difficulties inherent in the Offensive and the seriousness of the general situation, but – he added – there was no other way out. He was counting on a full success, and therefore on a change of fortune. Whatever the Zone of Interior, and the armament industry in particular, had been able to produce, was being made available for the Offensive.

Thereupon, the two division commanders gave him a full account of what they had on their minds. When they raised objections about the far-reaching objective of the Offensive, and said, that a smaller but more certain success seemed preferable and would lessen the danger of again draining the combat strength of the panzer divisions and once more losing their cadre personnel, the Führer would not enter into these arguments since his decision in favor of the 'grand' plan was irrevocable. On the other hand, he agreed to a detailed discussion of the situation in the air. The generals insisted that, at least the attack forces, and above all the armored points, would have to be relieved of the pressure from the air. They described the low morale their troops were suffering from as a result of the enemy air superiority, and the doubts that were spreading whenever promises were being made. The Führer informed them that Reichsmarschall Göring was counting on committing 1,000 out of 3,000 available planes. The 1,000 planes would be in serviceable condition at the start of the Offensive. He added that, although the generals were aware of the fact that Göring was inclined to submit over-optimistic figures, one could certainly count on 800 planes, a number which will guarantee a really noticeable relief.

Furthermore, the generals insisted that they must be sufficiently equipped with tanks, materiel, ammunition, POL, and other necessary supplies. The Führer reassured them that they would receive what they needed.

During the discussion of the progress of the attack, the Führer was of the opinion that, after the breakthrough had been achieved, panzer divisions would be up against the American rear echelon troops from which no extensive resistance would have to be expected. The generals asserted that, in the preceding fighting in the Aachen area, and particularly in the vicinity of Vossenack, the Americans had shown themselves to be very tenacious fighting opponents. As to the morale of the Germans, they reported that they had observed a strong will to resist among the columns of the *Organization Todt* workers committed behind the West Wall, but, on the other hand, the local population seemed to be scared that they would now lose even their last possessions. For this reason, the desire seemed to prevail among the people, that the war be brought to an end as quickly as possible, whatever its final outcome might be. Thus, the troops, the morale of whom was altogether beyond reproach, were exposed not only to positive but also to negative pressure.

This conversation, during which the two division Commanders had ample opportunity to talk, lasted about half an hour. One of the effects of the 20 Jul 44 was, that the generals had to deposit their brief cases and leave their firearms in an antechamber.

The generals gathered for the two meetings at the command post of OB West and were taken by bus to Adlerhorst. The two speeches by the Führer were delivered at nightfall in one of the rooms in the barracks. He spoke for almost two hours. After a general introduction, he emphasized that he had done everything to guarantee the success of the coming Offensive. All available tanks, artillery, self-propelled assault guns, anti-tank, and other material had been brought up. The newly activated *volks grenadier* divisions, which were now to be committed, were outstanding in their morale and their equipment. Adequate air support was assured. Down to the last gallon of gasoline, everything not absolutely essential for its own fighting had been withdrawn from the Eastern Front. The Führer repeated in front of these generals that, after having made such extensive preparations for the Offensive, he expected a decisive turn in the War. He reminded them of the sufferings the Home Front was undergoing, and appealed to all of them to do their best in the coming struggle.

To anybody, who during the last few months had had no opportunity to talk to or even see the C-in-C of the Wehrmacht, and this was the case with the majority of the generals, the outward change, which had in the meantime taken place in him, was startling. He had suddenly grown old, his complexion looked unhealthy, he often stared vacantly, his back was bent, and his shoulders sunken, as if an invisible weight was crushing him. The most frightening impression, however, resulted from the tremble of his hands, which had become much more pronounced during the last few months. But, the speeches proved that, in spite of his physical condition, the Führer's energy and intelligence were entirely unimpaired.

The impressions, which these meetings made on the participants, were varied. Some of them felt encouraged by the realistic tone of the speech as well as by the strong confidence it inspired which made one forget the external impressions; others felt confirmed in their skepticism which was primarily based on the deficiencies in the preparations. Not even the high figures of the number of planes – the figures of 1,500, 3,000 and more were circulating during these last few days – which were supposed to be committed by the Luftwaffe, could deceive the skeptics. Some of them, also, were disappointed that they had not been given an opportunity of making a detailed report on their troubles and wishes. However, the Supreme Command, unwilling to make any further changes, had no time for such discussions. Although the Führer questioned one or two generals with regard to the condition of his troops and received the standard reply, that they were not yet in condition for the attack, he did not enter into details – especially, since he had already been informed by the two divisional commanders. He dismissed them without having had individual conversations with them. Genobst Jodl, who together with Genfldm Keitel and von Rundstedt assisted at these speeches, received the most urgent requests. While he promised stop-gap assistance, he also would not admit any alterations in the plan.

It ought to be once more recalled, that, in connection with these meetings, another discussion was held on the question of the secondary thrust from the north, which ended with its rejection on 12 Dec 44.

The fact, that the preparations could not be concluded on time in spite of all efforts, was being allowed for by several successive postponements of the start of the attack. During the conference, which had taken place in Berlin on 2 Dec 44, the Führer had still insisted on 10 Dec 44. When it became obvious that this dead line could not be met, OB West had suggested the later dates. On 7 Dec 44, he was informed that the second one, namely 14 Dec 44, had been chosen, but that the attack was to be advanced by one day in case of favorable weather conditions. On 10 Dec 44, OB West reported that the transfer of the units, which had not yet arrived, was proceeding without any delay worth mentioning, but that a number of railroad tracks had been blocked by air attacks. On 11 Dec 44, the Führer authorized the postponement of the attack date to 15 Dec 44. He added that a further postponement was to be avoided, if possible, but was not to be altogether excluded. On 12 Dec 44, the dead line was postponed to 16 Dec 44, but this date was finally adhered to. Thus, the preparations had been concluded.

On the day preceding the attack, on 15 Dec 44, the Führer informed Genfldm Model that he had taken his final decisions. All prerequisites for the success of the operation had been established. Its size and dimension now solely depended on the leadership during the course of the attack. Model had to renew his pledges to the Führer to unconditionally execute all orders and to ensure their execution down to the lowest echelon. Hitler denounced any deviation by the panzer units east of the Maas toward the north, which would correspond to the 'little' plan. He also ordered that the panzer units of Sixth Pz Army were to keep clear of the covering front LXVII Inf Corps was to build up along the line Monschau–Liège, so that they would not become involved in the fighting along this front. Furthermore, the entire roadnet on the right sector of Fifth Pz Army, if necessary, up to Namur, was to immediately be placed at the disposal of Sixth Pz Army, should Army have any difficulty in crossing in and near Namur. In addition, the Führer charged Model with the responsibility of avoiding any concentration of his tanks in the vicinity of Liège, as this would, of necessity, lead to the commitment of the panzer units east of the Maas. During the advance on Antwerp, the eastern flank was to seek cover behind the natural obstacle constituted by the Albert Canal, and was not to be built up farther west. The left wing of Fifteenth Army was to be reinforced to such a degree, that it would become unnecessary to use infantry divisions of Sixth Pz Army in the fighting near Simmerath, north of Monschau; unless this intrusion were observed, the defensive flank between Monschau and Liège would be weakened. If these directives for the conduct of operations were followed, a great success seemed assured.

Genfldm Model replied the same evening to the effect that he had transmitted the entire instructions to the Commanding Officer of Sixth Pz Army, and that all the efforts of Army Group would be directed toward the thrust on Antwerp. He again requested the transfer of 3 Pz Gren Div to Army Group reserves to ascertain that the advance of the panzer units of Sixth Pz Army not be delayed under any circumstances by armored enemy units east of the Maas. He recommended that this division should drive as quickly as possible toward Verviers in place of the advance elements of 3 Fs Div which had dropped out. *Volks grenadier* divisions would arrive too late. The 89 Inf Div had already been committed on the left wing of Fifteenth Army to bolster its strength. By doing so, the reorganization of Division had to be neglected and risks on the Roer front had to be taken. Furthermore, three assault gun brigades and one assault panzer battalion had been transferred from Fifteenth Army to support the northern flank of Sixth Pz Army [394 and 667 StuG Brigades and 217 Sturmpz Battalion which had only 8 operational assault guns and 8 Sturmpanzer IVs between them]. Their arrival was anticipated for 16 Dec 44. By the commitment of local reserves between Jülich and Düren, additional infantry forces would immediately become available. Finally, Model reported that, according to his own evaluation, the expenditure of time and POL in the Eifel would be twice the usual amount. Timely and adequate bringing up of supplies would be vital.

On 16 Dec 44, the Führer authorized the temporary commitment of 3 Pz Gren Div between Eupen and Liège, and also the transfer of 257 Volks Gren Div – which, until then, was part of OKW reserves. This Division was to immediately relieve 11 Pz Div which was pinned down in defensive fighting on the A Gp G sector. The 11 Pz Div was to be assembled and reorganized in the Bitburg area, and was to be part of OKW reserves.

On this day, at 0530, began Operation 'Watch on the Rhine', planned since Sep 44, or better yet, Operation 'Autumn Fog', which was being prepared since Oct 44. At 1545 the Führer briefed the Commander of A Gp G, Gen Pz Balck, in the scope and details of the operation. He pointed out that the expected success would completely change the entire situation in the West, and that all prerequisites for such a success had now been established. In order to obtain and safeguard the forces for the attack, he had taken into account that all the other fronts and theaters of war would have to make heavy contributions, and even face critical situations. He had to accept the loss of important terrain in the outpost area of the West Wall and even that of some of the West Wall fortifications in the A Gp G sector. But, as of today, not another foot of ground was to be yielded. Before long A Gp G would experience a considerable relief. Thus, the Führer ordered that the outpost area of the West Wall between Völklingen and Bitsche, on the Saar Front, be held under all circumstances, that no more pill boxes should be given up in the West Wall, and that those which had already fallen into enemy hands, should be retaken by carefully prepared actions of assault detachments. This was to be the mission of A Gp G, and the success of the entire operation would depend no less on its accomplishment than on the aggressive spirit of A Gp B.

Was there any justification for the expectations harbored by the Supreme Command? Were its estimates correct? Had its preparations been sufficient? These questions were answered by the events which transpired on the days following 16 Dec 44.

B. SPECIAL PROBLEMS OF THE PREPARATORY STAGE

I. The Enemy Situation and the Maintenance of Secrecy

1. THE ENEMY SITUATION

The observation and obtainment of information on the enemy situation were part of the mission of the Seventh Army which was in control of the entire frontal sector of the Offensive until shortly before the start of the attack. But, Seventh Army constantly kept in touch with the two panzer armies and supplied them with maps concerning the enemy situation. In order to obtain information, Army was, above all, dependent on its own front line reconnaissance which was being carried out by reconnaissance and combat patrols. It was forbidden to intensify their extent. Apart from that, the monitoring of enemy radio communications was an important source of information.

Since the enemy had occupied his front line in some sectors only by groups, individual reconnaissance patrols penetrated up to ten and 20 km into his front line, stayed there for one or two days, occasionally even for three days, and ascertained that no signs of any special operation were to be observed. By this method, those sectors of the enemy front were also being reconnoitered, the front line of which was not so easy to penetrate. After the end of Nov 44, this source of information dried up, since Army Group completely stopped all reconnaissance patrol activity to avoid that anyone taken prisoner by the enemy might give information on his observations in the German rear area.

This prohibition of Army Group had the disadvantage that the tactical employment of the troops for the breakthrough might be based on information which at the moment of the attack would no longer up up to date. But, in view of maintaining secrecy this had to be accepted.

The observation of enemy activities in the area farther to the rear was completely inadequate. Although the German troops had only just passed through this area in retreat, there was no network of agents in it, which was able to furnish the German Command with sufficient information on the enemy situation. On the other hand, information originating from local inhabitants who sided with the Germans proved useful. The German air reconnaissance was practically eliminated: under favorable weather conditions by enemy interdiction, and in bad weather on account of the weather itself. Besides, the widely dispersed enemy forces had concealed themselves so well, that no practical results could be obtained by this method. Seventh Army repeatedly insisted that aerial photographs of the attack sector be taken; but, this request could be granted only in the last days preceding the attack and then not even completely, because the Allied air superiority prevented complete execution of the reconnaissance missions.

On the basis of reports furnished by the higher command, the strategic reserves of the enemy were assumed to be mainly in the Champagne area [these were 101st and 82nd Airborne Divisions]. It was known that new divisions were constantly arriving from the United States, but the information on the details of their arrival was not always sufficient. It was presumed that the enemy intended to carry out his counterthrusts against the left flank with troops which were available in the Rheims, Sedan, and Charleville area. Attacks against the northern flank were anticipated from the Brussels, Liège and Namur area.

Above all, it was expected that the enemy would immediately withdraw troops from the battle on the Roer and from the Moselle front, that is, from the Third US Army sector. The available information resulted in the following picture of the enemy situations:

Three American divisions were assumed to be in the Elsenborn area; their disposition indicated that a thrust on the Urft dam was contemplated. Opposite the attack sector were approximately three divisions which had been replaced by divisions exhausted during the battle of the Roer (2, 4, and 28 US Inf Divs).* No considerable reserves were assumed to be in their rear area. On the contrary, the conviction prevailed that, once the breakthrough had been accomplished, the enemy forces up to the Maas would be weak, if this area were crossed before the enemy had time to bring up reserves.

One armored division was assumed to be north of Spa and this was considered the first combat group which could attack the right flank of Army.** Enemy tanks, which had been observed in front of the German center and left wing, were believed to be elements of combat commands, which had been distributed behind the front as emergency security forces; but, it was not considered as impossible, that these were armored battalions belonging to Army or even elements of an armored division the presence of which had been hitherto unknown.

In front of the left wing of Seventh Army, the presence of a strong artillery group had repeatedly been observed [US 422nd FA Grp]. It was situated in the Alttrier–Christnach area and, from time to time, it covered Trier with surprise fire. The area around Luxembourg was assumed to be a reorganization center. The presence of any considerable body of reserves was not suspected in this area.

The general situation indicated that in the First Army sector, adjacent to the left, renewed heavy attacks were to be expected. However, Seventh Army had no conclusive information of the stage or objective of the preparations the enemy was making. It was anticipated that Third US Army would probably withdraw forces from the front opposite A Gp G or would make them available behind its front, and commit them in the Luxembourg area. It was considered as less likely that the American leadership would attack on both sides of the road between Luxembourg–Diekirch; but, on the contrary, it was assumed that here only elements would be committed to provide cover for Luxembourg and the northern flank of Third US Army, and that the main forces would be brought up via Arlon–Neufchâteau in the general direction of Bastogne, in order to carry the attack against the southern flank of the German attack edge.

---

* Significantly missing in the German assessment was the newly arrived 99th and 106th Infantry Divisions. The disposition of the 106th would result in a tragic loss of the greater part of the division. The 99th would be instrumental in blunting the assault of the Sixth Pz Army. Ed.

** OB West maps show the 9th Armored Division was mistakenly thought to be north of Spa. Ed.

The Supreme Command was inclined to assume that the enemy would rather attempt to stop the attack by frontal opposition than by a counterattack from the flank, and that therefore no real resistance was to be anticipated before the Maas was reached. The great question was at what time powerful counter-attacks had to be anticipated. The Supreme Command was of the opinion that, after the initial surprise had been overcome, the enemy would first have to discern the extent and direction of the Offensive, and then decide how much further he could continue in his present attacks and attack plans. Thus, a certain time lag would intervene before the issuance of the first orders, all the more so if complete agreement could not immediately be reached among the Allies. If one added the time required by the troop movements proper, the result was that attacks by divisional formations were not to be expected – neither on the right nor on the left wing – before the third day after the start of the attack.

It was important for the launching of the breakthrough, that the enemy had no cohesive front line in the attack sector, but that his front consisted of a number of strong points echeloned in a depth of four to five kilometers. These strong points had been constructed mainly in the vicinity of roads and narrow clearings. They had been strongly fortified by wire entanglements and mine-fields. The strong points were supported by tanks and armored combat teams of five to six tanks which constituted reserves for a counterthrust.

In addition, it was being assumed that the tactics, which had been tested in the East and which consisted in encircling enemy strong points and continuing the advance before the rear area had been cleared, would be unfamiliar to the Americans, and that it could therefore be presumed that the remaining pockets of resistance would not hold out for long.

The course of the Offensive proved that the evaluation of the enemy situation proper had been correct, but that neither the leadership nor the troops of the enemy reacted in the presumed manner [i.e. the Allied leadership reacted much more rapidly than anticipated].

2. THE MAINTENANCE OF SECRECY, CAMOUFLAGE AND DECEPTION

A plan for an offensive, such as the one which was being prepared by the German Supreme Command, had no prospect of succeeding unless complete surprise was achieved. It was therefore of vital importance that only as many people should be initiated into the secret at each stage in the preparations as absolutely necessary. Also, each person must only be told whatever he had to know to perform his part in the preparations. It was of equal importance that the preparations, which could no longer be concealed, should be disguised in a way that they could not be interpreted as initial phase of an offensive. Thus, the maintenance of secrecy and camouflage were closely connected with one another.

a) The following measures for the maintenance of secrecy should be specified: Only those officers of OKW, and especially of the Wehrmacht Operations Staff, were initiated who absolutely had to be informed. They were required to give an oath of secrecy in writing. The same applied to the few draftsmen and secretaries whose assistance could not be dispensed with. At the conferences on the situation held by the Führer, only the officers working on the preparations stayed for the discussion of the plan for the Offensive. Although the other members of the staff at the Führer's headquarters in the field sensed that something was going on, they were nevertheless surprised by the start of the attack in the Ardennes. All orders and instructions, and also the corresponding messages, which were connected with the Offensive, were dispatched to the competent authorities by officers acting as couriers. Neither telephone nor teletype were to be used for type of communication because the lifting of the secret was to be anticipated, in spite of the scrambling of telephone conversations and the use of cryptograms. This, of course, entailed a considerable loss of time, because the same delays occured at OB West, A Gp B, the Armies, and finally also at corps level after the initiation of the participating Corps.

The subordinate command authorities maintained the secrecy along the same lines. Above all, care was taken that the exchange of radio messages should not exceed the usual average. As a special precaution, the Armies used a different code name for the Offensive in their communications with the Corps to the one employed in their messages to their ranking commands, while the Corps chose another one in their communications with their subordinate units. These code names were being changed every two weeks.

In addition, each command authority was only initiated to the extent absolutely essential for the preparations. The Armies, Corps, etc., barely knew which unit was to attack in the adjacent sector, and were not aware of the missions which had been given to the units beyond their immediate neighbors.

In order to avoid transmitting by courier the attack date, which it was customary to designate X-Day, it was preferred to use code letters which were automatically changed. There was another special code for the clock time.

The most important medium for maintaining secrecy was to delay the initiation to the latest possible moment. The initiation was echeloned in the following manner: On 11 Oct 44, some of the personnel of the Wehrmacht Operations Staff, and at the end of Oct 44, OB West and A Gp B. The Army Commanders were subsequently informed. Within the Army Staffs only the Commanding Officer, the C-of-S, the Ia, and one additional person were allowed to be initiated. The initiation of the Ic, the OQu, the Engineer, Signal and Senior Artillery Commanders only took place when it had become unavoidable, and Army Group had given its authorization.

The generals and chiefs of staff on corps level were not initiated until the end of Nov 44, the division commanders in Dec 44. The troops were informed on the evening before the start of the attack. At the same time it was to be avoided that groups of officers suddenly appeared with maps to reconnoiter the terrain, because the various commanders from division on down to battalion level might feel a natural urge to carry out very thorough reconnaissances. This information would have been of the greatest value to the newly arrived divisions as well as to those which had already previously been committed. Here again, disadvantages had to be tolerated in favor of the maintenance of secrecy. These officers, who were authorized to visit up front, had to wear the uniforms of the units committed along the corresponding sector.

The names of each person, who had been initiated, were listed; they were bound to secrecy and were informed that any offense was punishable by death. The general staff officers therefore preferred to do – whenever possible – all the necessary secretarial and draft work themselves, and carried the records on their persons, by day and by night.

b) It was impossible for any length of time to conceal the concentration of a fighting force composed of hundreds of thousands of men, the building up of enormous supplies, and all the other measures which were necessitated by the preparations. For this reason, the motto 'Watch on the Rhine' was chosen from the beginning, which meant, preparation for a counterattack against a break-through the enemy was expected to attempt into the plains of the Rhine. It has already been described, how the very first preparations, which were being kept secret even from OB West, had been carried out under this deceptive desig-nation, which had been established by an order dated 12 Oct 44, and how, until the last moment, the fundamental idea of this deception was maintained.

It was inevitable that this version of the plan proved inadequate to motivate the accumulation of forces which went so far beyond defensive preparations. For this reason, false rumors were being spread in addition. The Wehrmacht Operations Staff gave the corresponding instructions on 7 Dec 44. For instance, Fifth Pz Army circulated a rumor that an offensive was to take place near Trier during Jan/Feb 45. These rumors particularly grew around the special operation 'Greif' which was being prepared by Ostbf Skorzeny. From the different versions which circulated originated the rumor that he had been given the mission to capture General Eisenhower.

Special attention was devoted to the camouflage of the changes which had been made in the leadership, because their discovery would have provided the enemy with valuable clues.

The regrouping of the Armies, the insertion of A Gp H, and the changes in the chain of command were therefore disguised by the use of camouflage designations, and their true objective was hidden as long as possible, even from the Germans. In order to simulate the assembly of Sixth Pz Army northwest of Cologne, instructions were issued to Army to send out a corresponding radio traffic. In addition, in order to intensify this impression, troop movements were carried out in this area by daylight. For the purpose of camouflage, the real troop movements were restricted to the hours of darkness.

In order to further deceive the enemy, Sixth Pz Army was ordered by A Gp B to make apparent preparations for the assembly of a fictitious Twenty-Fifth Army in the München-Gladbach–Cologne–Düsseldorf area. Army was represented by small labor staffs and radio stations. Quarters were being prepared for Army in the villages, and the roads leading to the billeting areas were marked with signposts indicating camouflage designations. These designations were also used in radio messages sent out by Sixth Pz Army for the purpose of radio deception.

It was difficult to explain the necessary measures to those who had not been initiated. Thus, for instance, the road blocks, which had just been erected by the *Volksaufgebot* (peoples volunteer corps) – after the *gauleiters* (district commissars) had incited the people to a special effort – now had to be removed because they would have obstructed the assembly.

c) Some of the measures adopted both along and behind the front in order to prevent the army from prematurely discovering the concentration of troops, are given as examples. Reconnaissance patrol activities were not to be increased. At the end of Nov 44, they were stopped altogether. The artillery forces, which were being assembled, and the newly arrived staffs were not permitted to cross certain lines in a western direction. They were therefore unable to sufficiently reconnoiter the terrain before the attack – a disadvantage which especially affected the solution of technical problems by the engineers.

In order to check the danger presented by deserters, no troops hailing from Alsace, Lorraine or Luxembourg were committed along the front. In spite of all precautions, two Seventh Army soldiers deserted shortly before the start of the attack. This incident caused great anxiety, but – as it transpired afterwards – it did not result in serious consequences.

The greatest problem obviously was the maintenance of secrecy for the moving into the assembly areas. The wooded terrain of the Eifel greatly facilitated the concealment of the troops from air reconnaissance. The only difficulty was caused by the smoke from the fires, which had to be built for cooking and heating purposes, and which, in clear weather, might have led to the discovery of the presence of troops. For this reason, charcoal was distributed to the units.

In the assembly areas, the camouflage was being carried out with utmost care. A *'Tarnmeister'* (camouflage commander) was appointed for each village. Traffic was reduced to a minimum. Signs to indicate roads and to show the location of telephone and radio stations were not permitted. Special attention was to be paid to providing adequate camouflage for vehicles which had broken down, to avoid that the enemy draw conclusions in case he discovered a certain number of them in one place.

To cover up the noise of motor vehicles, low-flying planes were assigned to certain areas – a scheme which had already been tested in the East. For this purpose, the Luftwaffe was notified which sector of the assembly area had to be covered by the noise of aircraft engines during the following night. But the use of this type of camouflage was limited by the fact that the commitment of planes depended on the weather, especially because of the danger of icing, and that the sorties had to be co-ordinated with the quantities of POL available. Besides, it was to be anticipated that the enemy would after all recognize the difference between the sound of planes and the noise of tracked vehicles. In order to avoid all noises, it was attempted to use horse-drawn vehicles. But, this means of transportation was limited by the number of horses available. Also, it proved difficult to take back the horses along the crowded roads for their next haul. Anyhow, this expedient was out of question for the transport of heavy guns.

The Offensive proved that all these efforts had been entirely successful: The element of surprise, which the German Supreme Command had considered as one of the most essential prerequisites for the execution of its plans, was attained.

II. The Reorganization

1. THE REORGANIZATION OF THE TROOPS

In order to get an idea of the implications of the reorganization and the difficulties, which developed during the preparation, we shall consider the units of Sixth Pz Army, the reorganization of which was carried out closer to schedule than that of the other armies.

The order issued on 14 Sep 44, which provided for the initial organization of the Army Staff, was directly connected with the plan for the Offensive. The Staff was assembled in Bad Salzuflen; two thirds of the officers and men belonged to the *Heer*, because the Waffen-SS was short of qualified specialists. The Commanding Officer was Obstgrf and Genobst of the Waffen-SS Sepp Dietrich who had been in charge of Fifth Pz Army since the Falaise pocket.

The following units were subordinated to the newly activated Army: The I SS Pz Corps with 1 and 12 SS Pz Divs, II SS Pz Corps with 2 and 9 SS Pz Divs, and, in addition, Pz Lehr Div, which was part of the *Heer*. Army therefore consisted of staffs and units, which had already played a decisive role in the fighting in Normandy, but which had suffered heavy casualties due to continuous fighting. Nevertheless, it was not until Oct 44, and only after the Führer himself had insisted, that their remnants could be withdrawn from the West Wall and assembled in Westphalia. The withdrawal of the corps staffs took even longer and was not accomplished until mid-Nov 44. A suggestion by OB West to transfer Sixth Pz Army to the West to secure certain areas against potential enemy airborne landings, was rejected by the Führer on 13 Oct 44, because he did not want to upset the reorganization schedule of Army.

The period of quietude was being used for different purposes. First of all, the personnel strength of the divisions was being replenished and the replacements were being blended in with the existing cadre. Secondly, the tasks were being overhauled and the newly delivered tanks were being tested. Finally, the training, for which there had been no opportunity for months, was reestablished. It emphasized maneuverability and speed. For these units, which had been worn out by defensive fighting during recent months, it was of vital importance to resuscitate the notion that panzer divisions were destined for aggressive conduct of battle. Their training in night fighting and their coordination with various other arms of the service were of equal importance. A special task consisted in the training of drivers, the number of which had seriously diminished, because they had been committed as infantry men during the preceding battles. They had suffered high casualties during the fighting. Since the Offensive was to lead across a hilly terrain with bad and narrow roads, very much was to depend on their ability. However, their training was not as complete as had been intended, because of the very limited quantity of POL which was available for this purpose.

Army supervised the training and the reorganization which were being complemented by map exercises carried out by the officers staff. The training was nearly always based on the concept of a flank attack against a motorized enemy breakthrough. This plan was plausible to all the participants because the efforts of the Allies to thrust up to the Rhine were becoming more and more obvious. A Gp B held similar map exercises with its army staffs.

After the redistribution of the Western Front sectors on 5 Nov 44, Sixth Pz Army was subordinated to A Gp B on 6 Nov 44. On 2 Nov 44, Army had already reported that its reorganization had not been completed because of the delay in the bringing up of the necessary equipment. Since the assembly was to be accomplished by 20 Nov 44, Army could not be granted any further delay. Its transfer was therefore initiated after 8 Nov 44. Army, together with the four SS divisions, was transferred into the areas of Cologne–Rheydt–Jülich–Düren–Münstereifel–Ahrweiler–Bonn. The Pz Lehr Div was again separated from Army and transferred to the Hundsrück sector, east of Traben-Trabach on the Moselle, which was on the boundary between A Gps B and G. As mentioned in the description of the fighting in Lorraine and in Alsace, the division had to be employed before its reorganization had been completed, and had not regained its full combat strength by the time the Ardennes Offensive started.

In spite of the attacks on the railroad network in Western Germany and the Rhine bridges, and in spite of the great number of trains needed, troop movements generally went according to schedule. They were completed by 20

Nov 44. However, transports with troops, tanks, motor vehicles, etc, continued to arrive until well into the month of Dec 44.

The reorganization of the other divisions took place under considerably worse conditions. It had to be, almost exclusively, carried out in areas close to the front, and, in most cases of too short a duration. Furthermore, their reorganization was not carried out to the same degree as that of the SS panzer divisions which were given preferential treatment. Expedients were therefore commonplace.

2. THE REPLENISHMENT OF EQUIPMENT

On 27 Oct 44, the Führer decided that the armored strength of the divisions of Sixth Pz Army was to be doubled. This meant that the entire supply of tanks for the Eastern Front had to be temporarily suspended. Army subsequently received 250 new tanks. In addition, by order of the Führer, all motor vehicles and all armored vehicles, which accrued from the production lines and from the repair shops, were to be shipped to the Western Front after 1 Nov 44.

On 9 Dec 44, the Führer ordered the *Reichsführer*-SS [Heinrich Himmler] to collect 2,000 horses for Seventh Army. Also, the two divisions, which were being transferred from Norway, were ordered to turn over to the Panzer Armies one half of all their available motor vehicles. Furthermore, the two Armies were assigned additional newly manufactured motor vehicles, whereas the other armies had to content themselves with receiving repaired ones.

In summarizing, it might be said that, as far as equipment was concerned, the Western Front received preferential treatment in view of the Offensive. It was given preference over all other fronts, even over the Eastern Front. Even though the staffs in the field considered the supplies they were assigned as altogehter insufficient, the total deliveries constituted an astounding accomplishment, if one remembered, that this was the sixth year of war, and that the armament industry was working under the most difficult circumstances.

III. The Preparations for Supplies

The preparations of the supply services had to be accomplished under the same circumstances as the tactical preparations: the maintenance of strict secrecy was mandatory. The lower echelons were almost up to the last moment unaware of the objective of their activities. They were to believe that the different supplies were destined only for the defensive battle.

Due to the incessant air attacks in the Zone of the Interior, OKH, which was responsible for the supply services, decided to store the bulk of the supplies on the east bank of the Rhine. The location of the supplies therefore presented a problem: Would the necessary supplies be made ready on time and be fully available for the Offensive?

The preparations for the transfer of supplies to the west bank of the Rhine were at first to be undertaken by the armies and corps assigned to that sector. At the beginning of Dec 44, Sixth Pz Army took over the command of the supply functions for all the troops employed in its sector under the false pretense that the supply services of Seventh Army were insufficient for the long sector, and that the OQu group of Sixth Pz Army had to gain practical experience.

The supply troops, which had been newly assigned to Army, were moved to the west bank and distributed along the Rhine, whereas the OQu group was transferred to Brühl. Seventy Army supply troops were assigned to Sixth Pz Army to complement the available troops. Additional supply troops were to be committed only after the Offensive had been launched. The supplies for Fifth Pz Army were distributed correspondingly.

On 9 Dec 44, a final discussion was held at the command post of Sixth Pz Army in Münstereifel. Its subject was the moving up of supplies during the operation. The Ib of Army, Genmaj Alfred Toppe, was also present at this meeting, and there was another opportunity to inform the Supreme Command at which points the requisitioned supplies had not yet been delivered. Seventh Army was responsible for the initial stages in the distribution of the supplies.

The food supply arrangements did not present any special problems because they were no different from those which had proved adequate for preceding operations of a similar nature. However, from the very beginning, the main problem of logistics was, whether it would be possible to procure the quantities of ammunition and POL needed for an offensive of so wide a scope, and whether these stocks would be ready behind the front before the dead-line.

In mid-Oct 44, it had been estimated that 50 trains of ammunition would be needed for the Offensive. The armament industry had been able to deliver this quantity which was successfully moved up to the Western Front. Any shortage of ammunition, which occurred during the Offensive, was only temporary and restricted to certain areas.* The ammunition supply situation became unfavorable only after the Germans were forced to switch to the defensive.

The distribution of ammunition according to points of main effort was complicated by the fact that details of the attack plan were completed only at the last moment. Furthermore, it was uncertain until the last moment which batteries would actually be in position at the beginning of the attack. An additional factor of uncertainty was the bringing up of supplies over routes which were endangered by bombing attacks.

---

* Others disagreed; Gen Karl Thoholte, in charge of Army Group B, reported that the 1.5 units of ammunition (150 rounds per gun) was insufficient and that 12 units were needed for the first ten days of the attack. Gen Walter Staudinger with Sixth Pz Army felt that 5–6 units were necessary for an adequate artillery preparation and support in the first days alone. Ed.

The differences in caliber and the insufficient transportation space created additional difficulties, which pertained particularly to the *volks artillerie* corps; another problem was the shortage of prime movers for the guns. The panzer divisions therefore had to help out. This resulted in inevitable breakdowns which again created new problems.

The stocks of ammunition and POL were stored away from the roads in order to protect them from air attacks. But this scheme hampered operations during bad weather.

During the days preceding the Offensive, the expenditure of light and heavy field howitzer ammunition was restricted to a minimum so that, in sectors where no heavy fighting was taking place, the artillery was not allowed to fire more than a few rounds per gun per day.

The high expenditure during the Roer Battle had necessitated the diversion of ammunition from the OKW reserves; however, the stocks were readjusted by the timely replacement of the expended ammunition. As far as ammunitions were concerned, the fighting preceding the Offensive therefore did not affect its course. Three issues of ammunition had been prepared for the Offensive; the first was to be expended during the artillery fire, the second was to be carried along, and the third had been dispersed in dumps farther to the rear. But, nevertheless, the stocks of certain types of ammunition were too small, in some cases very much smaller than anticipated.

Genfldm Keitel was the man who was responsible for the quantities of POL, which were made available to Army Group for the Offensive, as well as for its procurement, transportation and storage. As C-of-S of OKW he had always been responsible for the distribution of POL. After the breakdown of the POL production in spring 1944, which was caused by the air attacks on the Rumanian oilfields and on the German distillation plants, he had kept a close watch on POL consumption. One order after another had been issued to enforce a reduction in the consumption and to prevent any unnecessary use of POL. On the other hand, the C-of-S of OKW attempted to promote to the greatest possible extent the use of substitutes, such as, for instance, the use of wood-gas generators on motor vehicles. *Reichsminister* Speer made similar efforts in the sphere of the war industries, such as the intensified exploitation of other oil-fields, and the dispersion of the synthetic gasoline production into smaller plants, etc. But, all these measures had not succeeded in preventing a reduction in the quantities of POL, needed for strategic purposes. Nevertheless, the plan of building up a POL reserve for OKW was being adhered to; this was all the more important the greater the shortage became. Thus, when it was first conceived in Sep 44, the plan for an offensive did not find OKW in a state of unpreparedness. It was estimated that approximately 10,000 tons of gasoline would be accumulated by 20 Oct 44.

The calculations, which had been made in connection with the first draft, showed an estimated consumption of approximately 17,000 cubic meters [equivalent to 4.49 million gallons]; the C-of-S of OKW was able to simultaneously report that, in spite of the intervening further deterioration in the POL production, it would be possible to raise the OKW reserves to the desired level by the time the attack was to start.

On 28 Oct 44, an order was issued concerning the establishment of POL reserves in the West. Its objective was to accumulate 2,500 cubic meters (660,000 gallons) of oil and 15,000 cubic meters (3.96 million gallons) of gasoline – thus, a total of 17,500 cubic meters (4.62 million gallons). It had occasionally been mentioned during the discussions of this problem that the capture of enemy POL stocks was to be expected; this factor had been of considerable importance during the campaign in the West and in Africa. But, this uncertain factor was not considered for the evaluation.

It was attempted to cut down the daily consumption of the entire Western Front to 500 cubic meters (132,000 gallons) in order to increase the OKW reserves. But, this proved to be impossible because the extension of the damages to the railroad network necessitated an increase in the consumption of POL. It was, above all, the American offensive in the Jülich–Düren area which threatened to upset the constitution of POL reserves. At that time, the daily consumption of the Western Front stood at 650 cubic meters (171,600 gallons). Genfldm Keitel received some very urgent requests to release POL stocks because the prevailing shortage was expected to have the most serious consequences. The C-of-S of OKW granted these requests only very slowly, and then only for the smallest possible quantities which amounted to only a few thousand cubic meters. Thus, it was after all possible to accumulate the 17,000 cubic meters which had been promised in the beginning.

The problem, which overshadowed the Offensive even before its start, was therefore not really the shortage of POL, but the timely delivery from the dumps to the units. By mid-Dec 44, only 7,500 cubic meters (1.98 million gallons) had been delivered to the Eifel assembly area. The balance was still west or even east of the Rhine.

The cause for this delay partly was with the transportation system, which had already been greatly restricted between the front and the river as far as the railroads were concerned, and which functioned only during the night as far as it pertained to road convoys. The latter were made up of worn-out trucks which had to be driven over bomb damaged roads. Another contributing cause was, that it was impossible to deliver the large quantities, which were needed, to an area into which long columns were already moving from all directions, and in which the problem of storage presented great difficulties, one of the main ones being camouflage. Another disturbing factor was the destruction of the Moselle bridge by direct hits.

At the start of the Offensive the situation was as follows:

Approximately 12,000 cubic meters (3.17 million gallons) of POL had been delivered to the Armies and their subordinate units. An additional 8,000 cubic meters (2.11 million gallons) were on the way or were being delivered. OKW had promised 3,000 cubic meters (792,000 gallons) as a reserve stock. An estimated 12–15,000 cubic meters (3.17–3.96 million gallons) were needed to advance the attack wedge from the Maas up to Antwerp. Thus, a contribution from captured supplies would have been needed for this part of the Offensive.

The individual panzer divisions were equipped with one and one half to two and one half issues. But, because almost twice the usual amount of POL was needed for every kilometer due to the hilly terrain with ice on the roads – a fact which had been proved by trial runs – one issue lasted only for 50 km. It was intended to deliver one additional issue per day. As demonstrated during the course of the Offensive, this schedule could not be adhered to due to the congestion of the few available roads; the result was that considerable delays were caused by shortage of POL.

Thus, the scope of the Offensive had – in reality – been limited in advance by the POL situation, which also hampered the preparations at every stage because of the enforced fuel conservation. But, the quantities needed for the first stage of the thrust had been procured. It was not, however, possible to deliver them sufficiently close to the front to make them immediately available, and it proved to be even less possible to assure their timely delivery during the course of the Offensive.

IV. The Preparations in the Signal Communications System

On account of the maintenance of secrecy, no new signal communication lines were to be laid before the corresponding positions were occupied. The civilian telephone traffic behind the front was stopped or monitored, wherever it continued.

During the weeks preceding the Offensive, a general radio silence was imposed on the newly arriving divisions. The additional radio stations therefore had no opportunity to check into their nets. Nor was it possible to test in advance the radio network which had been prepared for the Offensive. The volume of traffic communications were not to be increased. This also applied to the radio stations which had been established farther to the rear. Thus, the existing situation in the field of radio communications remained unchanged until the last moment before the Offensive.

Seventh Army, remembering the experiences in the East, was apprehensive because the new radio stations would not have checked into their nets, and because the radio operators would be out of practise. Army, therefore, exerted pressure on Army Group that this restriction should not be applied so rigidly, but only succeeded in obtaining a somewhat greater intensification of the artillery fire direction by radio control.

As anticipated, the command authorities encountered considerable difficulties during the first days of the attack due to the fact that the new radio stations had not checked into their nets. These difficulties were only gradually overcome.

V. The Assembly

In order to save POL, as few motor vehicles as possible were to be employed for the assembly. Thus, the vital question was, whether the railroads were still capable of taking over the important part which had been assigned to them during the assembly stage. Conveyance to the assembly area of one single panzer division meant the use of sixty trains or more. The Supreme Command, therefore, waited anxiously for the daily reports on the damages to the Western German railroad network, especially for those on damages to the switching yards, junctions, and railroad bridges. By the extreme efforts of all concerned and by the employment of reinforced repair crews it had been possible to avert the critical situation which had been threatening during the withdrawal to the West Wall. In Oct 44, and even more in Nov 44 – the decisive month for the assembly – the German measures benefited from the nights, which grew longer, and the weather, which was bad on many days. Thus, a daily average of 100 trains could reach the rear area of the Western Front during Dec 44.

The performance of the railroads deserves special praise. They had to dispatch more trains for the Ardennes Offensive than for the Campaign in the West in 1940 during which a great number of troops had been moved up by road marches. In spite of the loss of daytime work hours and of the days during which the flying weather was good, and in spite of the destructions, the trains arrived with only insignificant delays. It was to be considered really lucky that the attacks on the Rhine bridges had so far not met with any significant success, and also, that the bridges over the Moselle and the Ahr were still intact, with the exception of the one at Ellern. A secondary disadvantage of the air attacks against the railroad tracks was that the communications system of the railways was being disrupted. It was therefore often necessary to establish the location of trains by motorized search patrols.

The plan of securing the most important lines by flak was frustrated by the lack of sufficient forces. Nevertheless, all the troop transports, with few exceptions, arrived without casualties. The same applies to the detraining, because the troops had – as a result of the constant air attacks – good practise in concealment.

It has already been mentioned that the foregoing did not apply to the same extent to transports of materiel, and that, as a result of the delayed arrival or the non-arrival of equipment, many shortages still existed at the start of the Offensive.

Army Group assigned a staff, commanded by a Colonel of the General Staff, to coordinate the movements in its rear area. Corresponding organizations were established with each Army. All road marches, whether motorized or by foot, were carried out only during the night. The moving up and placing in position of artillery reinforcements constituted a special problem. The firing positions had been reconnoitered and established by the artillery commanders and special staffs – obviously, for defensive purposes. The moving up was not to begin before 8 Dec 44, and also was to take place exclusively during the night. In the often pathless, wooded terrain, and during the very dark and foggy hours of the night, it was not always easy to find the correct roads and gun emplacements which were not to be designated on maps. It was therefore quite natural that different units were making for the same positions. Until 10 Dec 44, the guns were only allowed to be moved up to a certain line which was approximately 6 km behind the front.

During the daytime, the only traffic permitted was that of essential staff cars, and even these could only circulate individually. Whenever any enemy night reconnaissance was suspected, all movements had to come to a complete standstill. If a movement was delayed and could not be completed before daybreak, the commander of each *marschgruppe* was supposed to distribute the troops in his column in different villages or wooded areas, and conceal them. Since the first enemy planes appeared at a more or less certain hour, the deadline for the accomplishment of these measures was well known.

At a certain time, circulation maps were distributed, marking damaged and dangerous points. But, for the purpose of maintaining secrecy, no signs were put up along the roads. Special breakdown crews were placed at difficult points, and the roads were divided into sections and placed in charge of special commanders who could telephone with one another and with the command authorities. Five days before the Offensive, only one-way traffic was allowed along the roads. Even generals were not exempted from this restriction.

In order not to excite enemy suspicion by the noise of motor engines during the quiet night, truck convoys were at first only allowed to drive up to 10 km distance of the front line. From there onward, the additional transportation had to be accomplished by horse drawn vehicles, or the equipment was moved up by the troops themselves. Near positions in the proximity of the front line, the wheels were covered with rags, straw, etc. Lamps were not to be fully lit, and not a word was to be spoken, an order which was very difficult to observe, since – as everyone knows – a change of position normally causes much noise and loud talk.

Because of lack of time and insufficient means of transportation, the frontal strip barred to motor vehicle convoys was reduced to 5–6 km after 10 Dec 44. As a precautionary measure, observation posts were established close to the front line; it was their mission to report whether the noises originating from transportation vehicles were audible. In addition, it was attempted to form a 'noise curtain' covering these movements with the help of low flying planes.'

In order to avoid leaving tracks, the positions of the artillery reinforcements, that is to say of a great number of batteries, were selected in the immediate vicinity of roads, and corresponding to the available camouflage possibilities. This situation prevented the construction of gun emplacements, because they would have been too easily recognizable. The base-line directions of the newly arrived batteries were transferred from those which already were in position.

The transport of ammunition into the firing positions was just as complicated as the moving up of the guns. The ammunition, also, could not be taken up to the firing positions, but had to be brought up to a line which was approximately 8 km from the German front line. Practically all the ammunition had to be hand-carried the last stretch of road, which was a very tiresome detail; however, the soldiers willingly performed this duty. By 13 Dec 44, almost all the artillery reinforcements had taken up well camouflaged positions.

The preparation of the equipment for the construction of emergency bridges required special consideration; these constructions were of the greatest importance in the Seventh Army sector. Particular care was taken in the assembly of the equipment, which was brought to the immediate vicinity of the banks of the Our and was concealed. The assembly of the parts had been practised in advance along the Prüm river. The reason given to the troops and to the civilian population was, that all the existing bridges were known to the enemy and that he would eliminate them immediately during an attack; for this reason, substitute bridges had to be prepared in time.

The infantry divisions were moved into their assembly areas starting 14 Dec 44. The same precautionary measures were being applied as those observed during the movements of the artillery.

The difficulties encountered on account of the assembly of Fifth Pz Army units in the Seventh Army area, and which consisted of the necessity of first moving Fifth Pz Army to the north while the Seventh Army units were being taken westward – these difficulties were eliminated on time by agreements between the two army staffs. The panzer divisions were moved into their assembly areas in two night marches beginning 12 Dec 44. These marches had to be carried out without lights, and all motor vehicles, which had not reached their assembly areas by daybreak, had to be concealed wherever they were. A very extensive traffic control service by military police had to be instituted for the execution of these movements. Repair and wrecking services had to be provided to prevent that broken down vehicles could be seen or had to be repaired on the roads during daytime.

The quartering areas selected for the panzer corps were within easy reach of the assembly areas assigned to them. The abundant woods facilitated the moving up and quartering of troops, and storing of ammunition and POL. The importance of traffic control went beyond the scope of the assembly stage. A smoothly operating traffic control system was to provide for unhampered movements of the panzer divisions also after the attack had started. In addition to the available military police forces – each panzer corps and each panzer division had one company – Sixth Pz Army was assigned a military police regiment of 300 men. Fifth Pz Army received a corresponding military police force.

In general, the assembly was completed according to plan by 2400, 15 Dec 44. It would have been preferable if the troops had had two or three days more for their adjustment to the terrain and the reconnaissance of better attack possibilities. But, all requests for a delay in the start of the Offensive were rejected by Army Group which, in turn, was constrained by strict orders from OKW.

VI. The Tactical Preparations

In order to prevent a premature start of the fighting from which an early alarm of the enemy would have resulted, Army Group had ordered that no troops were allowed to pass the line of the combat outposts before the start of the attack. This meant a complication in the launching of the attack because the two fronts were, in the various sectors, separated by different distances which at some points were very long. The consequence of this order was, that the attack units could not everywhere penetrate the enemy lines at the same time.

The launching of the tanks in the Fifth Pz and Seventh Army sectors was complicated by the necessity of waiting for the construction of bridges, and by the additional difficulties presented by the steep curves in the roads leading down to the river banks. At certain points, the turns in the roads were so narrow that each tank had to first reverse before it could negotiate the curve. The demolitions, which had been carried out at the very same points during the German retreat for the purpose of delaying the enemy advance toward the West Wall, now proved to be very disadvantageous. Thus, in this sector the tanks were prevented from starting off during the first day, whereas only some of them could take off on the second day. It has already been mentioned that the launching of the mobile units in the Sixth Pz Army Area also encountered great difficulties.

Army Group had six large repair shops at its disposal; they had been set up as distant as possible from cities and traffic junctions, and they were therefore only rarely subjected to air attacks. Their transfer was to be avoided, if possible, because it involved so many problems. Nevertheless, during the Offensive, two of them were moved up into the Clerf and St Vith area. But, the difficulties experienced in the maintenance and repair situation continued to exist in spite of these transfers.

All the artillery of A Gp B was placed under the command of the *Hoehere Artilleriekommandeur* (Senior Artillery Commander) 303 zbV, Genlt Karl

Thoholte. Seven *volks artillerie* corps, three *volks werfer* brigades, and a great number of separate battalions, which had a total strength of approximately 12 artillery brigades, were subordinated to him.* His mission was to provide equal distribution of the artillery forces among all three armies and the reserves, and to organize them in such a way that their fire power would be used most effectively. In addition, he was given the special mission of improving the equipment and training of his units, such as for example, the conditioning of the *volks artillerie* corps. Special emphasis was to be put on the employment of artillery observers in armored vehicles, an increase in radio equipment, data computers, thorough training in the use of these means of modern artillery combat and the setting up of artillery message centers. Also, an orientation course in directing heavy barrages was to be attended by all artillery commanders down to the rank of battalion commander. The following fundamental principles were established for the artillery forces subordinate to A Gp B: fire was to be by at least one brigade or even a larger unit, the artillery concentration was to be rapidly lifted, the units were to be prepared for a swift advance, constant liaison with the ranking command was to be maintained, and artillery forces were not to be split up by the assignment of special missions to individual battalions.

The command posts of each unit were established by the ranking command authorities in order to avoid interference. Although these positions were not to be be occupied until two days before the start of the attack, no particular difficulties arose from this delay. Each artillery battalion received a manual containing respective instructions, data on cooperation with the infantry, on approach roads and on positions, information on the weather and plans of fire.

An artillery preparation, lasting half an hour, was to precede the attack. If it were further extended, the enemy would have had time to take the first countermeasures. Also, the available stocks of ammunition would not have permitted an extension; even during these 30 minutes of preparation, intervals had to be made to save ammunition. Fifth Pz Army was the only one to desist from using this attack aid.

The artillery preparation was, first of all, to be directed against the enemy MLR, secondly, against his command posts, crossroads, villages, and strong points, and finally, in the course of the attack, against the rest of the rear area and the roads along which reserves might be brought up. A concentration of fire against the Elsenborn heights in the Sixth Pz Army sector had been under consideration. But, it was finally decided that the artillery strength was to be about equally distributed behind the entire Army front.

---

* Actually 7 *volks artillerie korps*, 8 *volks werfer* brigades, 17 heavy artillery batteries and two independent heavy artillery battalions as well as divisional guns and many flak tubes (1,660 artillery pieces, 957 *werfers* and 188 flak guns. Ed.

For the purpose of reconnoitering the enemy artillery, the observation batteries of Seventh Army were, after 28 Nov 44, complemented by the observation batteries of I and II SS Pz Corps. This measure proved to be of great value, but it nearly led to the revelation of the secret. On about 2 Dec 44, a strong American reconnaissance patrol penetrated up to the observation posts of the observation battery of I SS Pz Corps. Two men belonging to this battery were found to be missing. Apparently they were dead when they were captured by the Americans, or they refused to give any information, or else they were unable to do so. By the time the attack was due to start, an adequate picture of the enemy battery positions was available.

The available fire power was distributed in the following manner:

The *Nebelwerfer* (rocket launchers), which were the main attack weapons of the infantry, were emplaced along the same line as the heavy infantry weapons so that they could reach as far as possible into the enemy area. The infantry guns were being kept farther behind in order to preserve their ammunition for the subsequent attack when the artillery would be obliged to change positions. The main target of the field artillery was to be the most forward enemy line. Some medium and heavy batteries were assigned special targets in the rear area. Other batteries were to concentrate their fire on the main traffic arteries five minutes after fire had been opened, while different ones were assigned the mission of concentrating their fire on the presumable assembly areas of the reserves. Special measures had to be taken for the silencing of enemy batteries since it was not certain from which positions they would fire. Two German batteries were employed to each American one, wherever this was possible. Flak batteries were mainly being used for this purpose.

It was not expected that the heavy barrage would decisively hit the enemy installations and supply dumps since these were too widely dispersed within the attack sector. Thus, it became obvious that only a limited firing period, with emphasis on its psychological effect, could be taken into consideration. The secondary objective was to neutralize the enemy artillery as much as possible. Since conditions differed in the combat sectors of the three Armies, they were given permission to direct their barrages according to their individual situations.

VII. The Measures taken by the Luftwaffe

At the start of the Invasion, *Luftflotte* 3 (Third Air Fleet) – later redesignated *Luftwaffenkommando* West (Air Force Command West) – which was to provide protection for the West, had approximately 2,400 planes, 800 of which were fighter planes, while the others were reconnaissance, bombing, and transport planes. Considerable losses had resulted from their irresponsible commitment during the first days of fighting, so that the daily rate of commitment very soon dropped to 2–300 fighter planes. In Sep 44, the daily average of planes available for commitment was only about 200 fighter, 80 reconnaissance, and 70 bombing planes. To these should be added the fighters of *Luftflotte Reich* (Air Fleet Reich), the mission of which was the defense of the Reichs territory; however, *Luftflotte Reich* carried out part of its mission in the western approaches to the Reich. Approximately 4–500 batteries of flak artillery were in the West, including the Rhine defenses.

During this time, the strength of the Luftwaffe in the West, which had amounted to approximately 300,000 men in the beginning of Jun 44, had dropped to about 120,000 men as the result of casualties, reassignments, and incorporations into the *Heer*. Upon repeated requests by OB West, the reclassification of ground personnnel of the Luftwaffe, the strength of which was now out of proportion with the flying crews, was intensified during the autumn of 1944. The personnel were used as replacements for the infantry and *Fallschirmjäger* divisions.

A very important prerequisite for the Offensive, perhaps even the most important one, was that the Luftwaffe regain its striking power in the West. For this reason, the command authorities of the *Heer* insisted, whenever there was an opportunity, that the existing enemy air superiority be eliminated during the attack. They also requested that the German Luftwaffe support the fighting on the ground.

The Supreme Command believed that these requests could be fulfilled. The German fighter program, which concentrated the efforts of the war industries on the production of fighter planes, had meanwhile been started. It was expected that its realization would bring about a general change for the better in the Luftwaffe situation. As a matter of fact, the yearly production of planes was successfully boosted to 37,000 planes, in spite of the increasing bomb damages suffered by the aircraft industry. 33,000 of these planes were one and two-seat fighter planes. The new jet and rocket-propelled planes were expected to be particularly effective because of their ability to very rapidly climb to great altitudes, and because they were faster than the enemy planes. When the Offensive was at its first planning stage it was therefore expected that, at the time of the attack, air formations of such strength and equipped with planes of so high a quality would have been assembled, that the whole situation in the air would be transformed.

However, this hope was not to be fulfilled. The commitment of the new types of planes was delayed for a number of reasons, and the German inferiority in the air did not allow for keeping them back until a change in the fortunes of war could be obtained by a sudden commitment of major forces. On the contrary, they were employed a few at a time. Thus, only 60–80 planes of the types Me 262 and Arado 234 could be promised for commitment in the Offensive.

Even the assembly of a strategic reserve of normal type fighter planes proved to be impossible because the monthly losses during the second half of 1944 amounted to 2,295 planes on all fronts. This figure represented a total loss of 13,770 planes for the six months period, which was the equivalent of more than two thirds of the simultaneous plane production.

Thus, the target which had been set during the first stage of planning, was far from being reached at the start of the Offensive. But, in comparison with the preceding period, the forces available for the Offensive had considerably increased. As already mentioned, the Führer had informed the generals before the Offensive that they could count on a total of 800–1,000 sorties during the first days of the attack. These calculations had taken into account both the losses, which were to be expected, and the fact that, according to past experience, only a certain fraction of the available planes could be made ready for commitment.

One further detail of the preparations worth mentioning was the presence of Luftwaffe liaison officers on all staffs of the *Heer*, down to panzer division level, in order to ensure adequate cooperation.

Why only a fraction of the promised assistance was furnished during the course of the Offensive, with the result that the inferiority in the air, which had been the cause of so much apprehension on the part of the *Heer*, once again showed its full effect, is a question which can only be answered in a description of the Offensive proper.

APPENDIX 1

The Most Important Dates

Sep 44:

4   (Capture of Antwerp.)

6   Conference of Hitler with Genobst Jodl concerning a large-scale offensive after 1 Nov 44.

14   Issuance of the order for the initial organization of Sixth Pz Army and the reorganization of the SS panzer units.

17   (Airborne landings at Arnhem.)

approx 25 Conference of the Führer with Genfldm Keitel and Genobst Jodl with regard to an offensive; order for the draft of a plan for an attack in the direction of Antwerp.

Oct 44:

2   (Beginning of the attack against Aachen.)

8   Evaluation of forces by the *Heeres* staff.

11	Genobst Jodl submits his plan; the Führer orders further elaboration of the plan with certain modifications.
12	The C-of-S of OKW issues an order for the concentration of reserves against the danger of an enemy breakthrough.
15	Disengagement of the Staff of Fifth Pz Army from the Lorraine front (on 22 Oct 44, the Staff was committed in the Aachen sector).
21	Issuance of an order for the formation of reserves.
22	Initiation of Ostbf Skorzeny to the special Operation '*Greif*'.
25	Orders for the concentration of the new *volks grenadier* divisions.
28 (24?)	Initiation of the C-in-C West and the Commander of A Gp B, followed by that of their Army Commanders.
29	Initial organization of A Gp H which assumes the command in the Roermond–Sea Coast sector on 10 Nov 44.

Nov 44:

1	Written transmission of the basic outlines of the offensive plan to OB West.
2	Conference held by OB West with the Commander of A Gp B and the Army Commanders east of Krefeld. (The Breskens bridgehead is eliminated; beginning of the fighting in the Vossenack–Hürtgen Forest area, southeast of Aachen.)
3	Conference of the Commander of A Gp B with the Commander of Fifth Pz Army; development of the 'little' plan. Expression of opinion by OB West on the basic outlines of 1 Nov 44.
5	Order for the regrouping of the Western Front in conformity with the draft for the attack.
6	(End of resistance in Walcheren Island and subsequent clearance of the Schelde delta.)
7	(Start of the attack on Metz.)
8 and 9	Issuance of orders with reference to the continued control over the reserves by the Supreme Command.
9	(Evacuation of the Moordijk bridgehead, withdrawal to the lower Maas line.)
10	Issuance of the Führer order on the assembly and preparations for the attack.

16	(Beginning of the second Battle of Aachen – Battle on the Roer, which lasted until mid-Dec 44.)
17	Permission by the Führer to redistribute the forces in Holland.
18	Instructions from the Führer concerning the attack procedure. A Gp B submits its suggestions: new proposals tending toward the 'little' plan.
21	OB West continues his efforts in favor of the 'little' plan. (End of resistance in Metz: the French penetrate into Belfort; subsequent loss of southern Alsace.)
22	Provisional expression of opinion by OKW, including the rejection of the 'little' plan. (Loss of Eschweiler.)
23	(Capture of Strasbourg in spite of commitment of Pz Lehr Div.)
25	Final expression of opinion by OKW on the intentions of A Gp B.
26	Conference between Genobst Jodl and Genfldm von Rundstedt.
29	A Gp B issues the attack order for operation 'Autumn Fog'.
End of Nov 44	Transfer of the Führer's headquarters from East Prussia to Berlin.
Dec 44: 1 and after	Continuation of the Battle on the Roer.
2	Führer confers with Genfldm Model and the Army Commanders in the Berlin Reichs Chancellery. (Agreement on pending questions; renewed rejection of the 'little' plan; confirmation of the attack date for 10 Dec 44.)
5	(Loss of Kaiserslautern.)
7	Postponement of the Offensive to 14 Dec 44.
9	Final modifications to the order on operation 'Autumn Fog' dated 29 Nov 44.
10	(Penetration of American forces into Saargemünd.)
10 and 11	After transfer of the Führer's headquarters from Berlin to installation Adlerhorst near Ziegenberg (Hesse): Speeches by the Führer to the Army and Corps commanders and other generals.
11	Postponement of the offensive from 14 to 15 Dec 44.

12   Further postponement to 16 Dec 44.

13   (Withdrawal to the Maas line between Nijmegen and Roermond,
            owing to British attacks at Mejel and against the Venlo bridge-
            head.)

15   Führer issues last instructions to Genfldm Model.

16   0530: beginning of the Ardennes Offensive.

APPENDIX NO 2

The Attack Orders of the Three Armies Taking Part in the Ardennes Offensive

(Reconstructed in their outlines according to data furnished by the Army Chiefs of Staff.)

a) Sixth Pz Army

After strong artillery preparation, Sixth Pz Army will – on X-Day – break through the enemy front in the sector on both sides of Hollerath, and will relentlessly thrust across the Maas toward Antwerp. For this purpose, Army will make full use of its motorized forces and will disregard the protection of its flanks.

The following instructions are hereby issued for this purpose:

I SS Pz Corps will start its attack at 0600 on X-Day, and will break through the enemy position in the Monschau–Udenbreth–Losheim sector. Subsequently, 12 SS Pz Div will thrust on the right wing of Corps, with 1 SS Pz Div on the left wing. They will cross the Maas and continue their attack in the Liège–Huy sector. According to developments in the situation, it will thereafter be the mission of Corps to relentlessly pierce toward Antwerp by making full use of its motorized elements, or to be available for the protection of the right flank along the Albert Canal.

Carefully selected advance detachments, led by particularly daring commanders, will advance rapidly and capture the bridges in the Maas sector before their demolition by the enemy.

The following units will be subordinated to Corps: the 277 and 12 Volks Gren Divs, and 3 Fs Div.

After the breakthrough across the main defensive area of the enemy has been achieved, 3 Fs Div and 12 Volks Gren Div will again be subordinated to Army.

The **II SS Pz Corps** will be held in readiness in the rear of I SS Pz Corps and will immediately follow the latter during its advance. It is the mission of Corps to thrust – together with I SS Pz Corps – toward the Maas, cross the river, and then continue its advance on Antwerp, disregarding any enemy contact with its flanks. Liaison with I SS Pz Corps will constantly be maintained. Armored advance detachments will immediately follow the last combat elements of I SS Pz Corps. The Corps is therefore responsible for keeping open the roads of advance behind I SS Pz Corps.

On X-Day, **LXVII Inf Corps**, with 326 and 246 Volks Gren Divs, will break through the enemy positions on both sides of Monschau, will cross the road Mützenich–Elsenborn, then turn off to the north and west, and will build up a secure defensive front along the line Simmerath-Eupen–Limburg–Liège.

The 12 Volks Gren Div and 3 Fs Div will be committed west of Limburg for the purpose of prolonging the defensive front. Army will be responsible for moving up these divisions. Road blocks supported by armored detachments, will be established far to the north across the main roads and across the lines of communication leading from north to south. The hilly terrain around Elsenborn will be seized and firmly held.

A special order was issued for the artillery; it regulated the preparations, the support to be given during the attack, the additional duties, and the subordination of the artillery while the attack was progressing. Apart from its organic artillery, Army was assigned three *volks artillerie* corps, two *volks werfer* brigades, and three heavy artillery battalions. The artillery of the panzer corps was to take part in the preparations.

b) Fifth Pz Army

On 10 Dec 44, Fifth Pz Army issued extensive 'instructions on the assembly and fighting'. They were subdivided in a number of parts:

1) The enemy.

2) Intentions of Army Group and the adjacent units.

3) As follows (the reconstruction of the text can be considered as almost literal):

The mission of Fifth Pz Army is, to break through the enemy positions in the Olzheim–Gemünd sector under cover of darkness, and to thrust across the Maas on both sides of Namur up to Brussels.

The first objectives of the attack are the bridgeheads across the Maas. It is of vital importance to pierce any enemy resistance, to keep moving by day and by night, to relentlessly advance, disregarding prescribed routes of advance; if necessary, the advance will be continued dismounted and on foot. For this purpose, **LXVI Inf Corps**, with 18 and 62 Volks Gren Divs, was to execute a double envelopment of the enemy forces in the Schnee Eifel, and was to capture St Vith; then, Corps was to thrust on, echeloned in depth, reach the Maas, and cross the river in the Huy–Andenne sector, or else be moved to the left Army wing.

The **LVIII Pz Corps**, with 116 Pz Div and 560 Volks Gren Div, was to force the crossing of the Our on a wide front on both sides of Ouren, was to move up to the Maas via Houffalize, thrust across the Maas in the Andenne–Namur sector, and establish bridgeheads.

The **XLVII Pz Corps**, with 2 Pz Div and 26 Volks Gren Div, was to force the crossing of the Our on a wide front in the Dasburg–Gemünd sector, by-pass the Clerf sector, capture Bastogne, and finally, echeloned in depth, thrust toward and across the Maas in the vicinity and south of Namur.

The **Pz Lehr Div and Führer Begleit Brig** were, at first, to be held in readiness as Army reserves, and were to be launched for a rapid thrust toward the Maas as soon as one of the corps had succeeded in breaking through.

The other parts and enclosures of the instructions pertained to the boundaries, directives for the conduct of battle, the mission of the artillery and the engineers, the commitment of the Luftwaffe and Flak, signal communications, and the description of the terrain; they also contained special instructions for the supply services, the maintenance of secrecy and the camouflage measures; also, the plan for the assembly, a time schedule for the organization of the troops, a complete series of maps, and instructions on the location of the command posts.

c) Seventh Army

On X-Day, Seventh Army will cross the Our and Sauer, will break through the enemy front in the Vianden–Echternach sector, and its reinforced right wing will thrust toward the line Gedinne–Libramont–Martelange–Mersch–Wasserbillig in order to protect the southern flank of Fifth Pz Army. Army will gain ground beyond this line, will advance up to the Semois sector and the Luxembourg area, and will – by fluid conduct of battle – prevent an enemy thrust into the southern flank of Army Group.

The following instructions are hereby issued for this purpose:

The **LXXXV Inf Corps** will start its attack at 0600 on X-Day, will cross the Our, and will break through the enemy front in the Vianden–Ammeldingen sector. The 5 Fs Div on the right, and 352 Volks Gren Div on the left, will relentlessly thrust to the west, and turn off toward the line Gedinne–Libramont–Martelange–Mersch; there, their main forces will at first stay on the defensive. Mobile advance detachments will keep contact with the southern wing of Fifth Pz Army which will be advancing via Bastogne to the north of Corps. These detachments will advance beyond the objective of the operation up to the Semois, and block its main crossing points.

The **LXXX Inf Corps** will start its attack at 0600 on X-Day, cross the Our and Sauer, and will break through the enemy front in the Wallendorf–Echternach sector. The 276 Volks Gren Div on the right, and 212 Volks Gren Div on the left, will relentlessly thrust toward the Mersch–Wasserbillig line, and their main forces will stay on the defensive along this line. Mobile advance detachments will cross the Sauer, thrust into the Luxembourg area, and prevent the advance of enemy forces via Luxembourg. It is of vital importance that the enemy artillery positions in the Christnach–Alttrier area be rapidly neutralized. During the course of the attack, the *Bewachrungsbatallion* (penal battalion), which was committed on the Sauer front west of Trier, was to be held in readiness for the thrust across the Sauer.

The LIII Inf Corps was, at first, to remain available to Army.

3

Interview with
Generaloberst Alfred Jodl

Editor's Introduction

With regard to military affairs, no-one was closer to Hitler in late 1944 than Generaloberst Alfred Jodl. The interview with General Jodl is consequently of considerable historical importance. Jodl was the taciturn head of the German High Command of the Armed Forces (OKW), and the *Wehrmachtführungsstab*, the Armed Forces Operations Staff, which comprised Hitler's household military command center.

Jodl had been born in Bavaria on 10 May 1890, the heir to a long line of German officers. 'I can well say,' Jodl said of his career, 'that the military profession was in my blood.' Jodl worked hard at Nuremberg to show himself an apolitical soldier, stating that: 'The National Socialist Party I hardly knew and hardly noticed before the Munich Putsch.' In the early years he never attended any of the Nazi party functions or Hitler speeches. 'The appointment of Hitler was a complete surprise to me.' Later, in a small meeting with the General Staff, Jodl confided his doubts, but concluded: 'We must obey and do our duty as soldiers.' He would not be called upon until the war actually began.

> I was presented to the Führer by Field Marshal Keitel in the command train on 3 September 1939, when we were going to the Polish Eastern Front. That was the first day that I exchanged words with him ... [Confidence] came about very gradually. The Führer had a certain distrust of all General Staff officers, especially of the Army, as at that time he was still very skeptical toward the Wehrmacht as a whole. The relations between us varied a great deal. At first, until about the end of the campaign in the West, there was considerable reserve. Then his confidence in me increased more until August 1942. Then the first great crisis arose and his attitude towards me was caustic and unfriendly. That lasted until 30 January 1943. Then relations improved and were particularly good, sincere, after the Italian betrayal of 1943 had been warded off. The last year was characterized by numerous sharp altercations.[1]

Despite his efforts at Nuremberg to distance himself from Hitler, and regardless of his 'sharp altercations', by late 1944 Jodl had become a fixture at the *Führerhauptquartier*. He described the accommodations thus:

> The Führer's headquarters was a cross between a cloister and a concentration camp. There were numerous barbed wire fences and much barbed wire surrounding it. There were outposts on the roads leading to it to safeguard it. In

154

the middle was the so-called Security Ring Number 1. Permanent passes to enter this security ring were not given even to my staff, only to General Warlimont. Every guard had to check on each officer whom he did not know. Apart from reports on the situation, very little news from the outside world penetrated into this holy of holies ... Every day I made at least two reports on the situation ... The discussion of the situation and reporting on the military position was at the same time an issuing of orders. On the basis of the reports of the events, the Führer decided immediately what orders were to be given for the next few days. When my report was finished, I went into an adjoining room. There I immediately drew up the teletype messages and orders for the next few days, and while these reports on the situation were still going on, I read these drafts to the Führer for his approval. Warlimont then took them along to my staff where they were sent off ...[2]

While Jodl was acknowledged as the brains behind the OKW plans, others such as General von Manteuffel were inclined to discount their realism:

Keitel, Jodl and Warlimont had never been in the war ... Their lack of fighting experience tended to make them underrate practical difficulties, and encourage Hitler to believe that things could be done that were quite impossible ... I imagined that Hitler must realize that a rapid advance would not be possible under winter conditions and these limitations, but from what I have heard since, it is clear that Hitler thought the advance could go much quicker than it did. The Meuse could not possibly have been reached on the second or third day as Jodl expected. He and Keitel tended to encourage Hitler's optimistic illusions.[3]

The interview reproduced here, conducted by Major Hechler at Bad Mondorf in Luxembourg on 31 July 1945, was preserved as ETHINT-51. After the war the Historical Section described their impressions of the chain-smoking head of OKW:

He was fairly cold, exact, humorless and stiff in posture and personality. I was impressed by his grasp of details; for example, I started to apologize for one question regarding the American attempt to simulate the presence of an extra U.S. division in the south of the VIII Corps sector. Gen. Jodl said, 'Oh, that's all right, I can answer that question with candor; we didn't know anything about a simulated division, but we did know that a few days before the 16th of December you moved fresh troops in the north flank of the VIII Corps [106th Infantry Division].'

But it was perhaps the weight of damning documents with the signature 'J' that emanated from Hitler's headquarters, and the very close nature of his association with his master, that led Jodl to the gallows. At Nuremberg he steadfastly defended his record on the human rights issue, telling how as quick as he received word of atrocities on the Eastern Front and in the Ardennes, he readily communicated the unsavory news to his leader:

> I immediately reported any news of that kind to the Führer, and no-one could have stopped me from doing so. As an example, Obergruppenführer Fegelein told the Chief of the General Staff, Colonel Guderian, and Generaloberst Jodl of atrocities committed by the SS Brigade Kominiski in Warsaw. That is absolutely true. Ten minutes later I reported this fact to the Führer and he immediately ordered the dissolution of this brigade. When I heard of the shooting of 120 American prisoners near Malmédy, I immediately, on my own initiative, had an investigation started through the Commander West so as to report the result to the Führer . . .[4]

But all this forthrightness could not save him. As Jodl was executed at Nuremberg on 16 October 1946, the opinions expressed in these papers are a major source – along with Jodl's unpublished war diaries – for the perspective on the Ardennes offensive as seen from Hitler's headquarters.[5] After all, in the course of the interrogations Jodl acknowledged that the plan for the operation itself had formed in numerous detailed discussions between Hitler and himself. The very earliest indication of the ideas fermenting in the German leader's mind are in evidence in the trenchant notes Jodl made in his diary on 19 August. This was the day on which the disaster at Falaise, in Normandy, was in progress, and was only five days after Field Marshal Kluge, who was in command there, had killed himself, his suicide note begging Hitler to seek peace:

> 19 August: The Führer spoke of the material and personnel issues with the Chief of OKW, Chief Army Staff [General Buhle] and Speer . . . Prepare to take the offensive in November when the enemy air force cannot fly. Main point: some 25 divisions must be moved to the West in one to two months.[6]

The attack had to be launched 'in the West because the Russians had so many troops that even if we had succeeded in destroying thirty divisions, it would not have made any difference. On the other hand, if we destroyed 30 divisions in the West, it would amount to more than one third of the entire invasion army.' Jodl and Hitler firmly believed that with a successful offensive 'a decisive turning point in the Campaign in the West, and possibly of the entire war, could be achieved.'

However, as the preparations for the offensive continued, Jodl found that more and more compromises had to be accepted within the framework of the plan, and found himself leaning to the 'small solutions' proposed by Hitler's generals: 'The venture of the far-flung objective [Antwerp] is unalterable,' he wrote to General Westphal on 1 November, 'although the goal appears to be disproportionate to our available forces.'[7] Just before the attack, Jodl confided, 'I was filled with doubt.'

Over the weeks leading up to the attack, Jodl's diary records the myriad details that absorbed his attention as the great operation was prepared:

> 3 November: The Führer does not wish to give Tigers [Pz Kpfw VI tanks] to the mobile formations but to allot them in small units to the infantry ... The King Tigers are too heavy and are having chassis troubles.
>
> 18 November: All attacks to begin simultaneously or the enemy will get warning. Night attack only if the troops are fit for it. Armored sanding machines. Get all Alsatians out of the front line divisions.
>
> 28 November: Three blankets per man for the attacking troops in the West. Can they be transported? Boots. Get units to report.
>
> 6 December: Navy frogmen to be attached to the Sixth Panzer Army (Meuse canal).
>
> 8 December: 7,150 cubic meters of fuel available; a further 6,000 is on the way with 2,400 coming from the East. The remainder must be moved up urgently ...
>
> 12 December: Seventh Army is still short two bridging columns, a pioneer battalion from the East and, above all, rubber boats.[8]

After the war, Jodl was asked whether the German army could have succeeded in reaching Antwerp if they had possessed the reserves which were available in 1940:

> We would have needed many, many more reserves and correspondingly more aircraft, munitions and fuel. We did not have the other factors of superiority on a large scale. If we had had ten more good divisions, we might have thrown you over the Meuse, but how we could have held the big salient thus created is not clear. Our strategic position would have been worse rather than better.[9]

Notes

1. *Trial of Major War Criminals*, International War Tribunal, Nuremberg, 1948, vol.XV, p.294.
2. *ibid*, pp.295–6.
3. B.H. Liddell Hart, *The German Generals Talk*, Quill, New York, 1948. Actually, there was hope within Hitler's headquarters that the Meuse might be reached on the evening of the first day of the assault.
4. *Trial of Major War Criminals*, International War Tribunal, Nuremberg, 1948, vol.XV, p.298.
5. See also Generaloberst Alfred Jodl, 'Planning the Ardennes Offensive', ETHINT-50, and two documents by Herbert Büchs, 'An Interview with Maj. Herbert Büchs: The Ardennes Offensive', ETHINT-34, 1947, and 'The German Ardennes Offensive', A-977, n.d. Büchs was Luftwaffe aide to Jodl during the period of the offensive. Extensive comparison between the 1940 and 1944 operations can be found in R-44, Magna Bauer, 'Comparison Between the Planning for the German Ardennes Offensive in 1944 and Operation "Gelb" in 1940', April 1950, in OCMH files.

6. Jodl Diaries, National Archives, Record Group 242, Entry 166, MS# P-215.

7. *OB West, KTB Anlage 50*, pp.30–1, 1 November 1944.

8. Jodl Diaries, *op. cit*.

9. This, and all other quotations in this section from Jodl, originate from ETHINT-50, *op. cit*.

Interview with Generaloberst Alfred Jodl

1. Q: We captured maps indicating objectives and routes of advance, and it would appear that the Sixth Pz Army main axis of attack was directed through Liège. You said, however, that the plan was to bypass Liège.

A: The main axis was to avoid Liège; however, I cannot explain without knowing the maps to which you refer. Some infantry divisions were brought up behind Sixth Pz Army, and, consequently, were attached to it; however, it was not anticipated that this attachment would continue. When Sixth Pz Army reached the Monschau–Eupen line, the divisions were to come under Fifteenth Army control and act as a screen. If mobile forces of 'Sepp' Dietrich were aimed at Liège, then Dietrich should be shot for disobeying orders.

2. Q: One map shows two arrows passing around Liège, one to the north and one to the south. It looks as if their intention was to cut off the city.

A: Three infantry divisions were to make the initial breakthrough, after which the panzer divisions were to race to the Meuse. The Fifteenth Army was to drive north. One or perhaps two infantry divisions were to act as a screen toward Liège, and later operate under the control of the Fifteenth Army. That must be the reason for the arrows on the maps. No encirclement of Liège was planned. The line of the flanking screen would run Monschau–Eupen–Verviers–Liège since that was the strongest defense line. The exact positions, however, were not important; they could be behind or in front of that general line. Under no circumstances was there to be a major attack on Liège. With that restriction, matters were left to the commanders.

3. Q: What was the mission of Fifteenth Army – to screen the entire flank Monschau–Liège inclusive, but not attack Liège?

A: Yes, just to hold the line.

4. Q: Could the failure of Fifteenth Army to penetrate on the extreme north of the attack have caused 'Sepp' Dietrich to move the axis of his advance farther

north and thus do what Fifteenth Army failed to do, that is, reach the Monschau–Eupen–Liège line?

A: No. Dietrich actually did not change his direction of advance. The failure of the Fifteenth Army had no real effect on the movement of Sixth Pz Army, although, of course, that failure weakened the flank protection of Sixth Pz Army. Dietrich's advance was too slow, and the Allies attacked around Stavelot–Malmédy; but this came later. After the initial attempt to reach the Meuse failed, we had to turn north, meet the Allied attack, and try to take the Elsenborn heights in order to avoid being crushed. This, however, occurred four days after the initial attack.

5. Q: Did this change your plans with regard to Liège?

A: No.

6. Q: Did you believe, or did Hitler believe at any time, that 'Sepp' Dietrich was going too far north and too near Liège?

A: The routes were fixed in advance, i.e. big '*Rollbahnen*' for the mobile units farther west. The Leibstandarte Div (1 SS Pz Div) went as far west as it could. The mobile units actually did not go too far north. About 22 or 23 Dec 44, many units went farther north. For example, 3 or 15 Pz Gren Div was committed in the fighting farther north.* After the first three days of the Offensive, certain developments forced us to take definite action. There was no longer any choice involved other than to counter the movements of the enemy.

7. Q: Had you lost the initiative by this time by becoming involuntarily involved on the northern flank?

A: We wanted to repulse these attacks and drive farther north so as to gain a good defensive position on the Elsenborn heights.

8. Q: Were many forces of Sixth Pz Army committed on the northern flank in order to reach Elsenborn?

A: The Army sectors are correctly reproduced on your map. Elsenborn was in the Fifteenth Army zone and Malmédy in that of Sixth Pz Army. Elements of Sixth Pz Army were then involved, as you say.

---

* 15 Pz Gren Div was committed in the fighting around Bastogne at the close of December. Ed.

9. Q: Did this distract the drive of Sixth Pz Army to the west?

A: Yes. Time had been lost, and your forces had attacked from the north and forced us into a flank battle. Had we reached Huy, the attack would not have been so intense here. It would have been aimed toward the southwest, because our forces would have penetrated much farther northwest.

10. Q: Was Sixth Pz Army assigned the main effort in the Offensive?

A: Yes. That army was to deliver the strongest blow.

11. Q: Were there geographical or other reasons for this decision?

A: The main reason was that Sixth Pz Army had the shortest distance to cover in the drive toward the Meuse and Antwerp.

12. Q: Most of our reserves were around Aachen. Therefore, was not Sixth Pz Army more exposed to attack than Fifth Pz Army?

A: Yes. Sixth Pz Army was responsible for screening the entire attack (*Deckungsauftrag*), but this was to be left to the infantry when the mobile units spearheaded the drive toward Antwerp. These screening units later reverted to Fifteenth Army control.

13. Q: What date was fixed for the transfer of these screening units to Fifteenth Army?

A: As soon as the first spearheads reached the Meuse, the task of screening would be assumed by Fifteenth Army. Once Sixth Pz Army crossed the Meuse, it was not to concern itself any longer with the task of screening.

14. Q: Gen Manteuffel claims that the training and equipment of Fifth Pz Army was superior to that of Sixth Pz Army. Was this only his personal pride in his Army, or do you think there was an actual difference?

A: Let me see. He had Pz Lehr Div, the 2 and 9 Pz Divs, and the 21st and 29th [in fact only the Pz Lehr, 2 Pz and 116 Pz Divisions. – Ed.]. The 2 Pz and Pz Lehr Divs, the latter having been at the front a long time, were excellent divisions, perhaps better than any in Sixth Pz Army. The Hitlerjugend Div (12 SS Pz Div) had been terribly battered by the British around Caen. It had had a year's training and, perhaps, had been the best division in the Ukrainian fighting. Due to its losses, however, most of the personnel was inexperienced; therefore the Division was no longer as good as 2 Pz or Pz Lehr Divs.

15. Q: In spite of that, Sixth Pz Army was given the role?

A: Bearing in mind the routes, there was no alternative. Sixth Pz Army occupied positions in the north, while Pz Lehr and 2 Pz Divs were farther south. There was a certain political interference in the conduct of the War; some things were done of which I would not have approved on purely professional grounds. Shifting all these divisions around might have caused trouble. The divisions would have had to cross each other and there would have been confusion which would have been followed by political recriminations.

The eventual line positions resulted from the locations of assembly areas and were, therefore, automatic. The Sixth Pz Army had been near Paderborn, Pz Lehr Div somewhere near Marburg, and 2 Pz Div west of Mainz. We had no choice other than to commit them in that relative order.

16. Q: Was the northernmost army given the main effort because it was an SS army?

A: The northernmost group was nearest the Meuse; it was mandatory to assign them the main effort. The fact that it was an SS army did not influence this decision.

17. Q: Had transportation been a less difficult problem, would you have made Fifth Pz and Sixth Pz Armies change places despite possible political recriminations?

A: I usually apply the principle of assigning the main effort to the best troops, if I can afford to do so. An even more important principle is to apply the most expeditious solution and not lose any time. In this particular situation, I could not have done anything else. Hitler did not decide which divisions were to be attached to each Army; I made that decision. Exercising general staff principles, I had to assign the divisions which were to carry out the attack, and put our units into action with as little friction as possible. There was enough friction as it was.

18. Q: What kind of friction?

A: By interchanging divisional areas, each division would have had to make an unnecessarily long march, thereby wasting time. People would have said there was some political motivation behind it.

Hitler ordered that Sixth Pz Army be employed; that is clear. The actual commitment of this Army, however, was my decision and not Hitler's. I might have picked other good Army or SS divisions; in fact, Sixth Pz Army did not have good divisions.

The only real weakness in the SS divisions was the training of the staff and senior officers (some of the company-grade officers were really excellent). These divisions, however, had been committed in all the major battles, and had suffered most of the losses. We were not in a position to analyze the origin and composition of each division too closely. Perhaps some of Fifth Pz Army divisions were better than the SS divisions, but this was not obvious.

Toward the end of the War, the SS no longer depended on volunteers and drafted many men. These draftees, the Catholic farmers from Upper Bavaria for example, had a different philosophy from the SS and performed less capably in SS uniform than they would have in Army uniforms. In addition, they feared they would be shot by the Russians upon capture. The attitude of the public toward SS troops was different from its attitude toward Army troops, and the troops felt it; so, the SS divisions lost some of their value.

19. Q: When you say that Fifth Pz Army was making greater progress, was there any idea of shifting the main effort to that Army?

A: Yes, certainly. The main effort was shifted to Fifth Pz Army to the extent that we gave it all the OKW reserves and also sent Führer Gren and Führer Begleit Brigades behind the center of that Army. When it became evident that Fifth Pz Army was advancing faster, we gave it our entire support. During the action, troops were thrown in wherever the opportunity was presented. Generally, reserves would be sent to whichever army advanced the faster. Model used the troops as the tactics of the battle dictated.

20. Q: Did Model dissipate these OKW reserves by his tactical employment of them?

A: No. He used them correctly. The fluid advance of Fifth Pz Army stopped and became entangled in a big battle when your counterattack developed. These reserves had to be thrown in then to hold the line.

21. Q: When were the OKW reserves employed?

A: For several days after approximately 21 Dec 44. OKW reserves were committed as they arrived. Two infantry divisions were also attached to Seventh Army from OKW reserve.

22. Q: After you had reached Antwerp, and had cut the British supply line, etc, what would your future offensive plans have been?

A: Because a larger force would have been necessary, we would have taken more reserves from the entire front. We calculated that the Allies would be incapable of launching an attack in any other sector of the front. We would have moved troops from every Army sector and initiated concentric attacks against Aachen from Monschau, Maastricht, and Holland. With their supply lines cut, we would crush your forces in the Aachen pocket. This was the only method which seemed promising. We could defeat those strong forces only by cutting off their supplies.

23. Q: If Antwerp had been captured, do you feel that you could have won the War in the West?

A: Had we taken Antwerp, the situation would have been difficult for the Allies. It is hard to say whether we could have destroyed the forces in the pocket or whether you, using your entire air force could have supplied them by air. In any event, it would have made a terrific impression on political, military, and public opinion. Even with captured fuel and supplies, I doubt whether we could have reconquered France, because we did not have the supplies, munitions, or troops for a major campaign in that country. In addition, the Russians launched their attack on 12 Jan 45 and we would have had to withdraw troops from the West. Still, it would have been a major set-back for you and you would have required many months to effect your recovery. You had many divisions in the United States which were not yet ready. We had all the divisions being organized in the United States, and those which were operating in the West, in Italy, and in the Far East plotted on our war maps. In fact, there was no special secrecy on your part in these matters.

24. Q: In general, when did you feel that the War in the West was lost for Germany?

A: The War was already lost in the West at the time of the breakthrough at Avranches and the beginning of the war of movement in France.

25. Q: What specific results did the failure of the German Seventh Army to broaden the base of the salient in the Echternach–Luxembourg area have on the Offensive? The attack of Seventh Army does not appear to have been vigorously pushed. Did this force Fifth Pz Army to use routes in the zone of Sixth Pz Army?

A: No. It was not necessary; they had their own sectors. Seventh Army should have gone farther forward, but this did not retard the advance of Fifth Pz Army at all.

26. Q: What was the background of the failure of Seventh Army to attack more strongly?

A: The Army was numerically weakest and received the smallest allocations of *Heeres* artillery, etc. Except for the 560th Volks Gren Div [sic], its divisions were not very good.* It also had to cross very difficult terrain.

27. Q: Had they succeeded in broadening the base of the salient as Hitler had insisted, would that have changed the picture of the Offensive in any way?

A: No, not in general. A broader attack would have required more divisions and we had no more available. We would have liked to give Seventh Army a panzer division, but we did not have it.

28. Q: Did this affect the routes taken in the advance?

A: No. There was no threat to the left flank of Fifth Pz Army until it reached Bastogne.

29. Q: The German Nineteenth Army was in a pocket at Colmar. Why were reinforcements sent down there and not to the Ardennes? What relationship did the 'Colmar Pocket' have to the Ardennes Offensive?

A: No fresh divisions were committed at Colmar. The 2 Geb Div was committed there after the Ardennes Offensive. The 269th Inf Div was already there (it had come from Norway). We sent only assault-gun battalions. No division was ever sent down to Colmar which could have been sent to the Ardennes, although that Army was always appealing for more help.

30. Q: Was it a definite part of the plan to exert pressure in the south to prevent reinforcement from this area?

A: Yes, that was the idea. The French took over and US troops were being taken out. It was our aim to keep the US troops tied down in the south until after the Ardennes Offensive so as to force you to commit your reserves and keep you from preparing a major offensive.

31. Q: Were there any specific instructions as to the type of pressure to exert in the pocket area?

---

* Jodl probably means 212th Volks Gren Div, which was generally considered the best division in the army. Ed.

A: Yes. Himmler was down on the Upper Rhine Front – his first practical front command. He had assumed command before the Ardennes Offensive, having succeeded Balck. The 'Colmar Pocket' under Himmler was directly under OKW by Nov 44 and not under any army group.

32. Q: Were any special instructions given him at the time of the Ardennes Offensive?

A: Yes. He was to fix your troops as much as possible by small actions, and was to hold his bridgehead at all costs.

33. Q: Did these instructions change in the course of the Ardennes Offensive?

A: The instructions were not changed; they remained the same. Himmler was still in command at the end of Jan 45.

34. Q: Did the activity of the troops in Alsace contribute to the success of the Ardennes Offensive?

A: Perhaps fewer troops were moved north for the American counterattack than would have gone had we not held the pocket. We probably did delay the movement of US troops to the Ardennes, but, in general, it did not affect things. It did not affect the speed of our advance insofar as the breakthrough was concerned. In general, there was no connection.

35. Q: You knew the Gen Patton's Army was down on the Moselle. Did you plan to attack south of Trier after Patton moved up to counterattack in the Ardennes? Gen Patton, fearing an attack by the German Seventh Army, moved four armored divisions behind this front.

A: No. There was no such plan by Seventh Army. It might have been possible later, but we were not in a position to do it at that time. There was one general attack north of Strasbourg, but by 14 Jan 45 we had already issued orders to relinquish the nine panzer units and three infantry divisions to the Eastern Front.

36. Q: What individual in the German Army can give a complete statement of Gen Model's rejected plan for the offensive in the Aachen region?

A: Krebs, his Chief of Staff, or Obst ig Reichhelm, a young and capable officer. Reichhelm was with Twelfth Army (Wenck) and is probably in US hands as a result of my negotiations at Flensburg. Our contact with them had been severed.

37. **Q:** What do you think of the vigor with which Rundstedt prosecuted the Offensive?

A: He worked out the operation excellently and his leadership was very good. He knew the purpose of the Offensive perfectly, and caused no difficulties for the staff. He made his authority respected. He was an intellectually superior, well-trained officer. He did not waste time on details, which he left to Genlt Westphal, and kept the primary objective in view. Because of his age, however, he was not so well fitted to spur men on to superhuman efforts in an adverse situation. For such a task, Model, or Rommel in his better days, would have been more successful. Rundstedt always enjoyed complete authority and had an excellent head for operations. He had studied in the old school.

38. **Q:** Rundstedt has said that the forces assembled for the Offensive were too small. You said you had ample forces and that the roads were the main problem.

A: If we had had more troops, we would not have penetrated any faster. He had to leave the troops he had behind and not put them into the front line. Had he had a larger force at the time of the big battle that then developed, we should have done better, but the surprise breakthrough to and over the Meuse did not depend on more troops. With a slower advance, which is what actually happened, we could not have got across the Meuse regardless of the number of troops. More troops would only have meant a bigger mess than the one we got into, and, anyway, Rundstedt was unable to use the troops he had in reserve due to the condition of the roads.

39. **Q:** Could you have gotten through to Antwerp with the reserves you had in 1940?

A: We would have needed many, many more reserves and correspondingly more aircraft, munitions, and fuel. We did not have the other factors of superiority on a large scale. If we had had ten more good divisions, we might have thrown you over the Meuse, but how we could have held the big salient thus created is not clear. Our strategic position would have been worse rather than better. We would have had too large a front and, in addition, we had to send troops to the Eastern Front. Only good roads, fast movement, and a complete surprise could have helped us. For this, more troops would have been no help.

40. **Q:** At one time you said that by 10 Dec 44 all of the forces had been

brought up for the attack; however, in another statement you said that 16 Dec 44 was the earliest moment at which an attack could be made. What is the reason for the discrepancy?

A: The railroad movement of the first wave was completed on 10 Dec 44, but not the movement on foot into the prepared positions, which took until 16 Dec 44 to complete. The railhead of Sixth Pz Army, from which they moved up by road, was west of the Rhine in the Köln–Bonn–Euskirchen area. The other troops of Fifth Pz Army used the Moselle railroads and detrained at Wittlich and Trier. We estimated six days would be required to complete the move following detraining; this movement went off as planned. Although the weather was favorable and foggy, all movements were made at night.

41. Q: Had the troops been briefed at this time as to the purposes of the attack?

A: No. We told them that they were being assembled in a preparation for a counterattack on the flank of a major British attack toward Köln and Düsseldorf, and an American move from Aachen.

42. Q: When did company officers learn of the real plan?

A: Not until 15 Dec 44, the day before the attack; regimental commanders knew a little sooner. Divisional commanders knew three or four days earlier. The disclosure was echeloned.

43. Q: Besides the handicap of artillery officers in not being able to reconnoiter terrain, were there any other handicaps caused by delaying the briefing until the last moment?

A: I heard only from the artillery. I do not remember any other special case.

44. Q: Were there any indications immediately before the Offensive that we were ignorant of your intentions? How did you know you were going to achieve surprise?

A: The best indication was that no reinforcements were made in your sector. Everything remained as it was before.

45. Q: What was your reaction to the movement of 106 Inf Div (US) into the Schnee Eifel?

A: We believed that a relief was being made, and not that another division was being moved in.

46. Q: Was the moving in of a 'green' division also a sign that we would be caught by surprise?

A: I told the Führer on the first day of the attack that surprise had been achieved completely ('*Ich habe dem Führer am ersten Tage des Angriffs berichtet, dass die Uberraschung voellig gelungen ist.*'). In so many previous cases, surprise had been spoiled at the last minute. In 1942, for example, an observation plane, carrying complete plans for the attack on Voronezh, was captured by the Russians. We learned of this and, knowing it did not extend to our intentions following the capture of Voronezh, persisted in the plan. We then moved south, however, instead of toward Moscow as the Russians expected, and the attack was still successful.

After this incident, we ordered that only information absolutely necessary be described in plans and orders. For example, an Army would be informed as to what the adjacent division on each side was doing, but not the activity of the entire adjacent Army.

47. Q: Was any change in plan made when you discovered that 106 Inf Div (US) was very 'green'? For example, was there any greater effort around St Vith?

A: No. Nothing was changed in the original plan.

48. Q: Did you know that 28 Inf Div (US), located south of 106 Inf Div (US), and 4 Armd Div (US), which was directly south of the 28th, had been badly battered in the Hürtgen Forest before being moved into that sector?

A: We knew that. We considered them to be battle-worn divisions.

49. Q: Did you know that our 9 Armd Div, which was supporting the line in that sector, had yet to see combat?

A: Yes. All these things had been factors leading to our decision that this was a weak spot in your line.

50. Q: Did you know the command post of VIII Corps (US) was in Bastogne?

A: No.

51. Q: Or that the command post of First US Army was in Spa?

A: We did not know exactly where it was.

52. Q: did you know that you nearly captured a big gasoline dump near Spa?

A: No. We did not realize were were so near a dump. Although you sent few radio messages, we did manage to keep track of the movement of your divisions. Your Army Headquarters sent few messages, but we did intercept divisional orders indicating movements by their reference to preparations to move large numbers of trucks along the roads.

53. Q: On 3 Dec 44, Hitler is supposed to have made a speech at St Ingbert promising a big German attack within two weeks.

A: There is such a place in the Saar or Pfalz, but we were in Berlin on 3 Dec 44, as was Hitler. He never left there again until he went to Ziegenberg.

54. Q: Were there any Hitler speeches prior to the Offensive predicting or promising it?

A: Only the speech made privately to the commanders in Ziegenberg a couple of days before the Offensive was launched. [In fact there were two: on 11 and 12 December. – Ed.]

55. Q: You stated that the second most important reason for the failure of the Offensive was the tough resistance around St Vith. Did this resistance force the German High Command to move its main axis of advance to the south with special attention to the Bastogne area?

A: No! I have already answered that. We had issued orders embodying the principle of by-passing strongpoints and capturing them later. Maj Johann Meyer, Hitler's Army Adjutant, was with Fifth Pz Army and telephoned me from that Army's Headquarters that he had contradictory orders. Although the original order, in principle, was to bypass places like Bastogne, he had received an order from Genfldm Model to take Bastogne as quickly as possible. He wanted my decision. I replied that the original orders of Hitler still held, and that he should by-pass Bastogne, reach the Meuse, and only then take Bastogne. As it later was clear that we would not reach the Meuse, the order was then given to take Bastogne and the main attack on the town begun.

56. Q: Was Bastogne essential because it commanded a number of routes?

A: Yes, but that was later, when the Allied counterattack was made. Still later, Bastogne became an important point as a big pocket behind our rear when you were attacking. It was not so important at the beginning.

57. Q: Was its capture a matter of prestige with Hitler after the 101 Abn Div (US) distinguished themselves in its defense?

A: No. Hitler hated 'prestige' as a factor in military operations (*'Er hasste immer den Begriff "prestige" in militärischen Handlungen'*).

58. Q: Someone has characterized Bastogne as an *'absoluter Schlüsselpunkt'* ('absolute keypoint'). Is this correct?

A: Later, yes. But we could advance farther west without taking it, and, in fact, nearly reached Dinant (with a panzer reconnaissance unit); so it was not really a key position. St Vith was more of a key position, as it blocked the road and we could not by-pass it as we did Bastogne.

59. Q: Was St Vith also important because it was a big rail communications center?

A: Yes.

60. Q: Did the defense of St Vith handicap you and compel a change of plan?

A: Perhaps. Because of it, II SS Pz Corps was moved down behind Fifth Pz Army.

61. Q: When did you decide on this?

A: About 19 Dec 44.

62. Q: You remarked that no reliance was to be placed on captured American supplies, especially gasoline. How do you explain the numerous captured orders referring to the necessity for units to secure American supplies in order to continue their forward movements?

A: No such order came to us. Maybe the troops wanted some souvenirs or cigarettes. The troops always tried to get cars. Also, it was convenient to capture gasoline instead of hauling it up from the rear. There were many prime movers being used, for example, to bring bridge-building materials to the front, but we had enough material ready for our purpose. The Offensive did not depend on capturing enemy materials and supplies.

63. Q: In your original plan, was there any discussion of the use of captured American supplies?

A: Yes. We discussed it, naturally. We estimated that when we reached the Meuse, we would find supplies we could use (food and fuel).

64. Q: Did the success of the Offensive depend on securing American supplies?

A: No. Of course, an army supplies itself in war time, and everyone picks up things. Every noncommissioned officer was driving a vehicle around, and we were worried about the waste of gasoline. All these vehicles were supposed to be turned in, but this was hard to enforce. When a division asked for 120 trains instead of its normal 62, we knew it had stuffed itself with booty of all kinds.

65. Q: We caught some of your tanks and assault-guns out of gasoline near the village of Celles and punished them severely. Do you remember this incident?

A: A reconnaissance battalion of 2 Pz Div was completely lost at Celles, east of Dinant.

66. Q: Does this indicate insufficiency of gasoline?

A: No. They were impatient and ran ahead of their supplies in the hope of reaching Dinant, or perhaps their supply column was destroyed by air attack. You would have to ask the unit commander.

67. Q: In your planning, you felt you had provided adequate supplies?

A: Yes. We consumed more than we had calculated by using low gear on bad roads, but there was always gasoline nearby, as is proved by our later retreat under our own power. The nine panzer units retreated on their own gasoline. Celles was a special case.*

68. Q: You state you expected to reach the Meuse on the first day. As that is 80 km at the closest point, how was this possible, especially as the armor was not immediately committed?

---

* Numerous testimony by other German commanders refute Jodl's opinion here. Obtaining fuel was a very serious problem for all German motorized formations right from the start. Ed.

A: Armor, generally, was not thrown in until 17 Dec 44, but reconnaissance units could have got through a hole in the line to the Meuse. Once behind your three divisions, there was nothing to stop them. We often executed maneuvers like this.

69. Q: Which route would you follow in such a dash – the road to Huy?

A: The Huy route, via Malmédy–Stavelot–Trois Ponts–Werbomont–Ouffet–Stree, was the most important. To reach Malmédy, we used the route Stadt-kyll–Scheid–Malmédy. This was the route of 1 SS Pz Div (Leibstandarte -- SS Adolf Hitler).*

70. Q: Were they not committed only late on the first or early on the second day?

A: I cannot say exactly. They were not moving the first day. I don't know why. It is true, but I do not know the reason. By moving night and day, 80 km was the maximum expectation. I expected them to reach the Meuse by the second day if everything went fairly well.

71. Q: Were there any other columns farther south that were expected to reach the Meuse as early as that?

A: The 12 SS Pz Div was to take the Prüm–St Vith–Vielsalm–Odeigne–Bomal-Ocquier–Andenne route, which 'Sepp' Dietrich believed could be done on the second day.** We wanted to have as many spearheads as possible race forward so that they would have more chance of finding an undestroyed bridge and thus increase our chances of getting across.

72. Q: Were elements of Fifth Pz Army expected to reach the Meuse on the second day?

A: We calculated it would take them longer – at least one and one-half days longer than Sixth Pz Army.

73. Q: Could you tell us about your plans regarding the city of Luxembourg? Why was it ruled out? What emphasis was placed on it?

---

* 1 SS Pz Div's route did not go through Malmédy. Jodl has the routes confused. Ed.
** In fact the route was to be Losheimergrabon–Büllingen–Waimes–Malmédy–Spa–Esneux, reaching the Meuse south of Liège at Clermont. Ed.

A: We considered an advance of the flanking screen as far down as Luxembourg, but we felt that Seventh Army was too weak and we would be satisfied if we could get as far down as a point half-way between Echternach and Luxembourg. Hitler wanted to throw in an assault group west of Trier and one northwest of Echternach to make a pincers movement around Echternach. It was discussed, but we did not adopt this plan. Model said the Seventh Army was too weak and, therefore, should be kept concentrated between Echternach and Diekirch. He said it had insufficient artillery to split into two forces and would need GHQ artillery. In addition, he felt it could not take all these points. I agreed and the plan was dropped.

74. Q: Was there any revival of this idea later?

A: No, not again.

75. Q: Who would know about plans for the accumulation of supplies of fuel, transport, etc, for the German Army for the Offensive?

A: Obst von John, *Oberquartiermeister* OB West.

76. Q: Who were Buhle and Thomale?

A: Gen Buhle is familiar with supply of weapons (and not fuel). He was *Chef des Heeresstabes* in OKW. Genmaj Thomale was concerned with the state of panzer forces, including SS panzer troops. He knows all about supply of tanks, and the organization and the equipment of panzer units.

77. Q: Who would know most about fuel?

A: Genfldm Keitel worked especially on that. His specialist was Obstlt Dereser. He was concerned with the allotment of fuel on all fronts.

78. Q: With what other aspects of the Ardennes Offensive would Keitel be familiar?

A: Practically none, except for fuel priorities. He only knows about fuel up to the point when it reached OB West. As to the allocation of fuel from there to the army groups, Obst von John would know most.

79. Q: Several times you referred to the two Führer Escort *Divisions*. According to our Order of Battle information, both of these units were brigades. We would like some additional information on these formations if you can give us any.

A: They arrived as brigades and were then filled up during the Offensive and expanded into divisions.

80. Q: Can any specific date be fixed for the change?

A: They were called divisions even before the Offensive, though, for example, one had no supply trains and received its supplies from another panzer division or from Army. They lacked many things. Hitler wanted to copy the Russian and Chinese practice of giving a unit the next higher title – for example, calling a strong company a battalion, a strong regiment a brigade. The Russians used storm brigades and even armies. Over a long period this had an effect. You see divisions on the map and forget that they are not really divisions. It has a propaganda effect. The practice originated in the Russian Revolution. Hitler liked giving smaller units larger titles prematurely. The two units were practically brigades when the Offensive started. They really became divisions only when they reached the Eastern Front, although they did get reinforcements during the Offensive. The soldiers were sober and did not like this idea of inflated titles, but the Party was exploiting political experience.

81. Q: When did Hitler and his party leave Berlin for Ziegenberg?

A: On 12 Dec 44, Hitler got off a camouflaged train between Halle and Munich during the night, and proceeded by motor to Ziegenberg. Fifty officers and guards accompanied him.

82. Q: What was the plan of attack from Metz northward toward Belgium, which was considered prior to the launching of the Ardennes Offensive?

A: The attack was to be from Metz and commanded by Gen Blaskowitz. There also was a plan to attack into that area from the northeast near Trier. These plans were only briefly discussed. Blaskowitz was to hold the Plateau de Langres bridgehead as a favorable point from which to launch an attack to the north. After four days, the idea had to be dropped as the chance was lost when the bridgehead was crushed and the troops forced to retreat to the Moselle. Before the Ardennes Offensive, the other idea of an attack to the south was discussed, but was then abandoned in favor of the drive on Antwerp.

83. Q: On 17 Dec 44, Gen Patton was angry that he was not allowed to carry through his plans to attack the Siegfried Line with Third US Army. Did you calculate that Patton might get through south of the Ardennes, south of Luxembourg?

A: No. We did not expect it, as we did not think he would attack the West Wall.

84. Q: What was your reason for not fearing such an attack?

A: You could not have won the West Wall *quickly*, and also, we had reserves to the east for an attack on Hagenau which could have been committed to stop you. We also figured that your forces would be drawn farther north toward the Ardennes.

85. Q: If Gen Patton had attacked the West Wall on 10 Dec 44, would that have disturbed your plans for the Ardennes Offensive?

A: Yes, it probably would have. There would have been a big cry for reinforcements by the Army defending that area. A Gp G had been divided into the Upper Rhine front, under Himmler, with Nineteenth Army, and the Saar Front, under Balck, with First Army.

86. Q: If an attack had been made on 10 Dec 44, would you have pulled out forces, reserves, etc, from those collected for the Ardennes Offensive?

A: We should have done so very unwillingly. I would have tried not to do so. Of course, if there had been a breakthrough of the West Wall, we would have had to send them reinforcements.

87. Q: What divisions did you have along the Siegfried Line near the Saar during the first two weeks of Dec 44?

A: Your map showing the divisions in the Saar is rather accurate. The 6 SS Geb Div also arrived from Norway about that time. It came originally from Rovaniemi in Finland. It was not in position yet. The 7 Fs Div was brought down later, and 10 SS Div was brought down to the Saar to Lauterbourg [in January] and attacked toward Hagenau. This was about the situation at the beginning of Dec 44.

88. Q: Did you expect an attack there by our Third Army?

A: No. In any case, we planned to attack there later from both sides of the salient. We wanted to advance through Saverne over the Vosges and 'cut off the corner'. This was the attack of 1 Jan 45.

89. Q: Were there any reinforcements provided for the attack of 1 Jan 45?

A: Yes. The 6 SS Geb, 7 Fs, and 10 SS Pz Divs.

90. Q: Where did you get these reinforcements?

A: The 7 Fs Div came from the Venlo area, and 10 SS Pz Div from a reserve area farther north of Düren. It moved to Prüm with 15 Pz Gren Div and then to the attack on Hagenau.

91. Q: Were these units committed in the Ardennes Offensive?

A: I do not believe 10 SS Pz Div was committed in the Ardennes Offensive.

4

Interview with Generalfeldmarschall Gerd von Rundstedt

Editor's Introduction

Generalfeldmarschall Gerd von Rundstedt was an important figure within the planning of the German Ardennes Offensive – in particular because he objected so vehemently to it. As a military realist von Rundstedt set himself against the idea at an early stage: 'If old von Moltke thought I had planned this offensive,' he told interrogators, 'he would turn over in his grave.' In the summer of 1945, a series of questions regarding the Ardennes Offensive were forwarded by the ETO Historical Section for the attention of von Rundstedt, who was in British custody in England. The original document, ETHINT-47, dated 3 August 1945 was forwarded by von Rundstedt to Captain Robert Merraim later that year.

A venerable product of the Prussian old school, von Rundstedt was a throwback to the German military aristocracy of the Great War.[1] By 1944 he had been a soldier for fifty years – his seventieth birthday took place just weeks before the planned offensive. 'He was excessively modest,' his chief of staff, General von Blumentritt, remembered, 'and was too reserved. He led a simple life and was indifferent to money or possessions.' He smoked too much, enjoyed drink, and was something of a Francophile. 'He chose to speak French in France during the occupation and was affable to inferiors and extravagantly polite to noble women ... and even to insignificant people.'[2] But his relationship with Hitler – who he sometimes referred to sarcastically as 'that corporal' – had been stormy throughout the conflict and he had been relieved of command for an outburst to Generalfeldmarschall Wilhelm Keitel during the disastrous Normandy Campaign. (His answer to the question of what to do in response to Patton's breakout at Avranches had been: 'Make peace, you fools!') But for his last great gamble Hitler desired a noble and respected military figure with which to inspire his forces. He brought the venerable old field marshal back in the autumn of 1944. He was in nominal command of all the German armed forces in the West – *Oberbefehlshaber West* (OB West). Let in on the plan, von Rundstedt argued long and hard for a more reasonable alternative; and in spite of a relationship with his younger Army Group B subordinate which was 'cool to say the least', Rundstedt found himself in agreement with Model in a protracted attempt to sway Hitler from his unrealistic goal of Antwerp. However, the reality of von Rundstedt's influence over events was quite another matter:

I strongly objected to the fact that this stupid operation in the Ardennes is sometimes called the 'Rundstedt Offensive'. That is a complete misnomer. I had

nothing to do with it. It came to me as an order complete in the last detail ...
When I was first told about the proposed offensive in the Ardennes, I protested
as vigorously as I could. The forces at our disposal were much too weak for such
far-reaching objectives. I suggested that my own plan against the Aachen salient
be used instead, but the suggestion was turned down, as were all my other
objections. It was only up to me to obey. It was a nonsensical operation, and the
most stupid part of it was the setting up of Antwerp as the target. If we reached
the Meuse we should have got down on our knees and thanked God – let alone
try to reach Antwerp![3]

As to his claimed lack of influence on the operation, von Rundstedt told Liddell
Hart that 'the only troops I was allowed to move were the two guards outside
my own headquarters.'[4]

Notes

1. For background, see Günther von Blumentritt, *Von Rundstedt*, Odhams Press Ltd, London,
1952; also Siegfried Westphal, *Herr in Fesseln*, Athenaum-Verlag, Bonn, 1950. Generalleutnant
Siegfried Westphal served in the Ardennes as Rundstedt's able chief of staff. Westphal had
proved himself in offensive operations, mainly under General Erwin Rommel in North Africa,
where he had earned a reputation for efficiency and effectiveness.
2. Günther von Blumentritt, 'Three Marshals, National Character and the July 20 Complex', B-
344, n.d.
3. Milton Shulman, *Defeat in the West*, E.P. Dutton, New York, 1948. Major Shulman served in
the intelligence section of the First Canadian Army, carrying out interrogations of important
German commanders in September 1945.
4. One very important historical resource is available as a series of records amassed by OB West
during the preparations for the operation. Available from the National Archives as microfilm T-
311, Rolls 17–20, the documents show specific organization and material strength for many of
the formations being assembled for the attack.

Interview with Generalfeldmarschall Gerd von Rundstedt

1. Q: When was the idea of the Ardennes Offensive first broached? What factors were decisive in the choice of 16 Dec 44 as the date for the launching of the offensive? Were any of these factors:

    a. The attack of First US Army against the Roer dams;

    b. The threat of the forthcoming offensive of Third US Army on the West Wall, which was to begin 19 Dec 44;

    c. Situation and possibility of an offensive on the Eastern Front;

    d. Considerations of a military nature, or from the point of view of war morale?

A: At the beginning of Nov 44, orders were given and plans and the date communicated by the German High Command to Genfldm Model and his three Army Commanders (Manteuffel, Dietrich, and Brandenberger, commanding Fifth Pz, Sixth Pz, and Seventh Armies, respectively). Although 1 Dec 44 was chosen as a probable date of launching the Offensive, it already was obvious at that time that the date could not be met. The date of 16 Dec 44, therefore, was proposed. The reason for this postponement was that the build-up of sufficient stocks of war material of all kinds, especially fuel, was yet incomplete. In addition, the Sixth Pz Army, which was spread out in the neighborhood of Bad Salzuflen, had to be collected from both sides of the Rhine and reassembled.

    The attack of the US Army on the line of the Roer was without influence on the situation, as was the expected attack of the Third US Army on the West Wall; furthermore, this plan of the Americans was unknown to us at the time. The situation on the Eastern Front played no role in our plan of offensive, nor was the Offensive undertaken with a view of improving the morale of the Army.

2. Q: Which were the separate final and direct targets of the Offensive, according to the last orders given? In the case of Antwerp being the objective and a wedge being inserted in the Allied lines, do you mean that with the available forces a success could have been expected, or did you expect only to reach the Meuse?

A: The Führer's wish was for a large-scale offensive beyond the Meuse above Liège and directed against Antwerp, with the purpose of cutting off the rear communications of the English and Americans and, by this means, perhaps changing the whole course of the War. Hitler stated that upon his own responsibility he had assumed a great risk on the Eastern Front and that he had called upon every man possible for this Offensive.

In complete accord with Genfldm Model, Genfldm von Rundstedt proposed the so called 'Small Solution' for the Offensive, which means that he wished for a pincer movement offensive. This was to have been made against an arc beginning east of Aix-la-Chapelle and south of Maastricht, with the Fifth Pz and Sixth Pz Armies moving from Monschau and Eifel across the Ardennes and east of Liège. This 'Small Solution' was rejected by the Führer. In the opinion of Genfldm von Rundstedt, success for the end in view was impossible due to the insufficient forces, material, and fuel at his disposal. Genfldm von Rundstedt considered success more likely only on the east of the Meuse River, and even then only if a German attack were judged opportune, which he did not believe to be the case.

3. Q: Did the German High Command plan to divert troops toward the south and make a surprise attack on the Third US Army flank? Did such an intention exist at the time plans for the Offensive were drawn up or develop during the course of the Offensive?

A: The solution of the Führer, 'a great offensive', required very large forces for adequate protection against an enemy counteroffensive directed against both sides of the wedge. This counteroffensive, furthermore, had to be expected to develop very shortly following our attack. In addition, it would be necessary to prepare very strong supporting panzer and infantry divisions to reinforce the offensives. These forces were entirely lacking.

It was a serious error to reinforce the right wing at the expense of the left wing, and to subordinate this right wing to Sixth Pz Army; this mistake was paid for later at great cost. In this last effort, it was necessary to employ selected Army leaders and not inexperienced SS commanders.

4. Q: What measures were taken to render inefficient the enemy intelligence service and to keep secret the preparation and concentration of Fifth Pz and Sixth Pz Armies?

A: A general radio silence was ordered, and the military moves and concentrations of Fifth Pz and Sixth Pz Armies were kept extremely secret. The troops and civil population were informed that these divisions were being held in readiness for the expected great enemy offensive west of the Rhine, and that they would be placed as reserve units for Fifteenth and Seventh Armies and under the control of the Western High Command (OB West). All of the artillery was never employed for defense purposes, and only the artillery regiments of each assault division, on the last two nights, were used as direct reinforcement for the advance movement.

5. Q: When drawing up plans for the Offensive, what concentration of forces was considered to be the minimum necessary? Was this minimum met or was it surpassed? When did the troops take up their positions, and when was this movement completed? Were the available reserves considered sufficient?

A: As already mentioned, the forces promised in the first order of OKW, in view of the 'great solution' (target Antwerp) were too weak and, as a last resource, would be just sufficient to insure the success of the 'Small Solution'. And even of these promised forces, four divisions, including 11 Pz and 17 SS Pz Gren Div, had not arrived in time for the launching of the Offensive.

The movement in the rear of Fifteenth and Seventh Armies began in the middle of Nov 44. The movement of Sixth Pz Army had already started at the beginning of Nov 44, as had that of the newly reassembled and organized divisions of the Home War Territory.

The available reserves were considered too weak, even for the 'Small Solution', especially in view of the task of Seventh Army whose mission was protecting the south wing of Fifth Pz Army.

Additional forces were requested verbally and in writing by Genfldm von Rundstedt, but the Führer and OKW paid no attention to these requests. In this way, OKW practically assumed the responsibility for carrying out the operation.

The last orders of OKW were declared by the Führer to be 'immutable'. OKW and Genfldm Model both received details and elaborate orders, which they had only to transmit to their subordinates. The same procedure was maintained during the execution of the Offensive and, in addition, sermons and orders from the High Command were continually received.

6. Q: An additional attack was envisaged for Fifteenth Army. If this was the case, why was it abandoned? Was it to enable all available forces to concentrate for an attack across the Eifel? Do you believe today that this decision was right? What was the objective of the offensive in Alsace? Was it really launched in connection with the Ardennes Offensive? It appears difficult to reconcile this attack far in the south with the abandoned Maastricht plan. What is your general opinion on this matter? Was this offensive in Alsace to be connected in any way with the advance in the Ardennes?

A: It is true, as already mentioned, that an offensive by a Corps of Fifteenth Army had been planned. It was to have been conducted by XII SS Inf Corps, which had withdrawn from the region of Sittard, and was to have been directed against Maastricht. The offensive was to have been launched by Fifth Pz and Sixth Pz Armies about four days after their arrival. The attack, however, did not take place because the Fifth Pz and Sixth Pz Armies plus seven divisions of the Army were withdrawn from the anticipated forces. In addition, the forces which were intended to reinforce Fifteenth Army were sent further south.

The decision that II SS Pz Corps should intervene would have been suitable had the promised troops and the other three armies arrived in full strength; even so, however, this move would only have been suitable for the proposed 'Small Solution'.

The attack on northern Lorraine and Alsace was planned for 31 Dec 44 to prevent the enemy from withdrawing even more of his forces to the north. The attack, however, was postponed for several days. The strategic objectives of this attack had no connection with the Ardennes Offensive. The purpose was to cut off and annihilate the enemy forces east of Saverne.

It was impossible to bring up troops, especially mobile units, from the south because the two Pz Divisions were not yet re-organized, and also because of the lack of fuel and the aerial superiority of the enemy prevented us from transporting them.

7. **Q:** What fuel supplies had you been able to collect? Was the German High Command able to feed this Offensive from its own stocks if the American depots could not be seized? How much fuel and other important material ought to have been seized to insure the continuation of the Offensive? Were you in possession of exact knowledge of places where the Allies had their most important stocks? Parts of I SS Pz Corps penetrated the south border of a storage plant of 3,000,000 gallons of fuel near Spa.

A: OKW demanded five consumption units (*Verbrauchssatz* (VS), fuel necessary to move any given unit 100 km) as the necessary fuel supply; however, even at the beginning of the Offensive, no more than one or two units were available. The remainder was to be delivered to our troops during the Offensive from our own fuel reserves east of the Rhine. We could not count on booty from the American fuel depot, as we were not yet in possession of details regarding its location. The storage of fuel at Spa was not yet known.

8. **Q:** If the plan of the Offensive took into consideration that the last objective might not be reached, how long did the German High Command believe the Allies would need to overcome the disturbing effects of the Offensive and make a counterattack themselves?

A: OKW counted on a success sufficient to force the Allies themselves to launch an offensive within three months. OKW and Genfldm Model were also of the opinion that the Allies which were undisturbed in their positions would, with large forces taken from the north, south, and interior of France, launch an attack much earlier against the thin divisions protecting our flanks.

9. Q: Did the heavy air attacks of 24 and 25 Dec 55 have an important effect upon the German lines of communication, especially in holding up the Offensive?

A: After 24 Dec 44, heavy air attacks made impossible almost all daytime transport, either of troops or of their supplies. Even regrouping of troops in occupied positions was rendered extremely difficult by the bombardment.

10. Q: Why was II SS Pz Corps kept in reserve until 23 Dec 44? Do you believe today that it would have been better to send this Corps to reinforce Fifth Pz Army in the south, since the focal point of the Offensive had gravitated there?

A: The center of gravity was situated on the south wing, that is, on the passage of Fifth Pz Army and II SS Pz Corps could have been employed there with great effect. This idea gained support when Sixth Pz Army which could not advance to its point of attack and the SS Pz Corps had extraordinary difficulty in advancing. The reasons for this latter situation were improper deployment by the commanders of Sixth SS Pz Army, difficulties of the terrain, lack of fuel, and the air activity of the enemy.

11. Q: At what time during the counteroffensive did it become obvious that it would be impossible to pursue the original objective and that it would be necessary to reserve and take up the defense of territory already gained? At what time did it become evident that a retreat from the whole Ardennes sector would be necessary?

A: On the third day of the Offensive, it became obvious that the goal could no longer be pursued. OKW, however, calculating that Fifth Pz Army, with its left wing on the Meuse, could advance north and carry Sixth Pz Army along in its attack, insisted upon reaching the Meuse. About 24 Dec 44, it was deemed necessary to make preparations to defend the territory gained. The defense was not to be made in the Marche–Rochefort–St Hubert salient, but at a strong point on the Houffalize line east of Bastogne.

OKW insisted that Fifth Pz Army continue the attack with the reserves which had been placed at its disposal in the meantime (3 and 15 Pz Gren Divs,

9 Pz Div and one Volks Gren Div). Retreat from the crescent in the Ardennes became necessary, however, when Fifth Pz Army was attacked from the north and from the south by superior forces. The last possible moment for this retreat was on 2 Jan 45, when attacks against Huy and Marche and against the south wing in the neighborhood of Bastogne became more and more fierce. In the opinion of OKW, a systematic withdrawal should have been made by the end of Dec 44 at the latest in order to reform an advantageous front on and close to the German frontier. The reiterated order of the Führer to 'stay and hold' advanced positions (à la Stalingrad) caused very heavy losses of armored fighting vehicles and artillery which could not be withdrawn. Here were the germs of the later collapse on the Western Front.

12. Q: In the German High Command plan of offensive, how much importance was attached to St Vith and Bastogne? Did the fact that St Vith was taken too late increase the importance of the capture of Bastogne?

A: The loss of Bastogne was of the greatest importance. Bastogne should have been reached by Fifth Pz Army on the first day of the Offensive. This Army, however, bypassed Bastogne on the north and south several days later with many divisions. Bastogne should have been occupied by the divisions of the second wave (11 Pz Div and 17 SS Pz Gren Div), but these, OKW did not send.

While the Allies continually reinforced their troops, supplied them, and closed in Bastogne from the air, our own Luftwaffe was unable to cooperate with the urgently requested bombardment of Bastogne. St Vith was captured 24 hours later than anticipated in the plan of the Offensive. This delay influenced operations, especially as it resulted in Fifth Pz Army's left wing becoming more exposed than before.

13. Q: Why did I SS Pz Corps fail in the Monschau–Malmédy sector?

A: The Sixth Pz Army, unlike Fifth Pz Army, was never up to full strength, and was unable to advance to its points of attack. This held up other corps on the roads of communication. [In fact 6th Pz Army was better up to strength than 5th Pz Army, but its traffic control was poor. – Ed.]

14. Q: Were the countermeasures taken by the Allies executed more quickly than expected by the German High Command?

A: The Allied countermovements were made more quickly than expected by OKW, with the reasons being the high mobility of the enemy forces (which had abundant fuel at their disposal), the excellent road net, and their absolute domination of the air. (See answer to Question 8.)

15. Q: What methods were employed to obtain exact knowledge of the distribution of Allied troops in the Ardennes? In what measure were the Germans satisfied with information given by civilian agents when obtaining material and information?

A: The supposed grouping of enemy forces in the Ardennes sector, as supplied by the Ic (Intelligence) service, corresponded exactly with the real situation. I am unaware as to what degree agents played a role.

16. Q: Did the Germans believe, when they mistook a limited withdrawal for a great retreat, that the XVIII Abn Corps (US) was so weakened on 24 Dec 44 that a break in the front toward Liège would be possible? What knowledge had the Germans of the feigned movement of VIII Corps (US) at the beginning of Dec 44?

A: Both movements remained unknown.

17. Q: What degree of importance was assigned by the Germans to the following factors which contributed to the failure of the German counter-offensive in the Ardennes, and in what order of importance would you place them:
   a. The failure to take St Vith in time, before the construction of a strong line of defense by the Allies on the north flank of the breach point;
   b. The good flying weather, on and about 24 Dec 44, which enabled the Allies to fully exploit their superiority in the air;
   c. The failure to take Bastogne;
   d. The failure to capture large Allied stocks of fuel and war material;
   e. The ability of the Allied High Command to rush reinforcement to threatened positions;
   f. The failure of the 'Greif' enterprise;
   g. Other factors.

A: The failure of the Offensive may be attributed to the following reasons:
   a. The chief fact was the improper grouping (by the High Command) of troops and the insufficient number of divisions placed at the disposal of the army commanders;
   b. Inadequate fuel supplies and unsatisfactory transportation;
   c. The absolute air supremacy of the Allies in the Offensive and rear sectors was a decisive factor and, later, the failure to occupy Bastogne played a most important role;
   d. The numerous reserves of the Allies, their good road net, their high class

motorization and important reserves of fuel and ammunition were decisive factors.

The '*Greif*' enterprise was directed by the SS Chief Head Office, and depended neither upon OKW nor A Gp B. The plans and their execution were not even communicated to OKW.

5

Generalfeldmarschall Walther Model and Army Group B

Interview with Oberst Thuisko von Metzsch

Editor's Introduction

For the historian in search of first-hand German perspectives on the Ardennes operation, the echelon with scantiest coverage is Army Group B, which was handled during the battle by General Walther Model and his chief of Staff Hans Krebs.[1] Model was a hard commander. A Prussian, he entered the German Army in 1909 at the age of eighteen. His leadership qualities took him to the rank of brigadier general between the wars, when he commanded the 4th Corps. Further advancement followed rapidly during the Second World War, and Model reached the rank of field marshal on 1 March 1944. His reputation as Hitler's 'fireman' was cemented when he took over Army Group Center in June 1944 amid the cataclysm of a massive Russian assault, and somehow organized a cohesive defense. Later he was called on to take over the faltering command of both OB West and Army Group B, which subsequently managed to hold on the German border during the fall of 1944 as the plans for the Ardennes Offensive were formed.

Although a staunch supporter of National Socialism and strongly obedient to Hitler and OKW, Model did not hide the fact that he considered the Ardennes Offensive a desperate operation. Several weeks prior to its start he had sounded a prophetic warning regarding *Die Wacht Am Rhein*:

> Should the attack be stopped at the Meuse due to lack of reserves, *the only result will be a bulge in the line and not the destruction of sizeable enemy forces* ... The far outstretched flanks, particularly in the south, will only invite enemy counter-attacks.[2]

In concert with von Rundstedt and von Manteuffel, he attempted to alter the ambitious German plan into something he believed stood at least some chance of success. But this was of no avail; 'There will be absolutely no change in the present intentions,' Hitler told him just before O-Tag. In the chaotic last days before the attack, he confided in Oberst von der Heydte – in charge of a desperate night parachute operation – that he gave the offensive only a ten per cent chance of success. And from late fall onwards, Model, who had regularly indulged in wine, increased his consumption to two bottles of Cognac a night. 'He turned alcoholic,' General Rudolf von Gersdorff observed.

Model killed himself just before the end of the conflict ('a field marshal does

192

not become a prisoner'), and Hans Krebs died in the last chaotic days of fighting around Hitler's bunker in Berlin, in April 1945. Consequently this seldom-seen interview with Thuisko von Metzsch, who served as aide to General Krebs, is invaluable.[3] Krebs himself was relatively uninspiring. He had served as Model's chief of staff in a number of other commands on the eastern front and had risen on his superior's coat-tails. His military tasks were generally on the staff level, and he had no experience as a field commander beyond some involvement in defensive operations — most recently during the apocalyptic summer with Army Group Center in Russia. But despite his lack of experience, Krebs' post during the Ardennes Offensive was an important one; and as Krebs' aide, von Metzsch was witness to momentous events.

Metzsch was a descendant of a distinguished family of Saxon soldiers, and found himself drafted into the German army in 1937 at the age of 20. For two years he served with the 7th Machine Gun Battalion, which evolved into an armored reconnaissance unit. In 1941 he was transferred to serve as an aide to the chief of staff of Headquarters *Militärbefehlshaber Frankreich*, General Hans Speidel. During the following year he was transferred to the 24th Panzer Division and was seriously wounded in the fierce fighting around Stalingrad. In March 1943 he returned to his assignment with General Speidel, who at the time was directing the German offensive at Kharkov. Later in the summer of 1944, Speidel and Metzsch were assigned to Army Group B, to co-ordinate the German response to the Normandy landings. Even after Speidel was relieved of command, Metzsch stayed on in the position.

Though he had little respect for Hans Krebs, Metzsch's views as an eye-witness present at Army Group B throughout the Ardennes operations are an invaluable source regarding the personalities as well as the operations of this echelon. His interviewer, Charles von Lüttichau, from the Office of the Chief of Military History (OCMH), described him as 'most co-operative in supplying the requested information.' The interview, which took place in May 1952, is held on file at OCMH and classified as manuscript R-10. It contains the original excerpts from the diary von Metzsch kept (against orders) at Army Group B. Although terse, his description of events between 16 and 27 December provides an unusual insight into early German expectations and the realization of ultimate failure:

16 Dec. Attack jumps off at 0535. Good progress at first, afternoon stop. Surprise was a success, advanced three to five kilometers.
17 Dec. 1st SS Panzer Division broke through to the west. Additional gains in terrain in Fifth Panzer Army. Seventh Army making slow headway.
18 Dec. Breakthrough at Stavelot and to the east of Bastogne. Krinkelt captured in heavy fighting.
19 Dec. Sixth Panzer Army involved in defensive fighting. Spearheads 20 km

beyond Stavelot. Fifth Panzer Army advanced past St. Vith. Seventh Army makes progress. 8,000 prisoners; 100 tanks captured or destroyed.

20 Dec. Breakthrough of Fifth Panzer Army widened. Bastogne encircled. Ourthe River reached. Krinkelt lost temporarily. The situation is beginning to get bad.

21 Dec. Heavy defensive fighting in Sixth Panzer Army. Kampfgruppe [Peiper] pushed back. Spearheads of Fifth Panzer Army advanced past La Roche and reached Marche to St. Hubert. 18,000 prisoners so far.

22 Dec. Advance of Fifth Panzer Army to outskirts of Marche. St. Hubert captured. Sixth Panzer Army engaged in defensive battle. Enemy attacks at Seventh Army.

23 Dec. Spearheads reach within five kilometers from the Meuse near Dinant. Heavy enemy attacks against the left wing [Seventh Army] causing penetrations and losses.

24 Dec. Defensive fighting in Sixth Panzer Army and Seventh Army. No significant changes in Fifth Panzer Army. Christmas ceremony with Model – lukewarm.

25 Dec. Heavy defensive fighting in Seventh Army. Slow progress of Fifth Panzer Army's attack. Beginning of a breakthrough attempt by Sixth Panzer Army. Heaviest enemy air activity.

26 Dec. Fierce defensive battle of Seventh Army continues. Spearheads in front of Dinant wiped out. Sixth Panzer Army drives ahead. Bastogne still not captured.

27 Dec. Distressing day. Setbacks in Seventh Army. Spearheads being withdrawn. Enemy forces corridor to Bastogne.

Notes

1. Although no accounts by the leaders of Army Group B exist perhaps the most important single German document as a primary record of the German operations is the Army Group B *Kriegstagebuch* for December 1944. This invaluable record is available from the Bundesarchiv as RH 19/IV-84, 85 and 86.

2. Memorandum from a conference with OB West on 23 November 1944, *OB West, KTB Andage 50*, vol. II, pp. 30–2. The emphasis is Model's own, from the original text.

3. Some additional interviews were carried out with members of Army Group B's services: Helmut Tholholte, 'Army Group B Artillery', B-311, 1946, and Richard Wirtz, 'Army Group Engineers', B-172; Anton Staubwasser, 'Army Group B Intelligence Estimate', B-675; Oberst Günther Reichhelm, 'Army Group B, Oct 15 1944–45', B-701; also 'The Ardennes Offensive', C.S.D.I.C.(UK) G.R.G.G. 330(C), 1 August 1945, held at OCMH files with an interview of Generalleutnant Kurt Kruse of the artillery command of Army Group B.

Generalfeldmarschall Walther Model and Army Group B: Interview with Thuisko von Metzsch

I. Field Marshal Model and his Headquarters

Field marshal Walter Model was extremely outspoken and straightforward. Once he had made up his mind he would not deviate from a taken course. His actions were based on strong convictions. The fact that they were identical with the Party line and the ideas of Hitler had made him an outstanding general in his master's opinion. His actions were easily predictable. Model was of high personal integrity and loyal to his superiors. He would never desert the cause. In his relations with others he was cold and impersonal, entirely matter of fact. He never stepped out of this reserve.

Model was ambitious. The closest he could get to being relaxed was the display of a sarcastic humor. He liked to tell tall stories and occasionally crack a joke in an epigrammatic manner. He enjoyed smoking and drinking French red wine with his close aides. During these regular evening sessions the situation was discussed and decisions were made. As a rule the Chief of Staff, General Hans Krebs, the operations officer, Colonel Reichhelm and one or two other aides were present.

In the treatment of his staff and commanders in the field Model was frequently brutal. The only exception to this rule was the Commanding General of Fifth Panzer Army, von Manteuffel. Model respected Manteuffel's ability and valor. He instinctively recognized that Manteuffel would not tolerate the insults Model habitually inflicted upon others. The general rule seemed to be: the higher the rank, the rougher the treatment. Model's rudeness increased in direct proportion with the rank. Worst off were the generals in his own headquarters such as the chiefs of communications, transport, artillery etc. It was a matter of record that these specialists could never compete with the field marshal who was nearly always better informed and gifted with a better memory. Lower ranking officers of army group headquarters were in a similar position. They lived under the constant threat of being courtmartialled. Whenever something went wrong they were blamed, although they were in many instances not responsible for the trouble. Army and corps commanders were no better off and received the same degrading treatment. All headquarters' operations were badly hampered by the fact that Model actually knew, or claimed to know, more about a specific case or operation than anyone else. On the other hand, he had an instinctive knowledge of the needs and expectations of the individual soldier and had a perfect approach to handling them just right.

Model was aided in his leadership by the advantage of a fabulous memory for the smallest details. From personal observation he had a clear conception of every battalion in his army group, where it was fighting, its qualities, weapons, replacement situation 'down to five grenadiers he had ordered to be transferred from one unit to another'. He would personally check on the execution of his orders, e.g. whether the 'five men' had arrived at their destination or not.

Personally, he was without fear. He knew instinctively where the most critical spot would be and saw to it to be there in person when the crisis arose. A 'master of improvisation', he would find the answer to meet an emergency. He thus had established his reputation, and had made his career.

The effectiveness of his leadership was due to his specialized knowledge of the situation which he gained through his daily visits to the front. His appreciation of the situation was based on experience and clear judgement as a field commander. He would execute his intentions and decisions with energy and untiring perseverance. At all times he supervised the execution of the orders he had given. He never forgot anything.

His weakness was evident in his relations with the OKW and Hitler. He was what Metzsch termed 'a wild Nazi'. Although he would make proposals and stand for them in discussions with the High Command, he basically always executed the orders he received even if he had been overruled. He did not meddle in strategic decisions. 'The strategy was laid down by Hitler and Jodl, OB West relayed the orders, and Model compassed the tactical execution.'

Another weakness was his eager compliance with the application of the institution of special courts [*Sondergerichte*]. Whenever there occurred blunders or failures he would immediately order special courts' procedures to investigate and try the case. He did this in anticipation of any action which might be ordered by Hitler. Consequently, when inquiries came from above he was always able to report that he had already acted.

Model's cooperation with the Party was good. He had introduced the *NSFO* [*National Sozialistischer Führungs Offizier*, Nazi indoctrination officer] in his headquarters, a position which had not been filled prior to his arrival. He held close contact with the *Gauleiters* of the army group's communications zone. To improve his relations with Himmler he requested him to assign an SS officer as one of his personal aides. Considering Model's loyalty to the Nazi Party, it becomes understandable why he had officers and men of his command who were accused of defeatism, tried immediately, and in many instances shot.

Only during the last months of the war Model underwent an inner change of his views on Hitler personally. Von Metzsch indicated that this change began on 11 December 1944, when Model met Hitler for the first time after he had assumed the command of Army Group B. The meeting took place on the occasion of the conference Hitler had called for all generals participating in the Ardennes Offensive. 'Model's high opinion of Hitler from then on gradually fell to pieces. He was particularly struck by the impression Hitler made, which was pitiful. Especially after the Ardennes Offensive had started he began to make disrespectful remarks about Hitler to his chief of staff and operations officer. Von Metzsch in turn heard about this change through Colonel Reichhelm. The reasons for the metamorphosis were 'Hitler's lies' and the 'failure of the Ardennes Offensive'. Hitler in his lengthy address to the generals had said that should the offensive fail he would have to make peace. The offensive was meant to gain time to arrange for peace talks. This was the impression the generals and troops engaged in the offensive had, when their attack jumped off. However, after the offensive had failed and was not followed by an armistice the dis-illusionment, even in the ranks of the SS, was all the greater. Model lost his faith in Hitler completely during the last weeks in the Ruhr pocket. The scorched earth orders issued by Hitler during the last phase of the war contributed to this reversal of attitude. The motive for Model's suicide could not be given by Metzsch. However, the collapse of everything in which Model had believed may offer a clue to this mystery.

Before General Hans Krebs was appointed Chief of Staff, Army Group B, he had been Chief of Staff of Army Group Center in Russia. He was short and fat, baldheaded and pig-eyed. He wore glasses. Shorter than Model, who was short himself, his appearance was anything but martial. He was conceited, altogether a yes-man, a shrewd operator, and deceitful. He had no opinions of his own, and was a convinced Nazi. He liked comfort, and even a certain amount of what would appear as luxury when compared to the prevailing situation of this last phase of the war. Despite these obvious shortcomings Model was appreciative of his chief of staff. Indeed, these very characteristics made Krebs a pliable tool in Model's hands. Since the field marshal was a proficient General Staff officer himself he actually increased his own responsibilities by assuming some of the prerogatives of the chief of staff. Despite the fact that Krebs was not an out-standing man he had a way of getting along well with his superiors. The fact that General Burgdorf, Hitler's adjutant and Chief of Army Personnel, was his close friend made Krebs' position strong. Although he never commanded troops in battle and had only had General Staff experience he had made his way to the top. He was over-ambitious to the point of meanness. He undoubtedly was quite able to discharge the duties of the chief of staff, and had grown into the position as time went on. Model frequently bypassed Krebs in favor of the Operations Officer, Colonel Reichhelm. With him he discussed and planned tactical details of all operations often without consulting the chief of staff. All-in-all, Krebs was a dislikeable personality.

Colonel Reichhelm, operations officer, was Model's favorite. Born 1918, he was representative for the officers of the new German Army. He had, in other words, gone through the indoctrination of the Hitler Youth and was a staunch follower of the Nazi ideology and Hitler. He maintained his enthusiasm to the very end, when he nursed the idea of joining the Werewolf organization in order to continue the war after the collapse of the regular army. He stemmed from a noted family, was bright, ambitious, and hardworking. His General Staff career started when he was assigned to headquarters of Model's division in the east. He had gone through the short training course in General Staff work. Thereafter he was assigned to Ninth Army in the east as G-2, or General Staff Officer for Organization and Personnel. Reichhelm made his first appearance at Head-quarters Army Group B at Krefeld sometime in October 1944. Model had requested his transfer to replace Colonel von Tempelhoff [15 October 44, 201 File].

Next to his chief of staff and operations officer the group of aides whose duty it was to escort the field marshal to the front was in closest contact with him. Although Model was quite short, he liked to be surrounded by tall aides, all of them well over six feet tall. The group was headed by Klaus Liebrecht, who had served Model in this position from the time when he was division commander to the bitter end, covering a period of three to four years. Liebrecht was with Model when he shot himself, and also buried him. He probably knew him better than anyone else. Other members of this escort team were a Count Stolberg, who was killed later in the war, a 1st Lieutenant von Seidel, and the above mentioned SS Major, Springer, who had joined headquarters at Krefeld. The latter was described as a most unpleasant character. One aide would not have been sufficient for Model who used to wear out four of them easily. The duties of his aides would vary from accompanying the field marshal on his daily trips, to special missions with corps and divisions. In these cases the aides were sent to crucial points on the battle scene and had to report to Model personally on every detail of the developments. It also happened that they were then completely forgotten and thus got a chance to catch up on some sleep. Model's personal escort convoy under the command of Liebrecht consisted of one armored car, one medium personnel carrier, two Mercedes sedans, and two BMW sedans.

Delegation of responsibilities, and division of workload, as well as the reporting system in Headquarters Army Group B was organized in the following way: Model was an early riser. Regularly, at 0600 hours he would depart from headquarters for the front in his command car with a small escort. Only the chief of staff and Reichhelm would know where he was going. His appearance at the front always came as a surprise to the armies and corps he visited. At corps and division headquarters Model would be met by army and corps commanders as soon as they had heard of his arrival. Model would conduct all operations from the front line; 'one can state that Model directed the battle in person.' This meant that all directives given to the army group from higher echelons had to be telephoned to some corps headquarters or even division headquarters. Top Secret security information was consequently discussed quite openly over the telephone in utter disregard of security regulations. After hearing the latest orders, Model made his decisions immediately. In so doing he was aided by his exceptional grasp of the situation. As a rule Model returned to his headquarters at 1800–1900 hours. He had dinner with the chief of staff and the operations officer and one or two aides. The group would then retire to the hunting room and the discussions would continue in front of the fireplace. In the course of the evening the entire situation was reviewed and the decisions were made for the operations of the next day.

Before Model left in the early morning he would have a short discussion with Reichhelm, who would give him the latest situation reports. After his arrival at the front Model would immediately call Krebs or Reichhelm and from then on stay in constant telephone contact with them. In order to stand the breathtaking pace of Model's day, Krebs and Reichhelm worked on a schedule. Krebs attended the night sessions, while Reichhelm was on duty in the morning. The routine work was handled by Krebs during the day, he also concentrated on the dealings with higher echelons, while Reichhelm concerned himself more with the lower ones and the contact with the field marshal.

The system of reporting of Army Group B was as follows: in general, estimates of the situation and reports to higher echelons were drafted by the Chief of Staff or by Reichhelm. It is important to note that von Metzsch said that the reports on the situation at the front took between six and twelve hours to reach the army group. Consequently its estimates and reports were based on a situation which had often become obsolete. In rendering the final version in the evening the personal impressions of the field marshal and of special observers were considered.

As a rule an aide would telephone the morning situation report to OB West at 0700 hours. It reflected the developments of the night and was very short consisting mainly of 'nothing special to report'. The important personalities having worked long hours during the night were mostly still sleeping at this hour.

At 0900 hours the intermediate report was made. Model had long since left the headquarters and often had arrived at the front by this time. At 1200 hours the noon report was relayed to OB West. Thereafter Hitler's orders, coming directly from the *Führerhauptquartier* conference, started pouring in. As soon as Krebs had received them, he telephoned them to Model, making suggestions which were either accepted or immediately changed by Model. The telephone conversations always resulted in precise orders and decisions. The evening situation report, containing the tactical situation at the front as of approximately 1400–1500 hours, was regularly supplemented later by spot reports as they came in. The daily report covered the actions of the day and was sent off by teletype during the night.

All the above mentioned reports, which were made on the phone, were also confirmed by teletype later. The business of reporting, receiving, and giving orders was, however, transacted on the telephone. The standard German term was 'Fernendlich voraus'. In addition to the above mentioned schedule numerous telephone calls were received from OB West and WFSt (Jodl). Von Metzsch contends that these calls came in practically every hour.

Army Group B applied the principle of extreme caution in its orienting of higher echelons. Frequently the slightest indication of success was interpreted by WFSt as a local victory and reported to Hitler in this sense. When the teletypes reached WFSt, they frequently failed to confirm the rosy picture which had been drawn at Hitler's headquarters. This fact resulted in reproaches and questions why the 'successes' which had been 'reported' on the phone were not contained in the written report. The blame was always placed on the army group. As a result, army group made no more reports to higher echelons which had not been put into writing. In addition several witnesses would listen in on the conversations and take them down as a matter of precaution.

As the situation at the front deteriorated, the precautionary measures increased proportionately. The climax was reached when the orders to disengage Sixth Panzer Army were received on 8 January 1945. The execution of the order was difficult and was aggravated by the fact that WFSt concerned itself with such details as individual guns, assault guns, and tanks.

The relations between Army Group B and OB West were cool to say the least. The dualism of the two headquarters caused a lot of competitive resentment and animosity. The controversy dated back to the days of the invasion, when OB West was mainly concerned with administration and logistics, while Army Group B had the function of forward echelon, directly responsible to OKW/WFSt in strategic matters. During the period of personal union of the OB West and Commanding General Army Group B, competitive animosity grew to the point where either headquarters felt the other was superfluous and could be dispensed with.

The functions of Headquarters OB West changed with the withdrawal, when von Rundstedt again accepted the command of the western front on 5 September 1944. At this point Headquarters Army Group B was assigned to OB West, and von Rundstedt nominally at least, assumed strategic command.

In reality, however, strategic command was exercised by Jodl and Hitler. Army Group B regarded OB West as a relay station. The strategic initiative originated at the WFSt level, the tactical one at the army group level. Von

Rundstedt rarely took the initiative. Consequently, matters were thrashed out between Jodl and Model. This state of affairs was not beneficial to the co-operation of the rival headquarters.

As long as General Speidel was Chief of Staff of Army Group B he got along well with General Blumentritt of OB West. Later, after Krebs and Westphal had taken over the respective positions, relations deteriorated. The fact that Westphal was conceited, disagreeable and not liked, did not improve the situation.

Officers of forward echelon, Headquarters Army Group B, did not live like Spartans as one might assume. Living conditions were agreeable. Nevertheless, the hectic routine and the disgraceful treatment most members of the staff had to endure made life most unpleasant. Von Metzsch claimed that at times headquarters resembled a madhouse.

The Ardennes Offensive and Army Group B

During the planning period for the Ardennes Offensive, the headquarters were located at Fichtenhain, south of Krefeld, on the premises of a former institution for alcoholics. There were a number of larger buildings which were taken over by forward echelon. Fichtenhain was a pleasant place, surrounded by woods. The fact that it was an alcoholics' institution had, in von Metzsch's words, no effect on the drinking habits of headquarters' personnel.

The first meeting between von Rundstedt, Westphal and Model was held at Fichtenhain. It was the first discussion dealing with the planned offensive. The date was probably 27 October. Generals Westphal and Krebs had been briefed by Hitler between 22–24 October, 1944.

A second meeting between Rundstedt, Westphal, Rundstedt's son, who served as aide to his father and was a historian, and Model and Krebs was held at Toennisstein, early in November. Von Metzsch was present during part of the conversations which lasted for two or three hours. Von Metzsch believes that this meeting was called as a result of the first operation draft submitted by Army Group B, after the return of the chiefs of staff from Hitler's headquarters. This first draft was based on the concept that the main effort to be made by Sixth Panzer Army, would be in the center, while Fifth Panzer Army would attack on the right wing. Toennisstein had been chosen for this meeting for reasons of security.

The first meeting with the commanding generals of the participating armies was also held at Fichtenhain in early November. Metzsch recalled that 'Sepp' Dietrich, Commanding General, Sixth Panzer Army, was also present. The date for this conference could not be established during the interview.

On 11 December 1944, forward echelon Headquarters Army Group B moved to Münstereifel. Forward echelon occupied the so-called *Lager* [camp] Steinbach, which had served as headquarters to the Commander in Chief of the

German Army during the preparatory phase of the Campaign in the West, 1939–40. *Lager* Steinbach consisted of the hunting lodge of the German industrialist Werner Karp, a number of temporary buildings, and of a few bunkers. Model's quarters were at the lodge, together with a few of his closest aides. Two elderly servants of Herr Karp, ran the household. The main living room with its open fireplace was the stage for practically all staff meetings, discussions and decisions. Culprits were summoned to this room and dressed down here. It was also the backdrop for the nightly sessions, and wining and dining. The only big map exercise, rehearsed on a sandbox model of the Ardennes terrain, was staged in one of the bunkers two or three weeks before the offensive started. Attending were all commanding generals of armies and corps, their chiefs of staff, the communications, artillery and transport generals, as well as the Luftwaffe generals. Headquarters remained at Münsterifel *Lager* Steinbach throughout the main phases of the Offensive. During the Offensive *Lager* Steinbach was once bombed, which caused a few casualties. However, only the bunker area was hit. The bombing did not affect the operations of headquarters.

In January 1945 headquarters were moved to Toennisstein, north of the Laacher Sea. Toennisstein was a resort and watering place close to the famous holy shrine of Maria Laach. Forward echelon was housed in a resort hotel. Model and his closest entourage occupied the residence of the hotel owner. Connected with this private house was a temporary building which housed the operations division. The other sections were dispersed in the town and vicinity.

Idea and Preparations

The idea of a strategic counterthrust as it was realized in the Ardennes Offensive, had existed in all echelons ever since the Allied invasion. However, all attempts prior to the Ardennes were frustrated due to the fact that the Allies struck first every time. In making proposals for counterattacks Army Group B had to be extremely careful. There was at all times a real danger that troops pulled out of the front lines to make such a counterattack would be redeployed to the eastern front. In fear of such action of the OKW (Jodl) the army group abstained from making suggestions for counterattacks whenever the situation in the east was critical.

Despite the fact that the idea to strike back was old, the Ardennes Offensive when ordered by Hitler, came as a complete surprise to Army Group B. The objective of the offensive was, von Metzsch contends, the destruction of the Allied forces in the Aachen salient. This was the concept of OB West and Army Group B, and in all probability also of Jodl. Hitler, however, extended the objective to include the capture of Antwerp. The reason for this decision was said to have been a political and psychological one. Hitler had in mind a psychological success which would lend itself to propagandistic exploitation.

Consequently the concept of a battle of annihilation in the Aachen area was traded for the gamble of Antwerp. The fact that OKW believed that Antwerp was the terminal of the pipeline may have played a role in Hitler's considerations. Metzsch believed that even Jodl was convinced that 'the label Antwerp was window-dressing.' OB West and the army group were profoundly skeptical in regard to the far-flung objective and would have preferred the 'smaller solution'. Considering the fact that there would be only thirty divisions at the most available for the thrust, Model never took Antwerp seriously. This negative attitude was, however, not voiced after Hitler remained adamant despite the plans of OB West and the army group to limit the offensive to an operation this side of the Meuse. The troops on the other hand took the objective very seriously. 'To cross the Meuse was a real objective.'

The planning stage. Hitler personally initiated the Chiefs of Staff of OB West and Army Group B. Thereafter, they were briefed by Jodl on the plan of the offensive. After General Krebs had returned to Fichtenhain, the army group worked out a first draft of the operations plan which was submitted to WFSt through command channels and accompanied by a map, order of battle, and a timetable. The plan ws submitted in the original only. No copies were retained. This first version of the operation proposed commitment of Manteuffel's Fifth Panzer Army on the right wing, 'Sepp' Dietrich's Sixth Panzer Army in the center, and Brandenberger's Seventh Army on the left.

Security measures during the planning stage. The only persons entrusted with the planning at Headquarters Army Group B were Model, Krebs, Reichhelm, and von Metzsch. Somewhat later the Chief of Administration and Supplies was initiated. Army commanders and their chiefs of staff were let in on the top secret plan on or around 5 November, 1944. Still later the corps commanders and their chiefs of staff were informed. All the others were informed by Hitler in two shifts during the conferences on 12 and 13 December. Everyone attending had to sign a statement acknowledging the fact of having been initiated and that he would not divulge any information to a third party under penalty of execution. The troops were informed on the last day before the offensive.

Fear that the German intentions had been recognized by the Allies. During the last two or three days before the attack jumped off Headquarters, Army Group B was under the impression that the Allies were in possession of information revealing to them the German intentions. This German suspicion was increased by the fact that U.S. air reconnaissance was especially intense over the assembly area. Furthermore, von Metzsch recalled a serious incident which occurred four or five days before the attack. A battalion commander was captured by the Allies. He carried in his pocket an order issued by a corps headquarters. The order dealt with assembly and attack. Issuance of such an order was strictly in violation of the security regulations. Von Metzsch believed that the army group received the news about this incident through radio intercept. The two facts mentioned above contributed most to the army group's fear that the plan had been detected. Apart from these cases it can be said that security measures were effective at least with respect to the Army.

Commitment of secret weapons was promised by Jodl four to six weeks prior to the offensive. Generally speaking headquarters took them for granted; in reality, however, they did not exist. Von Metzsch termed these promises as propaganda. Into the same category of promises made which were later on not kept, fell the assurances Hitler and WFSt gave in regard to the support of the Luftwaffe. For the first time the new jet planes were to be committed on a large scale. These hopes were crushed when their commitment resulted in failure. Model was disappointed when the promises were not kept. He was particularly disillusioned about the fuel situation; in the initial planning stages assurances were given which were later not fulfilled.

Special units and weapons. Independent commitment of Antiaircraft Artillery was out of the question. The main mission was to protect the advance and supply routes. Only in exceptional cases were antiaircraft units committed in support of ground actions.

Organization Todt regiments [two with each army] had the mission to keep the roads open for traffic. Their work was efficient and yielded good results. Without them the road situation would have been considerably more serious. Despite the untiring efforts of the *OT*, road repairs frequently took hours after Allied bombings.

Volks Artillerie Corps. The designation was a gross exaggeration. In reality they could not claim to be more than brigades. Their personnel situation was poor. Personnel consisted mainly of older age groups. Training and replacements were unsatisfactory.

Volks Grenadier Divisions were, generally speaking, in bad shape. Von Metzsch used the term 'scrap'. The only exception was the 12th Volks Grenadier Division, due to the fact that General Engel, the commanding general, had been commandant of Hitler's headquarters, and Hitler took a personal interest in his protégé.

V-Weapons. It proved impossible to integrate their employment adequately into the big effort. The missiles were unreliable, and frequently fell on German lines. However, such straying flying-bombs did not cause much damage. All told, approximately one hundred missiles were launched. Inspector General of V-Weapons was SS General Kammler. In summing up, von Metzsch indicated that V-Weapons had as little effect on the outcome of the Ardennes Offensive as the Luftwaffe.

Sturmbatallions [assault battalions], were spearhead battalions of first wave divisions. They were specially equipped and had their full complement of selected personnel. They enjoyed preferential treatment in regard to replacements. As a rule the assault guns of each division were attached to the assault battalion. Each division had only one assault battalion. Comparing them to peacetime standards the battalions were merely regular fully equipped units. For 1944, however, they were something exceptional. First wave divisions were fully equipped when they moved into their assembly areas.

11th Panzer Division was held in OKW reserve despite the fact that the army group wished to commit the division in accordance with the original operations plan. One regimental combat team was actually committed on 26 December 1944, on Seventh Army's extreme left wing in order to prevent a possible Allied penetration into the West Wall.

During the planning stage of the Ardennes Offensive the rehabilitation and replacement situation was pitiful. Supplies of ammunition and fuel were inadequate, but this was not a decisive factor. During the planning of the operation capture of Allied fuel dumps was not assumed. From the standpoint of logistics preparations were made to have the minimum quantities of fuel on hand to reach the ordered objectives without having to rely on captured supplies. However, the chance of such loot entered the considerations. The troops were not instructed to supply themselves from captured supplies. The army group hoped that possibly a second thrust could be made with captured fuel. This hope, however, never materialized. As it turned out, U.S. troops had large local fuel reserves. A considerable portion of these was captured by the panzer divisions of Fifth Panzer Army. Consequently it was a fact that the spearhead divisions made themselves independent of German supplies to a large extent and kept on the move with Allied fuel.*

During the dress rehearsal of the offensive, staged in a sandbox model of the Ardennes area, a number of flaws were detected in the execution of the operations plan. However, von Metzsch could not recall any details.

The Ardennes Offensive Proper

The prevailing attitude of Headquarters Army Group B in regard to the success of the planned offensive was: 'If it succeeds, it is a miracle.' When von Manteuffel achieved the breakthrough in his army sector the reaction was surprise. Nobody, it appears, had counted on success in Sixth Panzer Army's sector. When the attempt failed it was accepted as a prediction which had come true. On the first day of the offensive the objectives were reached in Fifth Panzer Army's sector. No reports were received from Sixth Panzer Army. On the second day Allied reports were intercepted revealing to the German command the positions reached by Sixth Panzer Army. These messages made it clear that the SS panzer divisions had not reached their objectives during the first day.

---

* While it is true that limited supplies were captured by 1 SS Panzer and 116th Panzer Divisions, this statement is not borne out by evidence. Ed.

With that the failure was evident.* Fifth Panzer Army fell behind schedule on the second day, although further progress was made. On the third day the SS had still not moved ahead as had been planned. Manteuffel by now had fallen way behind schedule. 'This being so, Army Group B came to the conclusion on this the third day that the "small solution" had failed.' Von Metzsch stated that he had listened in on telephone conversations between Model and von Rundstedt on one hand, and Model and Jodl on the other, during which the Commander of Army Group B indicated that in his appreciation of the situation the offensive had failed. Metzsch believed that these conversations took place in the evening of 18 December 1944.

Von Metzsch referred to the postwar account of the offensive as it is contained in Heinz Guderian, *Erinnerungen eines Soldaten* (Heidelberg, 1951), pp. 343 ff and 349. Metzsch claimed that Guderian's statements, in which he tells of visits to Hitler's headquarters and OB West, were correct [recorded in OB West KTB as having taken place on 20 and 26 December]. These visits reflected the estimate of the situation of the time, namely that the Meuse could not be reached after the third day of the offensive had gone by. In consequence thereof Guderian tried to pry lose divisions which he felt were urgently needed on the eastern front in order to check the expected new offensive of the Red Army. Von Metzsch believed that the Guderian visits can be interpreted as a symbol of failure.

Mr. von Metzsch was asked to comment on a telegram sent by Model at 2000 hours, 25 December 1944, to OB West. This telegram has puzzled the writer during the research on the offensive. The communication displays unwarranted optimism if taken at face value. The situation at the time was the following: Army Group B's intentions were to eliminate the Allied stronghold of Bastogne while at the same time attempting to widen the attack wedge by breaking through the Allied defense lines in the Marche–Hotton area. For this purpose army group had ordered a concentric attack on Bastogne for 25 December. On the same day II SS Panzer Corps of Sixth Panzer Army made its most determined effort to break through to the Erezée road junction and was stopped in this attempt in a tank battle in the area of Grandmenil. LVIII Panzer Corps was engaged in an attack aiming at the high ground in the Marche area. By the end of the day all of these efforts had failed.

Von Metzsch recalls that Model delivered a speech to headquarters personnel on the morning of 25 December (Christmas Day) on the lawn in front of his quarters. He spoke in the customary, optimistic manner expressing his belief in the ultimate victory. He then left for the front. During the day Krebs,

---

* The daily reports of Army Group B on December 16 and 17 do not reflect the pessimism that von Metzsch describes. Also, his personal diary describes a 'breakthrough by 1 SS Panzer Division at Stavelot' on December 17th and 18th. Ed.

presumably as usual, drafted an estimate of the situation, basing it on the offensive operations which were under way. Some hopes were attached to these efforts. When Model returned in the evening the results of the fighting of that day, spelling failure, could not have been in. Metzsch stated: 'This estimate of the situation could not have been based on the action report for the day.' Consequently, Metzsch believed that 'Model's hopes for a *tactical* success had been revived.' This could explain the passage of the report in which Model speaks of 'Great chances for success.' Another cause for the optimistic tenor of the report could have been the fact that Army Group B had been reprimanded for its pessimistic attitude of the third day of the operations. Now they were trying to erase that bad mark.

In summing up, von Metzsch held that the report 'was over optimistic and based upon an obsolete situation. Provided headquarters had been in possession of the true facts at the time the telegram was dispatched the estimate of the situation could still not have been entirely candid and honest due to the customary practice of embellishing reports. The document is therefore misleading.'

Supplies OKW and OB West had pledged did not arrive on time and in good condition. Army Group B had requested more, having based its demands on the schedule of daily objectives. These requests had, however, been reduced during the discussions of the planning period. Von Metzsch remarked in this context that it had become a practice to ask for more than was actually needed in anticipation of reductions. Supply difficulties affected transportation of supplies more than the movements of spearheads.

Transportation was a problem even before the offensive got started. The West German railroad system was badly damaged by Allied bombings. Transports across the Rhine bridges, however, were only temporarily interrupted. Allied bombing raids did not cause essential losses in matériel, but did slow down delivery of shipments. The majority of rail transfer points were on the west bank of the Rhine. From there and from the river ports supplies were hauled by truck columns. On this last leg of the tour delays were generally greater due to bad and narrow roads. The truck columns had to move during the night under adverse conditions. Day transports were prohibited in the entire area east and west of the Rhine. Allied raids in the areas of Manderscheid, Prüm, and Wittlich had delaying effects. The roads in the Eifel area were poor to begin with. They hd not been widened, as they had been in the sector further north, which had served as a staging area for the offensive of 1940.

There was little co-operation with the Luftwaffe. General Wilke was Luftwaffe liaison officer to Headquarters Army Group B. Luftwaffe commanders were present at the dress rehearsal mentioned above. In spite of the concentration of air power, the forces which could be mustered at the time proved to be inadequate for the tasks imposed on them. Allied air activity was practically unchallenged. As early as the first day of the offensive the troops started to complain about the lacking air support which had been promised to them. A lot of German tanks were disabled by Allied air attacks. On the German side only a few fighters were in the skies.

6

Hitler's Speech to his Generals
28 December 1944

Editor's Introduction

The stenographers at Hitler's Adlerhorst headquarters recorded that transcriptions of three speeches to his generals were recorded during the month of December 1944. The first two, on 11 and 12 December, were made at Ziegenberg to his assembled generals prior to launching the Ardennes Offensive. No record has survived of the speech of 11 December. A portion of his speech of 12 December was saved from the flames and captured at Berchtesgaden; the most pertinent parts of this residual portion are reproduced in this volume (see pp. 4–9). Unfortunately, the most relevant sections of his complete talk were lost, and the surviving long-winded preamble is one of the lessons in European history that Hitler would impart to his military commanders before speaking of the necessity for great sacrifice.

The final speech, that of 28 December, stands as perhaps the most valuable of the two surviving transcripts. For one thing, the entirety of 'Fragment 27' has survived, with the full range of Hitler's thinking revealed. More important, however, is its content. Coming, as it did, after the Ardennes venture had foundered, the speech gives Adolf Hitler's assessment of the offensive, and his impressions of its dynamics as well as reasons for each wrong turn. The justification for assembling another round of generals was as before: he was preparing to launch another offensive. This time, however, it was to be in Alsace-Lorraine and not the Ardennes, since the Allies had brought up large reserves to blunt his attack towards Antwerp. Operation *Nordwind* was to burst upon the U.S. Seventh Army and smash its way towards Strasbourg and the Saverne Gap.

The region's ownership was long disputed by France and Germany, having changed hands five times in the previous century. To bring it under German control once more, Hitler believed that newly assembled forces in Army Group G opposite Zweibrücken–Bitsche would find offensive freedom since the Americans had denuded their front to reinforce the Ardennes. Furthermore, a severe blow in the south might suddenly unlock the offensive effort stuck fast in the snowy woods of Belgium – or that was how Jodl and others within OKW attempted to justify yet another effort. The attack was to be made on 1 January 1945, attempting to achieve surprise yet again, and perhaps take advantage of American hangovers.

These speeches were extremely secret. After the 20 July plot against his life by a cabal of officers from the Army, Hitler was ever suspicious of the generals upon whom his military fate depended. Generalleutnant Fritz Bayerlein, who was to command the Panzer Lehr Division, described the paranoid atmosphere prevailing during the 12 December briefing:

It was at Ziegenberg that I found out about the offensive for the first time. After dinner we were told to attend a special briefing. We were stripped of all weapons and briefcases and loaded into buses and driven about the countryside for about half an hour. Finally, we were led into a large room which was surrounded by SS guards who watched our every move.

Then Hitler arrived, accompanied by Field Marshal Keitel and General Jodl. Hitler looked sick and broken and began to read from a long manuscript. The speech lasted for two hours, during which I felt most uneasy. The suspicious looks of the SS guards made me afraid to reach into my pocket for a handkerchief.

Hitler started off this briefing as if he were giving one of his birthday speeches. For about an hour he told us what he and the National Socialist party had done for Germany during the past twelve years. He then went into the details of the Ardennes Offensive, telling us what formations were involved and what they were to do. The object was to capture Antwerp in 14 days and at the same time trap Montgomery's 21st Army Group in Holland. The loss of so large a force would cause Canada to withdraw from the war and thoroughly discourage the United States about continuing the struggle.

Hitler also impressed us with the fact that if this offensive did not succeed, things would be extremely difficult for Germany. At this statement, Keitel and Jodl, who were sitting at the front table, nodded their heads approvingly. The Führer also promised us sufficient petrol, and a fighter support of 3,000 planes which would keep the Allies out of the skies. When Hitler had finished, von Rundstedt expressed his loyalty to the Führer on behalf of the generals and he assured him that this time they would not fail him.[1]

But like the Ardennes Offensive, the actual resolution of the *Nordwind* did not lead to the success Hitler demanded.[2] Perhaps most importantly to the Alsace operation, the Allies were warned by ULTRA of the intent of the German movements. On Sunday 1 January, the assault began, without artillery preparation, with limited gains of five miles. One battle group of the 17th SS Panzergrenadier Division managed to penetrate twice that far. But Allied response to the attack was swift and the *kampfgruppe* found itself nearly encircled in confused fighting. The divisional commander, SS-Standartenführer Hans Lingner, was taken prisoner on 9 January as the attack ground to a halt. Other jabs would be launched by other German forces hastily assembled in the salient, but by the end of the month the entire charade had played out with no lasting success for the German forces. On 14 January, the day before Hitler and his entourage left their headquarters in the West to return to Berlin, Schramm's

Operations Staff diary drearily admitted that 'the initiative in the area of the offensive has passed to the enemy.'

Returning from his speech to the assembled generals, Hitler had begun to read again the collected letters of his idol, Frederick the Great. He quoted one of these letters in a late-night discussion with General Wolfgang Thomale, his inspector of the panzer forces. Clearly, he found Frederick the Great's problems a reassuring mirror for his own increasingly desperate thinking:

> 'I started this war with the most wonderful army in Europe; today I've got a muck heap. I have no leaders anymore, my generals are incompetent, the officers are no commanders and the troops are wretched.' It was a devastating estimate. But nevertheless the man got through the war. What's more if you read the estimates of the Russian troops, they're wretched. But they carry on just the same. So the important things are eternal human qualities, the qualities which are really basic to the military profession. Military qualities don't show themselves in an exercise on a sand table. In the last analysis, they show themselves in the capacity to hold on, in perseverence and determination. That's the decisive factor in any victory. Genius is a will-o'-the-wisp unless it is founded in perseverence and fanatical determination . . .[3]

Notes

1. From a post-war interview with Generalleutnant Bayerlein. Milton Shulman, *Defeat in the West*, Dutton, 1948, pp. 230–1.

2. For a more complete description see D.S. Parker, 'War's Last Eruption,' *Military History Magazine: Great Battles*, September 1992, pp. 42–9.

3. This exchange, like each of the other two portions of Hitler's speeches, is excerpted from Fragment 30. Helmut Heiber (ed.), *Hitlers Lagebesprechungen: Die Protokollfragmente seiner militärischen Konferenzen 1942–1945*, Stuttgart, 1962.

Hitler's Speech to his Generals 28 December, 1944

Gentlemen: I have asked you to come here before an operation, the successful conclusion of which is vital for further blows in the West. Firstly, I want briefly to place this particular operation in its true context. I want to relate it to the overall situation that confronts us and to the problems which we face and which must be solved. Whether they develop in a happy or an unhappy fashion, solved they shall be, ending either in our favor or in our destruction. The German situation can be characterized in a few sentences.

As in the First World War, so in this war the question is not whether Germany will be graciously permitted by her enemies, in the event of their victory, some kind of existence, but whether Germany has the will to remain in existence or whether it will be destroyed. Unlike earlier wars of the seventeenth or eighteenth century, this war will decide neither a question of political organization nor a question of the adherence of a people or a tribe or a former federal state to the German Reich. What in the last analysis will be decided is the survival of the very essence of our German people, not survival of the German Reich but survival of the very essence of the German people. A victory for our enemies must 'bolshevize' Europe. What 'bolshevization' means for Germany everybody must and will realize. In contrast with earlier times, it is not now a question of a change in the form of our government. Changes in the form of government have taken place in the lives of peoples on innumerable occasions. They come and go. Here the survival of the very essence is involved. Essences are either preserved or they are removed. Preservation is our goal. The destruction of the essence under certain circumstances destroys the race forever.

Struggles such as are going on now have the character of clashes of philo-sophies of life *(Weltanschauungen)* and they frequently last a very long time. Therefore they are not comparable to the struggles of the time of Frederick the Great. Then the issue was whether, within the framework of the gradually crumbling and disintegrating Empire, a new great German power would emerge and whether this power would, so to speak, achieve recognition as a great European power. Today Germany no longer needs to prove herself a great European power – her importance as such is clear to everyone. The German Reich is now fighting an ideological war for its very existence. The winning of this war will, once and for all, stabilize this great power, which quantitatively

213

and qualitatively is already in existence. The loss of this war will destroy the German people and break it up. Parts of Germany will be evacuated.

A few weeks ago you heard Churchill say in the English Parliament that the whole of East Prussia and parts of Pomerania and Silesia would be given to Poland, who in turn would give something else to Russia.* Seven or ten or eleven million Germans would have to be transferred. Churchill hopes in any case to eliminate by air attack six or seven million, so that the population transfer would offer no great difficulties. This is today the sober statement of a leading statesman in a public body. In earlier times you would have regarded this as a propaganda argument, as a propaganda lie. Here it is said quite officially, though it by no means corresponds to what will actually happen, because, in the case of a German collapse, England would be unable to offer serious resistance to bolshevism anywhere.

That is pure theory. In these days when Mr. Churchill leaves Athens in humiliating failure and is unable to oppose bolshevism even on a small scale, he wants to give the impression that he is able to halt the advance of bolshevism at any frontier in Europe.** That is ridiculous fantasy. America can't do it. England can't do it. The only country whose fate will be decided in this war is Germany. She will be saved or, in the event of the loss of the war, she will perish.

I hasten to add, gentlemen, that from these statements of mine you are not to draw the conclusion that even remotely I envisage the loss of this war. In my life I have never learned to know the word 'capitulation,' and I am a self-made man. For me the situation in which we are today is nothing new. I have been in very different and much worse situations. I mention this only because I want you to understand why I pursue my aim with such fanaticism and why nothing can wear me down. As much as I may be tormented with worries and even physically shaken by them, nothing will make the slightest change in my decision to fight on until at last the scales tip to our side.

The objection that, with respect to such issues, we must think in sober military terms can best be refuted by taking a quick look at the great events of history. In the time after the battle of Cannae, everyone would, by sober military calculations, have been forced to the conclusion that Rome was lost.

---

* Hitler refers to Churchill's 15 December speech in the House of Commons in which the British leader, anticipating the end of the war, discussed the post-war Polish–Soviet frontier, saying that 'The Poles are free, so far as Russia and Great Britain are concerned, to extend their territories at the expense of Germany in the West.' He added that along with new borders there would be 'the total expulsion of Germans from the areas to be acquired by Poland in the West and North...'
** Winston Churchill had just departed from Athens after being unable to end the fighting between the opposing parties in Greece. The establishment of Archbishop Dasmaskinos as Regent was announced only after Churchill's return to London.

But, though abandoned by all her friends, betrayed by all her allies, the last army at her disposal lost, and the enemy at the gates, Rome was saved by the steadfastness of the Senate – not the Roman people, but the Senate, which means their leadership. We have a similar example in our own German history, not of the same world-wide significance, but tremendously important for the whole course of German history, for the later foundation of the German Reich was determined by this hero, was made possible by his historical achievement. I refer to the Seven Years War. As early as the third year countless military and political officials were convinced that the war could never be won. According to human calculations it should have been lost: 3,700,000 Prussians were pitched against about 52,000,000 Europeans. In spite of that, however, this war was won. Even in struggles of a world-wide nature the spirit is one of the decisive factors. It enables men to discover new ways out, and to mobilize new potentials. Above all, in such situations it is decisive to know that the enemy is made up of men of flesh and blood, of men who have nerves, and of men who do not fight for their very existence in the same sense that we do. That means that the enemy does not know, as we do, that this is a fight for existence. If the English should now lose this war, this would not be as decisive for them [as for Germany]. Neither would America lose its political racial essence. But Germany fights for her very existence. People are aware of this, you all realize. You need only look at today's German youth and compare them with the youth of the First World War. You need only look at the German cities and compare their attitude with that of the German people in the year 1918. Today the entire German people remain unshaken and will remain unshaken. In 1918 the German people capitulated without necessity. Now they realize the dangers of the situation and are aware of the problem with which we are confronted. That is what I wanted to say as a brief introduction before I discuss the purely military issues.

What is the military situation? Whoever studies the great world historical struggles which are known to us will very frequently find situations of a similar character, perhaps even situations much worse than the one with which we are confronted today. For we should not forget that even today we are defending a territory – German territory and [Germany's] Allied territory – which is essentially larger than Germany has ever been, and that we have at our disposal an armed force which even today unquestionably is the strongest on the earth. If anyone wants to get the overall situation into correct perspective, he should visualize the following: he should take by itself one of the world powers which are opposing us, Russia, England, or America. There can be no doubt that singly we could dispose of each of these states with ease. That not only is proof of the strength of the German people, but also of the strength of the German military force, which, of course, in the final analysis grows out of the strength of the German people, which cannot be imagined to exist in a vacuum.

In a military sense it is decisive that in the West we are moving from a sterile defensive to the offensive. The offensive alone will enable us to give once more to this war in the West a successful turn. To the extent to which the enemy succeeds in mobilizing his resources, defensive warfare would get us into a hopeless position within a calculable period of time. The offensive would not cost such sacrifice in blood as people generally assume – at least less in the future than at present. The view that under all circumstances an offensive would be more costly in blood than a defensive is wrong. We ourselves have had that experience. The battles that were most bloody and costly were in all cases our defensive battles. If we take into account the losses of the enemy and our own losses and if we include the numbers of war prisoners, offensive battles have always been favorable to us.

The same is true of the present offensive. If I imagine the total number of the divisions the enemy has thrown in here, and if I calculate his entire losses in prisoners alone (losses in prisoners are the same thing as losses in killed; the men are eliminated), and if I add his losses in blood to his losses in material, then if I compare them with our losses, there can be no doubt that even the brief offensive we have just undertaken has resulted in an immediate easing of the situation on the entire front. Although, unfortunately, the offensive has not resulted in the decisive success which might have been expected, a tremendous easing of the situation has occurred. The enemy has had to abandon all his plans for attack. He has been obliged to re-group all his forces. He has had to throw in again units that were fatigued. His operational plans have been completely upset. He is enormously criticized at home. It is a bad psychological moment for him. Already he has had to admit that there is no chance of the war being decided before August, perhaps not before the end of next year. That means a transformation of the entire situation such as nobody would have believed possible a fortnight ago. That is the net result of a battle in which a great part of our divisions has not even been committed. A considerable part of our Panzer divisions still follows in the rear or has been in combat for only a few days. I am convinced that the defensive would in the long run be unbearable for us. For the losses in blood of an enemy offensive will steadily decrease; commitments of material will increase. The enemy will not continue these monotonous assaults with men, for the criticism at home will on the one hand be decisive, and on the other, of course, the gradually improving flow of munitions and war material will have its decisive effect. To the same extent to which he repairs the harbors and solves his transportation problem he can accelerate the moving up of supplies as long as the stock piles suffice. He will become accustomed to the tactics that were actually employed at Aachen, namely concentrated artillery fire on a position, destruction of single pill boxes by fire from tanks, and then

occupation of a completely pulverized area by relatively weak infantry forces.*
In the long run his losses in manpower will be fewer than ours. During this time
he will demolish our rail system – slowly but surely – and will make transportation gradually impossible for us. We do not force him to use his bomber
squadrons over the battle front alone, but open to them the German homeland;
and in turn that will react upon the front because of decreases in delivery of
ammunition, of gasoline, of weapons, of tools, of motor cars, et cetera, and that
will have unfavorable effects upon the troops. In other words, the result of a
continuation of the present or former tactics which were forced upon us by
circumstances, because we were unable to attack earlier, might result in
extremely heavy losses in blood while the losses of the enemy would probably
decrease considerably.

Consequently, if possible, we shall abandon these tactics the moment we
believe that we have forces enough for offensive action. That is possible. The
result of the present first act of our offensive in the West has already been that
the Americans have been forced to move up something like 50 per cent of the
forces from their other fronts, that their other offensive formations, located
north and south of our breakthrough point, have been greatly weakened, that
the first English divisions are arriving, that the enemy is already moving up a
great part of his armored forces. I believe that eight or nine armored divisions,
of a total of fifteen, have been in action. That means that he has had to concentrate his forces there. In the sector in which we are now starting to attack,
lines have become extraordinarily thin. He has pulled out division after division
and now we must hurry in order to be able to annihilate a still larger number of
divisions – perhaps the enemy has left there only three or perhaps four – if we
have luck it may be five, but hardly six.**

I want to emphasize right away that the aims of all these offensives, which
will be delivered blow by blow (already I am preparing a third blow), is first the

---

* Hitler here refers to the American tactics in the siege of the German-held city of Aachen, which
ended on 21 October after only 13 days of street fighting, at a cost of about 1,400 casualties in
the 1st Infantry Division. This was considered relatively light for this form of city fighting.
During the battle, the U.S. Army employed great quantities of artillery to force out the German
defenders street by street and only moved in infantry after each block had received a thorough
pounding.
** A characteristically optimistic assessment by Hitler. SS-Standartenführer Hans Lingner took
part in Hitler's proposed *Nordwind* operation as a youthful commander of the 17th SS Panzergrenadier Division. His account is telling: 'When the breakthrough in the Ardennes had been
stopped by the Allies, it was realized that several Allied divisions had been sent north to aid the
Americans in their defense. It was therefore decided to launch an attack against what we felt was
sure to be a weak position. This offensive was only given very limited objectives and I believe it
was undertaken on the theory that an attack was the best means of defense. We apparently
miscalculated Allied strength in the Saar, for we were very surprised by the number of divisions
still opposing us. As a result the operation only achieved very limited success.' (Shulman, *Defeat in
the West*, p. 257.)

elimination of all American units south of the penetration points by annihilating them piece by piece, division by division. Then we shall see how we can establish a direct connection between this operation and the penetration point. The task of our forces at the penetration point is to tie down as many enemy forces as possible. The penetration point is at a spot vital for them. The crossing of the Meuse would be immensely dangerous for both the Americans and the English. An advance toward Antwerp would be catastrophic for them. The advance did not succeed, but we did succeed in one thing, namely in forcing them to concentrate all essential and available forces in order to localize the danger. That is our first positive gain. Now our task is to destroy the forces south of the penetration point, first by means of a number of single blows.

Thus the task set for this new offensive does not go beyond what is possible and can be achieved with our available forces. We are committing eight divisions. With the exception of one division which comes from Finland, seven are of course worn out from fighting, though parts of a few are rested; but the enemy who opposes us (if we have luck with five divisions, possibly only with four, possibly only with three) is not fresh either. He too is worn out, with the exception of one division which is stationed directly along the Rhine, and we shall have to see how it will prove itself, and with the exception of the 12th American Armored Division, which may not be committed at all, and which in any case is a new unit which has not yet been in combat. But the rest of the units on the enemy side are also worn out. We shall find a situation which we could not wish to be better.

If this operation succeeds it will lead to the destruction of a part of that group of divisions which confronts us south of the breakthrough point. The next operation will then follow immediately. It will be connected with a further push. I hope that in this way we shall first smash these American units in the south. Then we shall continue the attack and shall try to connect it with the real long-term operation itself.

Thus this second attack has an entirely clear objective – the destruction of the enemy forces. No questions of prestige are involved. It is not a question of gaining space. The exclusive aim is to destroy and eliminate the enemy forces wherever we find them. It is not even the task of this operation to liberate all Alsace. That would be wonderful. It would have an immense effect on the German people, a decisive effect on the world, immense psychological importance, a very depressing effect on the French people. But that is not what matters. As I said before, what matters is the destruction of the manpower of the enemy.

However, even in this operation, it will be necessary to pay attention to speed. That means, in my opinion, that we should take what can be taken quickly, like lightning, without being deflected from our proper target. Sometimes you cannot catch up in weeks what you failed to do, or missed doing, in three or four hours. A reconnaissance unit, or a small motorized unit, or an assault gun brigade, or a panzer battalion is sometimes able to cover in three or four hours 20 to 40 decisive kilometers which afterwards could not be gained in six weeks of battle. Unfortunately that is what we experienced in our first operation.

This [operation, the Ardennes Offensive] stood under a number of lucky as well as unlucky stars. A lucky omen was that we succeeded for the first time in keeping an operation secret – I may say for the first time since the fall of 1939, since we entered the war. A few bad things happened even here. One officer carrying a written order went up to the front and was snatched. Whether the enemy found the order and made use of this intelligence, or whether they did not believe it, cannot be established now. At any rate the order reached the enemy. However, thank heaven, it had no effect. At least no reports have come in from any quarter that the enemy was put on guard. That was a lucky omen.

The best omen of all was the development of the weather, which had been forecast by a young weather prophet who actually proved to have been right. This weather development gave us the possibility of camouflaging, though this had seemed hardly possible, the final assembly of the troops during the last two or three days, so that the enemy gained no insight. The same weather prophet, who again forecast the present weather with absolute certainty, has again proved to be right. Then there was the complete failure of the enemy air reconnaissance, partly because of the weather but partly also because of a certain existing conceit. Those people did not think it necessary to look around. They did not believe it at all likely that we could again take the initiative. Perhaps they were even influenced by the conviction that I am already dead or that, at any rate, I suffer from cancer and cannot any longer live and drink, so that they consider this danger also eliminated. They have lived exclusively in the thought of their own offensive.

A third factor has also to be added, namely the conviction that we could not possess the necessary forces. Gentlemen, here I want to tell you something immediately. Certainly our forces are not unlimited. It was an extremely bold venture to mobilize the forces for this offensive and for the coming blows, a venture which, of course, involved very grave risks. Hence if you read today that things are not going well in the south of the Eastern Front, in Hungary, you must know that as a matter of course we cannot be equally strong everywhere.* We have lost so many allies. Unfortunately, because of the treachery of our dear allies, we are forced to retire gradually to a narrower ring of barriers. Yet despite all this it has been possible on the whole to hold the Eastern Front. We shall stop the enemy advance in the south too. We shall close it off.

---

*Hitler alludes to the disastrous development in Budapest in late December 1944, when the Russians had broken into and encircled the city. Street fighting would continue until 13 February 1945, when 110,000 German prisoners would be captured.

Nevertheless it has been possible to organize numerous new divisions and to arm them, to reactivate old divisions and to rearm them, to reactivate Panzer divisions, to accumulate gasoline, and above all to get the air force into shape so that, weather permitting, it can be committed to a number of daylight flights and can come forward with new models which are able to make daylight attacks in the enemy's rear, and against which he has at present nothing to oppose. In other words, we have been able to reassemble enough in the way of artillery, mortars, tanks, and infantry divisions to restore the balance of forces in the West. That in itself is a miracle. It demanded continuous pushing and months of work and plugging, even with regard to the smallest detail. I am by no means satisfied yet. Every day shows that there is something which is not yet ready, which has not yet arrived. Just today I received the sad news that the needed 21 cm mortars, which I have kept after like the devil, probably still won't come. I still hope they will. It is a continuous struggle for weapons and men, for supplies and fuel, and God knows what. Of course this cannot go on forever. This offensive really must lead to a success.

If we succeed in cleaning up, at least half way, the situation in the West, and that must be our unalterable goal, then we should be able to rectify the situation with respect to iron ore, because we need not only the Saar territory, but most of all we need the Minotte.* This is a prerequisite. The more critical our situation in the rest of Europe, the more important is this iron ore region. We cannot continue this war for any length of time, we cannot continue to exist as a nation, without having bases of certain raw material at our disposal. That also is crucial. I hope this objective also will be reached in the course of these operations. The enemy did not think that possible. He was firmly convinced that we were at the end of our rope. That was a further, third, reason why initially we succeeded in our offensive.

Then difficulties arose. First of all, the terribly bad roads. Then the repairing of bridges took longer than anticipated. Here for the first time it became clear what it means to lose ten hours. To a Panzer division ten lost hours can mean, under certain circumstances, the loss of an entire operation. If you don't succeed in getting through in ten hours, you may not be able, under certain circumstances, to make that up in eight days. Speed, therefore, here means everything. That is one point.

The second was: because of the delays caused by bad roads, because of the destruction of certain bridges which could not be quickly repaired, we did not begin our offensive with the mobility that would have been desirable, but were heavily burdened with equipment and most of all with vehicles. Exactly why all these vehicles were taken along I do not know. It has even been claimed that the vehicles were taken along in order that everyone could carry with him what

---

* Hitler refers to the high grade iron ore from that area of the Lorraine.

he could grab. I do not know about that, but it is certain that we were encumbered with vehicles. In that respect we must learn from the Russians.

One primary fact was demonstrated at once. In this attack infantry divisions generally advanced quite as fast as Panzer divisions, and indeed sometimes faster, although these infantry divisions were advancing on foot. That reminds me of the year 1940 when, for instance, a division like the First Mountain Division, about which I had seriously worried whether it could catch up at all, suddenly whizzed along like a weasel. All of a sudden it reached the Aisne, nearly as quickly as our Panzer units. Quite a number of infantry divisions have given very good accounts of themselves, some of them young divisions, though they were really impeded in their own progress by the road jam caused by the Panzer units. They would have advanced faster if the roads had not been clogged by the Panzer units. One thing is clear, namely, that Panzer units which are fully motorized – I always hear it said that they are 75 to 80 per cent or 65 per cent motorized; that is usually too much because then everything is on the road and there are eight or ten men to a truck whereas formerly there were thirty – I say Panzer units can cover 100 kilometers per day, even 150, given free terrain. But I cannot remember that there has been one offensive when even for two or three days we have covered more than 50 or 60 kilometers. Generally at the end the pace has hardly exceeded that of the infantry units. The Panzer units made only short hops. They quickly took possession of something, but the advance units of the infantry division then had to close up.

As soon as a Panzer division cannot roll, excessive motorization becomes a burden. The vehicles cannot get off the roads and if, because of the danger from the air, they have to move at intervals, the final result is that some of the forces will not be in their places. Either the artillery, or the infantry, or the grenadiers won't get to the front. Actually the battle out front has been fought out by quite small spearheads. That happened in the fighting of the Army Group Model {Army Group B}, also of the 'Leibstandarte' {1st SS Panzer Division}. In the last analysis only the spearheads did the fighting. Only the spearheads of the 12th SS Panzer Division were in the battle, but a gigantic network of roads toward the rear was completely clogged and blocked. You could not get ahead and you could not get back ... Finally not even the fuel was brought up. The vehicles hardly moved. They actually let the motors idle. They let them keep running during the night in order to prevent damage from freezing, et cetera. The men kept warm that way too. An immense amount of gasoline is needed. Everywhere the roads were bad. You had to drive in first gear ...

We can really learn from the Russians. When today I get a report about a Russian road which leads to a front section where there are 36 infantry divisions and Panzer units, so many armored regiments, and so and so many other units, and when this report says that last night 1,000 vehicles were on the road, tonight 800, and then 1,200 and 300 vehicles, this report causes an alarm that runs through the whole Eastern Front, for it is understood to mean that an attack is imminent. Our Panzer divisions have 2,500, 3,000, 4,000, 4,500 trucks, and then they report that they are mobile only 60, 75, or 80 per cent. Quite by chance I found out about two Mountain Divisions, of which one had 1,800, the other 1,400 trucks. Those are Mountain Divisions. Of course, they will get plucked if they have not plucked themselves already. This development would not be so bad if we could afford all that and if we could operate in large open terrain. But at a time when you are hemmed in and crammed onto a few roads, this motorization can even be a misfortune. That is one of the reasons why the right wing first got entirely stuck – bad roads, obstacles because of bridges which could not be repaired in a short time, then thirdly the difficulty of coping with the masses of vehicles, then again the difficulty of the fuel supply, which, unlike in earlier offensives, could not be brought up by the Air Force, and then finally of course the threatened clearing of the weather.

We have to realize that the Air Force did a pretty good job. It has thrown itself into the offensive and has done everything that it could do considering the number of planes which can be committed and the kind of planes at our disposal. Nevertheless, in good weather it is impossible for us to give such protection in the air that no enemy planes can get in. In the case of such crammed roads, the roads then become mass graves for vehicles of all kinds. Nevertheless, we had immense luck, for when the good weather came the disentanglement was in general already getting under way.

As I said before, those were the unlucky moments among the lucky ones. Nevertheless, for a moment, the situation seemed to justify the hope that we could hold out. At the beginning I did not at all believe that the enemy would thin out his fronts to such an extent. Now that the thinning out has taken place it is time to draw the consequences at other parts of the front, and they must be drawn quickly. Here I must take up a very decisive consideration, namely the objections that can be raised to a continuation of this operation. The first objection is the old one, the forces are not yet strong enough. Here I can only say that you have to take advantage of the unique situation even at the risk of being not yet quite strong enough. We have committed very strong units. If circumstances had been somewhat more favorable, weaker units certainly would have achieved a greater success than the strong units in default of lucky circumstances. Thus yardsticks of strength are relative. The enemy, too, is not up to his full strength. He too has weaknesses.

Another argument always put forward is that a greater period of rest should be allowed. Gentlemen, speed is everything today. If we permit the enemy to regain his wits, then, in my opinion, we shall have lost half the chance we possessed. The year 1918 should be a warning to us. In 1918 the intervals between the various attacks were much too long. Reasons have been given why, but there can be no doubt that if the second offensive at Chemin des Dames had followed the first one sooner, the outcome would have been very different.* Connection with the wing of the first great assault group would have certainly been established via Compiègne, and a decisive turn might have occurred. Perhaps we might have reached the sea. Rest periods, therefore, are not always desirable.

Gentlemen, there is something else I want to emphasize. I have been in this business for eleven years, and during these eleven years I have never heard anybody report that everything was completely ready. On the contrary, during these eleven years a report usually arrived saying that the Navy requested urgently a delay for such and such a length of time because this and that should still be done and would be ready at such and such a date. Then when the Navy was ready, the Army had its say: 'It would be a great pity if we should do that now, because the Army is just about to introduce this and that thing and would like to wait for it.' When the Army was ready then the Air Force came forward and said: 'It is quite impossible to do that. Until the new model is introduced it is impossible to attack or to expose oneself to such a danger.' When finally the Air Force was ready the Navy came back and declared: 'The present submarine has not proved itself. A new type must be introduced and a new type cannot be ready before the year so and so.' We have never been ready. That has been true for every offensive.

The most tragic example perhaps was the fall of 1939. I wanted to attack in the West immediately but I was told that we were not ready.** Afterwards I was asked: 'Why did we not attack? You had only to give the order.' I then had to admit that a mistake had been made. We should have declared simply. 'We attack in the West on 15 November at the latest. That is final, no objection permitted.' Then we would have started action. I am convinced that we would have beaten France to a pulp that winter and would have been completely free in the West.

You are never entirely ready. That is plain. In our situation it is not even possible. The big problem is that when in theory you are ready, the things that were ready are no longer at your disposal but have been used somewhere else. Today we are not in a position to put divisions on ice. Everyone is watched with the eyes of Argus. If there is quiet, or no large-scale battle in the East for two weeks, then the commander of the Army Group in the West comes and says: 'There are unused Panzer units in the East, why do we not get them?' If there is quiet momentarily in the West, then the same commander, if in the East,

---

* In the last great German offensives of World War I, the assault from Chemin des Dames toward Soissons and Chateau Thierry took place in May 1918, two months after the key attack toward Amiens.
** Hitler refers to his debate with the German General Staff during the winter of 1939, about whether to invade France immediately after the conquest of Poland or wait until the following May.

would declare immediately: 'There is complete quiet in the West; we should get at least four to six Panzer divisions over here to the East.' As soon as I have a division free anywhere, other sections are already eyeing it. For myself I am really glad that the divisions are in existence at all. Now I am following the example of some clever Army or Army Group commanders. They never pull out any divisions but leave them all in, even if the divisional sectors at their front get very narrow, and then they declare: 'I have no divisions at free disposal, they are all committed.' Then it is up to me to unfreeze a division; otherwise I would never get one.

Therefore, I have to state that we do not have unlimited time at our disposal. Events march on. If I don't act quickly at one point, then somewhere else a situation may arise by which I am forced to send something away. Time is of value only if you make use of it.

Then a further worry is the problem of ammunition. I am convinced that we can afford the ammunition needed for this offensive, because experience shows that an offensive eats up less ammunition than a defensive. Furthermore the following consideration should be emphasized. It is generally believed that we are unable to equal our enemies' supply of ammunition. According to the reports of our troops, our reserve of ammunition in the West was . . . of that of the Allies. In the East our expenditure of ammunition is nearly 100 per cent greater than that of the Russians. Although you may sometimes hear it said that the Russians send over gigantic quantities of ammunition, the fact is that the German expenditure of ammunition is exactly 100 per cent higher than the Russian, and I do not count the ammunition we leave behind on retreats. That beats everything. So far as ammunition is concerned, we can afford this offensive. The real problem is transportation.

The fuel actually needed for this operation is available. That we shall get it there, there is no doubt. The general transportation situation is more difficult. Improvement in the transportation situation will depend on the extent to which each commander of a unit, each troop leader, examines conscientiously what he needs to take along and what is not absolutely essential. Everything that is taken along and is not absolutely necessary is not only a burden for the troops but a burden for the supply forces and a burden for the entire fuel situation, and that means a burden for the coming operation. I consider it important to ask oneself rigorously again and again: 'Is there anything that I do not absolutely need?'

The character and the honor of a Panzer division – whether an army or an SS division makes no difference – is not demeaned if its battalions march for once on foot. If they cannot close up because of a road jam, then they are compelled to march on foot anyway. They have to get up to the front under all circumstances. If this operation were headed for the Sahara or for Central Asia, I would say that I understood that you do not want to part with your vehicles, but this operation, which in any case will not extend for more than 50 to 60 kilometers, can be carried out on foot. The infantry has to do that anyway and has never known otherwise. The infantry accepts this as its God-appointed fate and its honorable duty, but Panzer units regard it as a kind of disgrace if suddenly some must for a while march on foot.

I believe this to be a decisive factor for the success of this operation. On the whole the plan of the operation is clear. I am in full agreement with the measures that have been taken. I particularly hope that we shall succeed in moving the right wing forward rapidly in order to open the way to Saverne and then to push into the plains of the Rhine and liquidate the American divisions. The destruction of these American divisions must be our goal. I further hope that by then the fuel situation will permit a re-grouping for a fresh assault and a further blow, as a result of which I confidently expect that additional American divisions will be destroyed by the growing forces on our side. For the number of our forces will by then have increased somewhat. I hope I can support this next attack with . . . additional divisions, one of them a very good one from Finland.

Unless the enterprise is cursed with bad luck from the beginning, it should, in my opinion, succeed. I do not need to explain to you a second time how much depends upon it. It will largely determine the success of the first operation. By carrying out the two operations, A and B, and by succeeding in them, the threat to our left flank will disappear automatically. We shall then immediately fight the third battle and smash the Americans completely. I am firmly convinced that we can then turn toward the left.

Our firm aim must be to clean up the situation in the West by offensive action. We must be fanatical in this aim. Perhaps there are some who will secretly object, saying, 'All right, but will it succeed?' Gentlemen, the same objection was raised in the year 1939. I was told in writing and verbally that the thing could not be done, that it was impossible. Even in the winter of 1940 I was told, 'That cannot be done. Why do we not stay within the West Wall? We have built the West Wall, why do we not let the enemy run against it and then perhaps attack him as a follow-up? But let him come first; we can perhaps advance afterwards. We hold these wonderful positions, why should we run unnecessary risks?' What would have happened to us if we had not attacked then? You have exactly the same situation today. Our relative strength is not less today than it was in 1939 or 1940. On the contrary, if, in two blows, we succeed in destroying both American groups, the balance will have shifted clearly and absolutely in our favor. After all I rely on the German soldier being aware of what he is fighting for.

Only one thing is not in our favor this time and that is the air situation. But that is why we are now forced, despite all hazards, to take advantage of the bad winter weather. The air situation forces us to action. I cannot wait till we have more favorable weather. I would prefer to delay matters somehow until spring.

Perhaps I could then organize another 10, 15, or 20 divisions, and we could then attack in spring. But, first of all, the enemy also will bring over 15 or 20 new divisions. Secondly, I do not know whether in the spring I shall be any more master of the air than I am now, but if I am then no more master of the air than now, the weather will give a decisive advantage to the enemy, whereas now there are at least several weeks during which carpet bombing of troop concentrations cannot take place. That means a lot.

How important it is to get an early decision you will realize from the following. The enemy has full knowledge of the flying bombs. He has already reconstructed them entirely. We know that. He has put them into production. Unquestionably, exactly as we are causing continuous disturbances to the English industrial regions through these flying bombs, so the enemy will be able almost to demolish the Ruhr area by the mass shooting of flying bombs. There is no protection against them. We cannot even fend them off with fighter planes. I do not want to talk about the rockets. There is no remedy against them at all. Everything, therefore, speaks in favor of cleaning up this situation before the enemy begins to use super-weapons of this kind.

The German people have breathed more freely during recent days. We must prevent this relief from being followed by lethargy – lethargy is the wrong word, I mean resignation. They have breathed again. The mere idea that we are on the offensive has had a cheering effect on the German people, and when this offensive is continued, when we have our first really great successes – and we shall have them – for our situation is not different from that of the Russians from 1941 to 1942, when, despite their most unfavorable situation, they maneuvered us slowly back by single offensive blows along the extended front on which we had passed over to the defensive. If the German people see such a development taking place here, you can be sure that they will make all sacrifices which are humanly possible. We shall obtain whatever we ask of them. Nothing will deter the nation, whether I order a new textile collection, or some other collection, or whether I call for men. The youth will come forward enthusiastically. The German people as a whole will react in a thoroughly positive manner. I must say the nation behaves as decently as could possibly be expected. There are no better people than our Germans. Individual bad incidents are just the exception that proves the rule.

Finally, I wish to appeal to you to support this operation with all your fire, with all your zest, and with all your energy. This also is a decisive operation. Its success will automatically result in the success of the next operation. The success of the second operation will automatically bring about the collapse of the threat on the left to our offensive. We shall actually have knocked away one half of the enemy's Western Front. Then we shall see what happens. I do not believe that in the long run he will be able to resist 45 German divisions which will then be ready. We shall yet master fate.

Since the date could be fixed for New Year's night I wish to say that I am grateful to all those who have done the gigantic work of preparation for this operation and who have also taken upon themselves the great risk of being responsible for it. I consider it a particularly good omen that this was possible. In German history New Year's night has always been of good military omen.* The enemy will consider New Year's night an unpleasant disturbance, because he celebrates not Christmas but the New Year. We cannot introduce the New Year in any better way than by such a blow. When on New Year's day the news spreads in Germany that the German offensive has been resumed at a new spot and that it is meeting with success, the German people will conclude that the old year was miserable at the end but that the new year has had a good beginning. That will be a good omen for the future. Gentlemen, I want to wish each of you, individually, good luck.

Gentlemen, there is one thing more. A prerequisite for the success of this operation is secrecy. Anyone who does not need to know about it should not know about it. Whoever does need to know about it should hear only what he needs to know. Whoever does need to know about it should not hear about it earlier than he needs to know. That is imperative. And nobody should be ordered up to the front who knows something about it and might be caught. That also is imperative.**

---

* Hitler is speaking of New Year's day 1814, when Prussian forces began the final battles against Napoleon after crossing the Rhine.

** At the end of Hitler's speech the stenographer recorded that Generalfeldmarschall von Rundstedt again spoke up to offer assurance of his loyalty: 'My Führer, in the name of all the assembled commanders I wish to give you the firm assurance on the part of leadership and troops that everything, absolutely everything, will be done to make this offensive a success. We ourselves know where in our first offensive we have made mistakes. We shall learn from them.'

Index